Mary, Woman from Galilee

A Novel
D.L. HAWKES

Mary, Woman of Galilee

Dedication

To the beautiful, holy women in my life: my mother, Lorraine, and my two grandmothers, Alma and Bertha, and my mother-in-law, Lyn—all women of great faith.

Foreword

Do you believe in angels, miracles, and eternal life? I do.

This is a work of fiction. It is a story about a girl living in Roman occupied Palestine during the first century. The time when Mary, Joseph and Jesus walked the earth. There is conflicting information regarding these biblical characters. We can only imagine the details.

The aim of this novel is to explore and flesh out everyday life during that time. To see Mary in her political, social, domestic, and cultural traditions, norms and mores. The story will span the life of three generations: Mary, her parents, and her life with Joseph and Jesus.

What was Mary's life experience? She was just a teenager when she was pregnant with Jesus. Her early story pales in comparison to the glorious marks she has left on the world after her Assumption. However, one cannot help but wonder how special Mary was. She was the "Theotokos"—the God-bearer! She was the woman chosen by God to bear the Divine person and to give Jesus his human nature. Imagine what it must have been like to hug and wipe the tears of your baby, secretly knowing that this was the Son of God! She was, at once, the mother of her Creator and of her Redeemer. She truly was blessed among women and would hold a place in heaven above all creatures.

In conclusion, my story intends to be a glorious and loving celebration of the mother of the Saviour. It is a novel, so please keep in mind that the story is from the imagination and not a scholarly piece of work. There may be many inaccuracies; however, I pray that you can enjoy it as a story of a beautiful woman from Galilee. Any errors and misinterpretations in this story are mine alone, with no intention of offending anybody's personal views or personal beliefs about Mary.

D.L. Hawkes

"Never be afraid of loving the blessed Virgin too much. You can never love her more than Jesus did."

Saint Maximilian Kolbe

Table of Contents

Prologue
Testament of Simeon

I, Simeon, High-Priest of the Temple of our Lord, have been a witness to a miracle. I am an old man, and my beard has grown grey and long. All my life, I have strived to live according to our laws—to be a good and devout man. The Holy Spirit came upon me and revealed to me that I should not see death before I had seen the Lord's Christ.[1]

Do you believe in miracles? This is a story of miracles, of Adonai's sacred plan for our salvation. Miracles happen when the power of the Lord overrides and overshadows many of our natural laws. Many of the events that took place occurred according to the words of our prophets. Much of this is a sacred mystery. I hardly understand it myself. Only those who rely on the wisdom of their soul will even begin to comprehend the miracle of a virgin giving birth to the Divine Messiah.

I, Simeon, knew this when his parents, Mary and Joseph, brought Jesus to my Temple for Presentation according to our customs and laws. I knew it immediately. His presence was like the strike of dawn, and all around him stood still, filled with pink light. I was filled with great joy and a singing in my head. I took the child up in my arms and blessed the Lord and proclaimed: "Lord, now let your servant depart in peace, according to your word; for my eyes have seen your salvation which you have prepared in the presence of all people, a light for revelation to the Gentiles, and for the glory to your people Israel." I blessed his parents and said to Mary, "Behold, this

---

[1] Taken from Luke: 2:25-27

child is set for the fall and rising of many in Israel and for a sign that is spoken against (and a sword will pierce through your own soul also), and that thoughts out of many hearts may be revealed."[2] Mary and Joseph marvelled at my words, but they were not entirely comforted. Mary, too, would be a very special person in the scheme for salvation of not only the Hebrews, but of the whole world. That also was prophesized.

This is a story of surprise, joy, sacrifice, labour, sorrow, and pain. It is the story of Mary, Mother of God. It is the story of the secrets of the universe and the promises of eternal life.

It is a tapestry woven by the Creator of the universe. The pathways, the warp and the weft, the colours and patterns, were imagined by our Lord Almighty to introduce us to the promised Saviour. Adonai is the Father of all life, and He is master of the universe. He knows all and is all. All is holy in His name.

Let us start from the very beginning, where the first of a chain of miracles happened. The story begins with a miraculous birth of a little girl, named Maryam, but everyone called her Mary. It falls during the reign of King Herod in Israel, ruled by Augustus, the Caesar of the Roman Empire. The story takes place, in great part, in Galilee. Our people are in great turmoil because of the foreign and pagan occupation of the Promised Land. The people want to be freed and liberated to follow the faith of Abraham, Jacob, and Isaac. Moses delivered them to this land, but they are still under the yoke of an unholy Roman landlord. We desperately needed a Messiah. Adonai promised us a Messiah. Little did they know that the time was near, and it all began in this humble village in the hills of Tabor near the Sea of Galilee.

---

[2] Luke: 2:34-36

Oh, there was talk—town talk. There always is. I should know. I hear it all the time. It is how the citizens of Judea and Galilee pass their time. Telling stories, spinning tales, and spreading gossip. Not everything is true, but it serves the purpose of spreading the news throughout the community. Myself, I listen to those who are closest to the people involved. It is up to us to decide what is truth, what is mystery, and what is miracle.

Chapter 1
Anna and Joachim

The moon was special this clear August night. It was full, it was bright, and it was blue. All the nocturnal creatures' songs were raised in festive celebration of a miraculous event that would happen soon. The crickets chirped, the doves cooed, and the breeze softly crooned. A vast, spangled, and milky veil of stars canopied a fair house in the hamlet of Cana in the hills of Galilee. There was holiness in the air. It was a night of miracles.

Shimmering moonglow flooded the village of Cana with a mystic light and illuminated a stone-walled hamlet with a normally bustling community that was now in quiet sleep. Only a few candles still burned in the mud-bricked houses and only the sound of mewling animals and a crying baby gently disturbed the peace that rested within the homes perched on this hillside in Galilee. This Jewish house had a wonderful view of the village of Nazareth in the valley below and the majestic breast-shaped Mount Tabor to the southeast. The moon's light enhanced the diaphanous veil of mist and made it brilliant and white, so that it brightened the Jezreel Valley. Between Cana and Nazareth was a patchwork of grain fields yielding wheat, flax, and barley, olives, and grapes. The hills were covered with tufts of grass and scruffy shrubs that fed the herds of goat and sheep. Their woolly bodies speckled the rocky ledges on the pasture knolls and took on the colour of the lunar beams. Trees of fig, pomegranate, olive, mulberry and sycamore shaded homes and courtyards.

This story centres on a home that was somewhat larger and richer than the typical village structure. This was the house of a wealthy, but generous, herdsman. This affluent Jew divided his worldly goods and harvest blessings in three ways: the needy orphans, widows and the poor, the worship of God, and the provision for his own household.

Inside the house, Anna and Joachim were breathing hard and short after making love. They lay side by side, holding hands between their bodies as they let the cool air dry the glow of their efforts. They rested there in tranquility to quiet their respiration and to calm their souls to serenity once again. As the moon caressed their bodies, the serene meditation of each was one of prayerful gratitude for their soul mate. The matchmaker had been inspired when she suggested a marriage between Anna and Joachim. Anna's parents had been unsure of the match at first, because they felt that their pure and educated daughter could do better than this poor herdsman. However, Anna fell in love with him like a lightning strike. He carved a bolt in her heart, and every time she saw him, her heart would leap with energy and glee. Her parents had hired the services of a 'shadchan'. This matchmaker would find an excellent husband for their daughter. Many a young man was happy to court Anna. They did not care if love was part of this marriage as all they needed was a pure, devout woman who could keep house and bear them children, especially sons. Anna, however, was looking for her 'bashert', her soul mate. She waited for Joachim.

Joachim knew that Anna was more than he deserved. She was the daughter of Stolanus and Emmarentia from the Tribe of Judah and the line of David, who lived in the manner of the Essenes. Anna's niece, daughter of her dear sister Sobe, was Elizabeth. Both Sobe and Anna had been educated in the Temple and had studied the Torah and learned to read and speak Greek as well as Hebrew.

Joachim had met Anna in a Bethlehem market when he was buying stock for the Passover. She was collecting water at the well. The minute he glanced into her gold-brown eyes, his whole being was filled with a bliss and delight that had never occurred before in his twenty seasons of life. Joachim fell in

2

love with Anna in that instant. It defied all reason. She had enchanted him and captured his heart. How was he going to captivate her and gain her in marriage? He, Joachim, was merely a humble and lowly labourer. Even though this herdsman was poorly educated, he too was of the tribe of Judah and the family of David. He had attended synagogue lessons to study the Torah, and he was able to recite much of Scripture by heart. Though poor, Joachim had inherited a small herd of sheep and goats from his parents, and he knew he was clever and shrewd. He was confident that he was a hard worker and now he had a reason to put all the gifts that the Adonai had given him to good use. He would need to make himself worthy of her and give himself entirely to her wellbeing and happiness. He made that pledge to himself and set out to achieve enough success to convince Anna's parents.

Joachim fell to his knees beside a table rock and prayed: "Lord, this is Joachim, your humble servant. You know who I am, Lord. And you know how thankful I am for your many blessings. I am not worthy of you or of the beautiful girl Anna, but only you can make me truly deserving of the love of both of you. For my part, I will portion out my blessings to those less fortunate."

With a generous heart, Joachim put his gifts to work, and he purchased goats. Goats had the advantage of eating anything, so the scruffy hill side and its sparser vegetation were adequate for them. He purchased a special breed of goat whose hair could be used for high-quality fabric fibre. His mohair goats not only provided milk and meat but also beautiful threads that when skillfully spun and woven, would make cloth so fine that only the rich could afford it. Using good husbandry practices, Joachim grew his herd. With prosperity in this area, Joachim bought land, fields for new herds of sheep. Soon, his industry provided him with success in his village and he became a wealthy man himself. For that, he was eternally grateful and sought to give back. People always remarked on his generous spirit and his kindness to those less fortunate

3

than himself. The town-talk would say: "That Joachim, he is so kind and he would give you the clothes off his back. To anybody. Blessed be Joachim. He is a good man."

Others would say, "How did he come by his wealth? He's nothing special. Perhaps he has cheated to get his plenty."

Town talk is always small talk.

In time, his success in business resulted in this beautiful but modest house. Modest, but still the biggest and the nicest in the village. He had stables and fenced animal yards. The house was richly fitted with carpets and furniture. His house had an upper storey, a beautiful roof-top, and enjoyed several rooms and one of the largest courtyards in that region of lower Galilee. It could boast of numerous trees that shaded the courtyard which canopied the yard, and which bowed in the middle to produce beautiful natural arches that provided shelter and food for the many birds which graced the yard with song. There was also an abundance of fruit trees, imparting a variety of fresh fruit for the table.

The moonbeams shone through the open window of this house and the sounds could finally be heard in the reflective silence of the bedroom. The couple were basking in the glow of their love. For Anna, Joachim had been the one. She had passed on six candidates that the matchmaker, the shadchan, had put forward. She had waited for her first love bolt to strike. Time had passed and the matchmaker, frustrated by her failed attempts, had inquired beyond the area of the Judean hills. She was told that there was a herdsman named Joachim, also called Heli, who had done very well for himself in Galilee. She would send word to him that he should forward his suit.

Anna could not believe her eyes when the suitor who presented himself to her father was none other than the man she had seen in the market that day. He was not a particularly handsome or muscular man, and he was somewhat clumsy and awkward at times. Nevertheless, he was attractive and alluring.

He made her laugh and he looked at her with such love and passion and she just knew in her depths that he was kind, gentle and had a huge heart. She saw, by the way he looked into her soul, that he was her bashert—her soul mate. Her heart always leaped with joy when she looked upon him.

The match was made. All parties agreed and Joachim promised to return with the bride price—the mohar. Anna's parents were of the Essene sect, and they lived a simple and austere lifestyle. They were satisfied to put aside the mohar for their old age or in the event that their daughter would be widowed.

Joachim came beautifully dressed for the betrothal. He brought many gifts for her father. His donkey was loaded with gifts from his harvest, and it was followed by a flock of sheep. Joachim, feeling so blessed for his lovely bride, gifted her parents with a wooden chest filled with shekels, jewels, and precious articles of the religious domain. The betrothal and the wedding ceremonies were subdued and restrained because it was not the practice of the Essenes to spend lavishly on worldly things. Anna, the nineteen-year-old bride, wore a simple linen dress with a plainly embroidered tunic and a simple crown of wildflowers which circled her head and anchored her diaphanous veil. Joachim could not believe that he could be more in love with her than at their first encounter.

Joachim took his bride back to Cana and installed her in his newly built home. There, they lived a spiritual and righteous life, always kind and generous to their place of worship and to the poor.

The two spouses became tranquil again. Joachim sensed that Anna was sad in her silence. He rolled her over to face him and noticed that she had a teardrop trickling down her cheek.

"You're awfully quiet, my love. Is something bothering you? Was I unkind in my amorous endeavours?" asked a worried Joachim.

"No, Jo. You are a very tender and giving lover. I am always the happiest when I am in your embrace. What troubles me is the usual thing: the shame of being barren and not giving you a son, or even a daughter for that matter."

"You know that my love for you is beyond all material things. I love you beyond reason and I thank the Lord for having given you to me—the soul of my soul," replied Joachim.

"I was nineteen when we got married. That was much later than many other girls. It took that long because I refused all the other suitors. I was waiting for you. No other man would do. I am not regretting my decision. I love you beyond earthly things as well. However, we have been married for twenty years and still, we have not been blessed with a child.

"The town-talk is cruel. I sometimes overhear them chatting: 'There goes Anna. She has got everything—nice husband and a beautiful house, but still, it is a shame that she is childless,' says Maraha.

"I wonder what she has done wrong for the Lord to punish her in this way,' says Naomi. And so it goes, every time I go into the market or at the well, I see them whispering to themselves and shaking their heads. It just makes me feel worse."

"I know. I sense the same thing with the men in the trade workshops or in the Temple. 'Poor Joachim is childless. He has nobody to inherit all his worldly goods. Such a shame. He has been so blessed in business,' they mutter to themselves, but I hear them."

Another tear streams down her face. "I feel like I have let you down, Joachim. The rhythm of my womanly cycles has altered, and I hardly need to separate myself during my lunar time. That is good because I do not need to stay away from you, but it also means that I am running out of time." Anna catches her whimper before she gives in to her full grief.

Joachim reminds her, "We are in the hands of Adonai. He is a compassionate God and he is mighty. He has always answered our prayers, but in his own time, Anna. You never know what he has planned for us. It might even be better than our most desirable dreams. May his will be done here with us, Anna."

"I know, Jo. You are the love of my life and I accept the will of the Lord if you are by my side. I bless the day that you became my husband. My love for you is deep into the essence of my soul. My feelings of love exist at a level that is truly sacred."

Anna caressed Joachim and their lips sought each other's, and they let themselves unite into one person again, with the Holy Spirit surrounding them in a sacrament of devotion, love, and passion.

Chapter 2
Anna

Anna awoke with the sounds of household chores of the morning going on in her house. She slowly opened her eyes and listened to the bleats of the goat being milked and the squawks of the chickens being fed and the mourning dove cooing in her nest, and of course the bray of the donkey for no reason at all except to get attention. The sounds of nature outside contrasted with the clunk of clay pots and the slam of the door when a servant returned from the well with an urn of water, and the splash that followed as water was poured into ewers, as well the conversations of the numerous servants as they prepared for the day's tasks. She had slept late, and the bright sun shone through the shutter cracks. Joachim was already up, directing the care of his flocks, herds, and the other animals. He had done well, her Jo, thought Anna. He was the wealthiest man in that part of Galilee. He owned a house in Nazareth as well, and he treated his workers with consideration and was very generous to all. Yet, they had not been blessed with a child. The sober thought immediately soured the moment and the pain of being childless still, after so many years of marriage to her dearly beloved.

"Well, enough of that," Anna said out loud.

She needed to rid herself of those regrets and put on the spirit of this beautiful day in gratitude for all the blessings she did have. She lifted her eyes toward the heavens and gave glory and gratitude to Adonai and asked for the grace to live out today as a good Hebrew woman. Her servant, Judith, came in with a basin of water and a cake of scented soap for her morning ablutions.

"Thank you, Judith. Is your master gone to the fields?"

"He was, Mam, but he has returned and he's enjoying his breakfast at the moment."

"Good, I must hurry, or I will miss him again."

"Yes, Mam, and he looks like he is preparing for a long journey."

"Oh, I wonder where."

"I'm sure I don't know, Mam."

Anna hurried down to the ground floor and smiled at Joachim who was eating dates, cheese, and bread, with goat's milk to wash it down. He did have packs and water skins ready for a long journey. She walked behind him and held him around the shoulders from behind in an affectionate hug. He turned and kissed her cheek.

"Looks like you are leaving, Jo."

"I would never leave without seeing you, my dear love."

"Where are you going?"

"I will bring some of my best animals to the Temple in offering in hopes for a child. It can't hurt."

Anna did not respond to that comment right away. She understood that Joachim, too, was desperate for a child.

"No, it can't hurt. We know that miracles can happen, Jo. Look at Sarah and Abraham and Hannah. Adonai saw fit to grace them with children even in their old age. We must have faith."

"But I will miss you, my Anna."

"And I, you, dear Joachim."

Anna sat with her husband and enjoyed the morning repast in a comfortable, loving silence. Soon, Joachim was all packed and ready for his journey. After an affectionate goodbye, he left, and Anna was left on her own in contemplation and prayer for his safe travel.

Judith entered the room to clean up the breakfast and to spread out the vegetables for the mid-day meal. "Are you just about done, Mam? I would like to get on with my work."

"Yes, Judith. I will head out to the garden to pray now and get out of your way."

Judith left. Anna got up and thought about her handmaid. She was not always a kind person, and Anna had witnessed some mean-spiritedness in her treatment of the other servants and of Anna herself. She apparently did not know her place as a servant, but Anna was a humble person who tolerated her behaviour because she could not put her out. Where would an unmarried woman go? The fate of women was not easy, for without a man, she would have no way to protect herself and live.

Judith returned and was carrying an ornate headband.

"Here, mistress, take this beautifully made headwear. It was given to me by my former mistress, but it is not lawful for me to put it on, forasmuch as I am a handmaid, and it hath a mark of royalty,"[3] asserted Judith.

"I do not deserve such a gift, Judith. Lo! I have done nothing, and the Lord hath greatly humbled me."

Much put out by the refusal, Judith lashed back: "How shall I curse thee, seeing the Lord hath shut up thy womb, to give thee no fruit in Israel. You should hear what the town talk is about you in the market and in the synagogue!"

---

[3] Quoted from The Protoevangelium of James, Chapter 2:2

Anna was stunned, silent. She had no reply for this cruel remark. Tears filled her eyes with grief and hurt. She turned, grabbed her mantle, and ran to the garden.

Judith regretted having been so callous and called to her mistress, "I shouldn't have said that. I am sorry, Mistress. It was unkind of me to be so brutally frank."

Anna's tears were in full flow by the time she reached the bench under the arbour of the lush garden. This bench was Anna's favourite place for solitude and reflection. It sat under the shade of the laurel tree. From that vantage, she looked upon an almond tree. However, because it was now the season of Elul, it was far too late for blossoms, and even the fruit had been harvested. Nevertheless, the garden had always been a place of solace, meditation, and prayer for her.

Apart from her barrenness, Anna had much to be thankful for. She had Joachim and he was wealthy and could provide her with this beautiful oasis. It was a large space filled with an abundance of trees such as acacia, cypress, cedar, pine and sycamore for shade, and pomegranate, plum, fig, date, orange, apricot, and apple trees for soft fruit and many nut trees. And, of course, no respectable garden would be without olive trees and grape vines.

The orchard was filled with the songs of the birds that rested and nested in the branches. She could talk to her heavenly master here, but she was too full of shame and sorrow to do so this morning. Her thoughts returned to the words of her handmaid. What had Judith said that wasn't true? Truthfully, she knew that there was a lot of town-talk. Too often, she had seen the ladies in the market or at the public well, look at her, whisper, and shake their heads. Oh, the shame of it. Why was her Lord letting this happen? What else could she do? Was she being punished for her pride and her distrust in the will of her Lord? In her shame, hurt and grief, Anna fell to her knees and bowed her head low and prayed:

"O God of our fathers, bless me, and hearken unto my prayer, as you did bless the womb of Sarah, and gave her a son, Isaac."[4]

A delightful song and movement caught her eye, and looking up in the direction of the sound, she saw a nest of sparrows in the laurel tree. The mother bird was returning to feed the four little open mouths. The mama bird looked so proud and beautiful as she dropped a bug in one of the mouths and flew off to hunt for another. In another moment of anguish, poor Anna lamented to herself, thinking:

Woe unto me, who begat me? And what womb brought me forth, for I am become a curse before the children of Israel, and I am reproached, and they have mocked me forth out of the Temple of the Lord? Anna remembered a verse from a Psalm: 'Even the sparrow finds a home, and the swallow a nest for herself, where she may lay her young, at your altars, O Lord of hosts, my King and my God.' Woe is me, she thought. Even these little birds can have their babes, and these trees bear fruit. All the creatures of the earth do their part. I contribute nothing to the world and to Israel. I am so full of shame. What have I done that you have not blessed me, Lord? Please hear my prayer and make me fruitful in your eyes. This I beg of you.

In a burst of light, the garden stood still. All creatures had become calm and serene. Even the baby birds stopped chirping for their mother. Her own mind and her heart quieted. Anna's reverie was interrupted suddenly by singing. She could not make out the words, but it was beautiful and unworldly. She opened her eyes and was blinded by a bright, shimmering light. She lowered her head and brought her arms to cover her head. The heavenly music continued to fill the air, but the bright lights dimmed, and an iridescent and diaphanous form

---

[4] Taken from Protoevangelium of James, Chapter 2

appeared. It had large wings and a glorious face. The angel placed his finger on his lips.

"Be not afraid, Anna." heralded the angel of the Lord. "Anna, the Lord has heard your prayer, and you will conceive and bear a child who will be spoken of in the whole world."

Anna was stunned, not quite understanding what she had just experienced. It came as a shock at first, but gradually, the words of the celestial being took hold and she began to smile. The full meaning came to her. Her whole being was filled with the spirit and a great ecstasy overcame her. She was told that she was going to be a mother.

"If I bring forth a male or female, I will bring this child for a gift unto the Lord my God, and it shall be ministering unto him all the days of its life."[5] Anna's heart sang the praises of the Lord, and she roused out of her revelation and wandered in joy and rhapsody in her garden with renewed energy and excitement.

---

[5] Taken from Protoevangelium of James, Chapter 3-4

Chapter 3
Joachim

After saying good-bye to his wife and hugging her especially long, Joachim sought out his head herdsman, Daniel, at his farmstead in Nazareth. Together, they selected fifty lambs and twenty kids.

"Make sure that they are excellent specimens, without blemishes or spots. Only the most perfect are good enough to present to my Lord, Adonai. Let us hasten," ordered the master of the house, "for we have much travel left in our day."

Joachim had made a quick decision last night, after seeing Anna's sorrow, to go to the Holy City. I need to present these animals to the priests, the assembly of elders, and the whole people, he thought. Hopefully, this will atone for my sins and bring about a blessing to my childless family.

It was with a hopeful spring in his step that Joachim set off, walking stick in hand and with his heavily laden donkey, on the long and treacherous journey to Jerusalem. His destination was seventy miles to the south, and he had travelled this route often enough to know that there were always dangers on the passage. First, he would need to choose the best course for the present circumstances. The way through Samaria was shorter and cooler, which would allow the animals to graze and rest. However, while shorter, this route was rife with the menace of hostilities. As Joachim was contemplating his future plans, one of the goat kids, who was determined to hone his skills to become the lead he-goat, took a run at Joachim. Joachim saw the wily kid from the corner of his eye and waited until the last second and suddenly moved to the side and the silly goat, expecting to hit the man, ran past him, unable to slow down. With no barrier to impact, the inexperienced animal tumbled head over tail and finally came to a stop in the dirt, in a cloud of dust. Joachim and Daniel laughed at the lesson learned by their young charge. However, they agreed that this little goat had courage and the potential to be a leader among his herd if only he could control his ego and his urges.

"We must give him a name. What shall we call him?" asked Joachim.

"How about, 'Charge'?" offered Daniel.

"More like an assault," quipped Joachim. "That's it, we'll call him: 'Assault'!"

Which route to take was still a question. Daniel and Joachim discussed the choices.

"The road through Samaria is shorter by a day," reported Daniel.

"That is true, but it is fraught with brigands, and you know the Samaritans are not our friends," responded Joachim.

"But you said we must make haste."

"Yes, that is true. The section from Jericho is quite difficult and easier to do without the animals."

"The road through Samaria will be cooler and more comfortable," added Daniel.

Joachim hesitated while his mind weighed the risks for both possible treks.

"There will be many people on the road making the voyage to Jerusalem. There is safety in numbers; let us take the route through enemy country, then. Make sure that you are well-armed, Daniel. There will be many a bandit interested in robbing us of our possessions."

"Not counting the dinars in your purse, Master."

"Yes, they seem to be able to smell money from quite a distance. Let us pray for a safe journey, eh, Daniel?" as he slapped his helper on the shoulder and gave him a nod to begin the trip.

Daniel and Joachim, set off loaded with their water skins, a knife and sling in their belt, and sturdy walking sticks. Joachim kept his purse hidden under his tunic. The donkey was loaded with provisions for the road and, because Joachim had the means, a tent to spend the nights. They continued walking the many miles toward the land of Judea, Joachim leading the donkey and Daniel herding the animals. They would spend their first night in Ginea. One man would sleep while the other kept watch. They had entered the Samarian region and they needed to be on the alert at all times. To pass the time while walking, and to calm the animals, the two men sang psalms of praise.

The work of walking and herding undisciplined young animals was exhausting. Thankfully, the way had been easy so far, with not too many people on their path. However, they were in Samaria now, and they worried about the way ahead. They set up camp early to let the animals graze on a patch of grass. They watered the animals at a nearby watering hole, made a small fire and had a meal of cheese, bread, figs and olives. They sat together under the canopy of stars that their Lord had hung just for them. The moon was clear and bright, and the two men talked like old friends about animals, crops, and pasturelands. They laughed together as they recounted stories about the animals and their humorous and sometimes troublesome antics. And then they slept in turns.

The sun was just dimly peeping over the hills, throwing a bright fan of light into a pink and coral sky. The men quickly drank from their skins and consumed the cakes and oranges that had been packed for their trek. They had been lucky, and the night had been quiet, for which they praised Adonai and thanked him for his care. They prayed for a safe journey, rounded up their charges, and headed off singing.

Just before sunset, they reached the community of Sychar. Being closer to a more populated area increased the risks. There was no watering hole, so they had to approach a public well to quench the thirst of their beasts and to refill their own water supplies. There was only one woman at the well, and they cautiously approached her with a greeting:

"Shalom, kind woman. We come to water our herds at this public well. We mean you no harm."

"Well, since there are two of you and only one of me, I can have no objection."

The two men went about their business without speaking to her.

"Are you Jews from the north?" she inquired. They nodded their heads in response but did not encourage her further.

"Are you staying nearby, gents?" asked the woman, placing the urn she had just filled onto her head.

"Yes, not far from the foot of Mount Gerizim," responded Joachim.

"Well, have a safe journey, Jews from the north." She began her climb up a stony road back to her home.

"It might not have been wise to tell her where we were staying, Master."

"You are probably right. Anna is always telling me that I am too friendly and trusting. However, the area is vast, and it should not be too hard to hide."

Daniel wondered how this wonderful and steadfast man could be so naïve. There were just the two of them; they had bleating and mewling animals, and how could they hide? He saw no caves around.

"Still, better to not make a fire tonight and keep extra vigil during our watch," suggested Daniel.

Thank goodness, the sky was cloudy this night and the moon was not as bright. They repeated their camp routines, only this time without the fire, and settled down for their well-deserved sleep. Joachim took the first watch. He had to use rocks to fend off a wolf who had been sniffing around, hoping the animals were not protected, but other than that scary but brief episode, he passed the watch to his trusted servant at the midpoint of the night.

Daniel had been on watch for about an hour. The stars were less interesting tonight as he felt a sense of alarm in his body. His heightened awareness was quite on peak alert when he heard a slight sound. He made a complete circle to see if anything stirred. Although he could not see or hear anything, his instincts screamed that there was something amiss. In a whispered alarm, he alerted Joachim sleeping in the tent. Just at that moment, two men crept out from behind a rock. One headed for Daniel with a knife, but Daniel was not caught unawares, and he was prepared with his own weapon. The shepherd was well-fed and well-muscled from his work with animals. He met the bandit with a surprising attack of his own. The two men danced around, making loud and threatening sounds at each other, taking stabs at the other's body. Daniel was fast and agile and was no stranger to a knife fight. He had encountered many before in local inns and drinking establishments. One feint to the right and a quick move to the left and the intruder found himself with one arm behind his back and a knife at his throat. Another quick movement and the brigand hit the ground with a thud, taking the air out of his lungs, and his knife was stripped from his hand. Daniel put his foot on his neck while he ordered him to put his hands on his back. Once the man had conceded, Daniel bound his hands together with a leather cord he had attached to his belt and secured him to a tree. Once the thief was secured, he looked up to see an unusual skirmish.

The second intruder had crept to the opening of the tent, where Joachim, just barely awake, prepared for a fight. The flap

18

of the tent had just been lifted by the thief when out of nowhere came Assault, the want-to-be ram. At full speed and with his small horns down, Assault bore down on his victim and charged right into his exposed rear end, knocking the unprepared fighter into the tent. The goat had no time to recover from his strike and followed the man into the tent. Bedlam broke lose and Joachim went down flat on his back, while the thief got propelled to the back of the tent, followed immediately by a very angry goat who scrambled to catch his feet inside the canvas dwelling. The tent collapsed on the lot of them, and Daniel hurried to rescue his master and the frightened little goat who was still jumping, ramming, and kicking the man who lay on top of Joachim. Daniel dislodged the fallen tent. Assault scrambled out of the place, bleating and leaping. Daniel grabbed the stunned bandit by the back of his tunic. He lifted him up and set him down on the ground, holding his knife in a place that boded no argument.

"Are you all right, Master?" asked Daniel.

"Yes, are you?" said Joachim as he clambered up to right himself. "At least I was attacked by a single man, and not a man and a goat at the same time!" chuckled Daniel.

"All is well, then?"

"All is well except what to do with these two idiots." "What were you going to do to us?" grilled Daniel.

"The woman at the well was my wife. She said that two strangers were camping in the vicinity, and they looked like they were prosperous and might have riches that we could relieve them of."

"We would have had them too, if it wasn't for that damn goat!" cried the other.

"You only wish it were so. Well, you are going to have a very sore posterior to finish the night."

"Tie him to another tree, Daniel. They'll see what is to become of them tomorrow."

Joachim fetched his bedroll and placed it outside the dilapidated tent and returned to his makeshift pallet to continue his rudely interrupted sleep. Daniel checked the lashings of the prisoners and resumed the watch.

The next morning, at sunrise, the two prisoners were allowed to relieve themselves and get some water and a little food.

"What should we do with these two fools, Master?" asked Daniel.

"Why did you set upon us, Samaritans?" asked Joachim of the most vocal thief.

"You Jews are scum. Because you are our enemy, your goods are fair game."

"Stealing is never good, no matter who it is."

"Well, if it wasn't for that goat, we would be long gone with your animals, tents, and dinars. You would be dead, food for the vultures."

Joachim scratched his head in thought and replied: "Adonai was good to us and because of that we will be kind to you and spare your lives. We leave you tied here. Remember when we next come by here that we could have killed the bread winners of your children but we were compassionate of heart. Hopefully, you will be as kind to others in return. As a seal of our intentions, we will gift you that goat," offered Joachim.

"Oh, no! You wouldn't be so cruel as to leave that monster with us!" cried the bandit.

"Yes, he is a good and smart goat. His name is Assault. He will serve you well, as he did us. Let him serve as a reminder of a sin forgiven. I will leave you a she-goat as well and that way, you can start a herd of your own. You can name her."

They were reattached to the trees and left to be found by people who would soon be looking for them. Daniel hobbled the two little goats and left them to graze near the robbers. One thief kept a wary eye on Assault; he was not quite sure if this was a gift or a curse.

Joachim and Daniel rounded up the other animals and set out on their way again. There were no further dramatic incidents on their journey, but they were approaching the Sabbath, and they needed to stop soon to observe it. As fortune would have it, they were within the time and distance to reach Joachim's good friend in Bethany. His name was Lazarus, and he had been friends with Joachim and Anna for years and had always offered hospitality to his family in their treks to Jerusalem. In the luxury of this sojourn, the travellers were able to rest, bathe and eat and drink with merriment. It would be very welcome to honour the Sabbath and to visit with their good friends once again.

"Shalom, Simon." Joachim saluted his friend's son with a big hug of greeting.

"Shalom, Joachim. Welcome to our home. We are glad that you can visit with us. Mother has been busy preparing food for the Sabbath, and it is good that you are here at this time."

After breaking bread in the morning with his friends the day after observing the holy day, Joachim and Daniel set out again for the Holy City. Today would be a short trip as Bethany was only about 40 minutes' walk from Jerusalem, but when the animals were factored in the calculation, they thought they would be at the Temple in about an hour.

As Joachim approached the Temple courtyard with his offering, he was met by the High Priest, Reuben[6]. Reuben was wearing all the trappings of a High Priest: the ephod and the jeweled breast plate with the names of the tribes of Israel, worn over breeches, tunic, and robe, complete with pomegranates and bells, and a linen girdle. The turban or mitre was encircled by a gold plate fastened by blue string. The embossed "*Holy unto the Lord*" was prominent on the plate on this 'tzitz'. According to the 'Good Book', "*It shall be on Aaron's forehead. And Aaron shall take away the guilt of the holy things which the sons of Israel consecrate, regarding all their holy gifts; and it shall always be on his forehead, so that they may be accepted before the Lord.*" Joachim understood that through the line of Aaron, the High Priest had the authority to pass judgment and that the tzitz could also atone for sin. It was reputed to have mystical powers. If the words of the plate reflected on the person's face, it would reflect righteousness. He examined the gold plate that is upon his forehead to see if there was a sign from Adonai. He saw no sin in himself.

"Shalom, Joachim, how nice to see you. Are you bringing us another offering? You have more than paid your tithe. How generous of you."

"Yes, Kohen Gadol, I bring this additional offering seeking a blessing from our Lord. For many years now, Anna and I have not been able to conceive a child and it pains us both."

"Yes, Joachim, you must have sinned indeed that you have not been blessed with a child, a son of Israel. That would be a better offering to our Lord, than more animal offerings," reproached the High Priest. "It is not meet for you first to bring your offerings, because you have not made seed in Israel."

---

[6] Other sources use the name 'Rubim'

Joachim was stunned, speechless. According to the High Priest, he had sinned because he had not provided Israel with offspring. He could not bear fruit for his nation and his Lord. He was refused atonement. He was filled with shame and grief. He turned around and left, distraught, with his head lowered. He could not face Anna with this news. He rejoined Daniel with a heavy heart.

"Things did not go well, Daniel. According to the High Priest, I am not worthy enough to be in the presence of Anna. Return home and take away the animals. I will take only a few for my survival. Tell my good wife that I have gone to grieve, pray and atone in solitude in the desert. I will fast and do with little food or drink."

Joachim, as a barren man, set off for the barren lands. He pitched his tent and fasted for forty days and forty nights. As this was now Elul, approaching the cooler and rainier fall season, Joachim endured the exposure to the cold in sacrifice. In his weakened state, Joachim felt more dependent on God and his need made him even more devout. In the void left by the lack of worldly sustenance, an angel came to him. The image was so strong and powerful that he was stricken with fear. The voice coming from the bright form was soft and soothing but spoke with authority. It assured him that the Lord had heard his prayer and accepted his sacrifices. The angel introduced himself as Gabriel and announced that Anna would bear a girl-child. He told Joachim that this child was going to be blessed among women. She was already in the womb of her mother. She was to be named Mary and be consecrated to the Lord. She was destined for great things by the power of the Holy Spirit. Then the image vanished, leaving splendour in its wake.

Once again, Joachim stood in stunned silence, only this time he was filled with awe. He raised his eyes towards heaven and recited a psalm of praise:

I will extol you, O Lord,

for you have drawn me up,

and did not let my foes rejoice over me.

O Lord my Lord, I cried to you for help

and you have healed me,

O Lord, you have brought up my soul from Sheol,

restored me to life from among those gone

down to the Pit.

You have turned my mourning into dancing.

You have loosed my sackcloth

and clothed me in gladness,

that my soul may praise you and not be silent.

O Lord my God, I will give thanks to you for ever.[7]

His face broke into a smile, and he leapt for joy. He had forgotten that he was feeble of body, and he fell flat on the stony ground. But he was laughing and rolling around in glee. Later, a passing traveller found him there sleeping with a happy expression on his countenance. The traveller shared food and water with Joachim and stayed with him until he was strong enough to travel. They travelled together to Bethlehem, where Joachim hoped to stay with his in-laws. The traveller carried on his own way.

Joachim was anxious to send a servant to fetch Anna so that he could share his revelation with her and her family.

---

[7] Psalm 30:1-6, 11-12

Chapter 4
Anna and Joachim

Unbeknownst to Joachim, Anna, having been visited by the Archangel Gabriel, had also wanted to share her news. Aware that Joachim had secluded himself in the wilderness in shame and penance near her homeland, she had decided to send messengers ahead to call him to her. She would meet him there to share her great news. She was with child at last! A baby! Their prayers had been answered. Even in her old age, she would be fruitful for the Lord and for Israel. Joachim would be so happy—thrilled was more like it!

The journey would be long, and she was not sure how long she would need to wait, so she sent a messenger ahead to alert her family that she was heading to Bethlehem to stay until Jo would return. She set out with an entourage of servants and gifts of woven woolens and linens for her family.

She had been visiting with her relatives for about two weeks when she decided to go to the Temple in Jerusalem to visit her dear sisters in faith, the Daughters of the Hebrews. These consecrated women led prayerful lives and served this holy place of worship by doing domestic and liturgical functions. In exchange, they would learn the Scriptures and Law. They were instructed in the Greek and Hebrew languages, and in reading, writing and household skills which prepared them for domestic life. Eventually, some would return home to get married. Others would return as older widows to continue to care for the Temple and mentor the next generation of young girls who came to the Temple to learn, devote themselves and pray to the Lord in his sacred place.

Many women who were there now had been cloistered with Anna as child noviciates. The young maidens, pious and educated, returned to their families once they had reached the age of puberty, to resume domestic life and embrace family life as wives and mothers, while some cared for their parents and extended family as spinsters. Other former virgins of the Temple, always part of the guild of the Daughters of the Hebrews, experienced, and no less educated, pious, and devoted, returned in their later stage of life as older widows or unmarried women and dedicated themselves to passing their knowledge, skills, and devotion to the young, consecrated neophytes.

Today was a beautiful, temperate day with a delightfully clear and blue sky, which was unusual during the rainy and cold month of Shevat. The atmosphere glowed with a golden hue which lent lustre to the pleasant afternoon that Anna had just shared with many of her dear friends: Susannah, Rebecca, Sephora, Abigea and Cael. They sat outside the Temple in the shade of a pine tree and beneath a terebinth tree leafless and waiting for the first burst of bloom in the spring season. While the women enjoyed mint tea and honey cakes with her, they shared their life stories and they were delighted that Anna's prayers had been answered and that she was about to undertake the role of motherhood, the Lord willing. They were kindred spirits. Theirs was a sisterhood, a communion based on religious experience together.

Susannah had passed on a new piece of embroidery to Anna. After their tearful farewells, Anna departed and dreamily meandered down the path from the Shushan Gate. She was humming in her reverie and examining her gift.

Joachim arrived at the home of his parents-in-law. They lived a very austere life in the fashion of the Essenes, but the street and house were tidy and well-swept. He rapped on the oaken door and waited. It soon opened.

"Shalom, Emerentia. Peace to this house," greeted Joachim.

"Joachim, greetings and shalom to you!" responded his mother-in-law, pleased to see him.

"I'm sorry for the intrusion on your serenity, but I am in grave need to see my wife and I'm afraid that I am not in fit condition to see anybody right at the moment. I desperately need a bath before I face any human being."

Emerentia, as she finally caught a whiff of the long-time unbathed body of a hermit shepherd, held her nose and made a grimace and turned her face away.

"Oh, Joachim, you do smell foul! You are right; you are not fit for man or beast. Let me get you a pitcher of water and you can wash the dust off your feet and hands and then we will proceed to give you a proper bath in the courtyard."

Stolanus came to the door with arms open, ready to hug his son-in-law and was halted at the door opening. "Whew, Joachim, you stink!"

"He must have left an odorous trail all through the village. Oh, the town-talk we will be subjected to. I can already hear it now," added his wife. "Tut, tut."

True to her word, Emerentia had a servant come out with pitcher, ewer, and towels for his brief and hurried ablutions to make him respectable enough to even pass through the house. Days of sand and animal stench clung to his hair, skin, and clothing. He was embarrassed at his stink and was very much looking forward to cleansing the dirt and the odorous shame from his body.

A short while later, when Joachim re-entered the living quarters with freshened appearance and fresh clothes provided by his in-laws, he felt like a new man, clean, respectable, and renewed.

"Well, you look much better, Joachim. Your hair is now brown and not the colour of clay. We had to burn your clothes. They were that bad," teased Stolanus.

"You have grown quite thin, and we will need to put some flesh on your bones. How do you fare?" inquired Emerentia.

"I am much lighter for having lost the clay and the stench. You, and I'm sure others, have my gratitude for the bath. The water was so dirty, you could have planted a crop of turnips!" quipped Joachim.

"You are always welcome in our home, Joachim. Besides, Anna would have our heads on a pike if we didn't offer you respite and hospitality. It is the way of the Jew." The family gathering included Maraha and her daughter Mary. Maraha was now a widow and was poor of health. She lived with her parents and was grateful for the kindness of her brothers. They joyfully sat on a carpet with plates full of olives, dried figs, cheese, and bread. Wine was imbibed to wash down the food, a rich delight indeed for someone who had lived on desert hill fare. Joachim took care not to eat too much, or too fast of the rich food after his long fast in the desert.

"Speaking of my wife, I need to go home and see her. However, with so many days in the hills with the herd, I dared not proceed without making myself respectable to her. Besides, nobody on the road could have stood to be near me— not even the dirtiest of shepherds or travellers. As well, I don't want some man eyeing my beautiful wife because they think I have been gone so long I must be dead. And I certainly shouldn't smell that way!"

"The Lord has blessed you, Joachim, because Anna is not in Galilee; she is here with us. Besides, it would take more than that to deter your dutiful and loving wife."

"Where, why did she not greet me? Is she well?" Joachim asked, his voice showing concern.

"Relax, Joachim. She is not here at the moment. She went to visit her Temple sisters in Jerusalem." replied Emerentia in a calming voice. "She will return soon."

"I cannot wait for her to come back here. I will go and find her. We shall feast because I have good news!"

"Did you have a successful business deal again, Joachim?" asked Maraha, his sister-in-law.

"You will need to wait until I come back. For now, I will sleep, and tomorrow I will see my beautiful wife."

The family let him go as they shook their heads and smiled. Such a crazy man, yet such a lovable fellow.

Chapter 5
Joachim and Anna in Jerusalem

The next morning, Joachim quickly made his way to the Temple, and he knew exactly at which gate he would find Anna. Having been a Temple vestal, she would easily find access to the Temple at the northeastern gate— the gate that was known as the Shushan and also called the Golden Gate. He headed over to that side of the Temple Mount. And there she was. He stopped and gazed at her form in the distance. She was splendid in her countenance. She was dressed in a red tunic, with gold embroidery on the collar, that descended to her waist where it was cinched by a golden rope. Her forest-green mantle and hood billowed in the breeze, making quite a vision. A single strand of grey curly hair escaped her hood and blew around her cheeks. He still could not believe how fortunate he was that such a beautiful woman loved him. God had truly blessed him with the love of Anna, his dear, dear beloved. It brought to mind verses from the Holy Scrolls called Song of Songs, supposedly written by King Solomon, the wise one.

Arise, my love, my dove, my fair one, and come away;

For the winter is past, the rain is over and gone. The flowers appear on the earth, the time of pruning has come, and the voice of the turtledove is heard in our land.

Oh, my dove, in the clefts of the rock, in the covert of the cliff, let me see your face, let me hear your voice, for your voice is sweet, and your face comely.[8]

"Anna!" he called to her.

---

[8] Song of Solomon 2:10-12, 14

Anna looked up and saw Joachim's profile in the distance. He had come. But so soon? She had just sent a message to him a couple of days ago. He must have already been on his way back. How she delighted in seeing him! How fortunate was she that he loved her as much as she loved him. He was a good provider and had a heart of gold. She was truly blessed. Her mind also went to a verse from Song of Songs:

The voice of my beloved!

Behold, he comes,

leaping upon the mountains,

bounding over the hills.

My beloved is like a gazelle, or a young stag. ...

Enough dreaming. She recklessly ran towards her husband as he was bounding up the mountain grade to meet her. They ran to each other's arms in laughter and elation. They held each other for a long time, just enjoying the presence and the scent of the other. When Joachim broke the hold, he put his forehead on Anna's and his hands on both sides of her face.

"Shalom, my beloved Anna. How you lighten my heart with your beauty!"

"Shalom, my wayward husband," said Anna with a smile.

"You can tease me today all you want, because I have great news!"

"As do I." and I did truly miss you. You go first," responded Anna.

"While I was secluded in the barren hillside, I was visited by an angel, named Gabriel, who bid me return home because the Lord had heard my prayers and that my spouse would be blessed with a daughter. He said that this little girl-baby would have eternal blessing from the Lord himself. She is to be called Mary, and we should consecrate her to the Almighty. Our daughter will be blessed among many and will accomplish miraculous things. Isn't that wonderful, Anna? We had better get working on making this baby right away, Anna."

"Wait, wait, my eager lover! I have news as well. Our child is already in my womb."

Joachim stumbled back with the shock of the news. "What? I'm in complete awe of what the Lord has accomplished. Tell me what happened, love, for I am too thrilled to do anything but listen."

Anna recounted how woeful she felt after Joachim had left. She felt unbelievably sad in her barrenness and the town-talk was getting worse.

"The village women were whispering loudly that I would never get pregnant with my husband away. What a shame, they would say. Even Judith was cruel in her judgement."

Anna recounted the despair she had experienced in the garden, witnessing the birds feeding their young. She admitted that she had broken down in prayer when, suddenly, out of the blue, an angel appeared before her. He, too, said his name was Gabriel."

"Indeed! The same angel as I encountered. He gets around, that fellow," responded Joachim with a wry smile.

"He told me that I was with child. I couldn't believe it! He gave me a similar message. I was both dumbfounded and thrilled at the same time. I felt like Hannah and her news about having Samuel in her old age. I just could not wait to see you and share the great news. Oh, Joachim, the Lord has been very kind and generous to us!"

"Let us go to the Temple to pray in thanksgiving and then see the High Priest and make our announcement to him in person. Won't he be surprised! And a little sheepish, I would hope."

They quietly sang psalms of thanks and praise all the way back to the Temple. Joachim merrily skipped ahead and clicked his heels together, on one side and then the other. He couldn't help himself.

Chapter 6
Joachim and Anna in Bethlehem

Joachim and Anna announced their good news to the extended family. Everybody seemed to be there: Anna's parents and sisters and their families. They even got a visit from Zacharias and Elizabeth who had travelled from Ein Karem to celebrate with them. Elizabeth was ten years younger than Anna. She was the daughter of Anna's uncle and aunt—a beloved second cousin. Elizabeth had been married to Zacharias for a decade and had not yet been blessed with a child. She was anxious to produce a son for Israel. This was of special concern and distress because her husband Zacharias was a Temple priest who aspired to be the High Priest one day. They were actually encouraged by the news that Anna had at last become fruitful. They were happy for her and Joachim. It gave them hope.

"Shalom, Elizabeth!" exclaimed Anna as she met her.

"Shalom, Anna. What wonderful news!"

"Yes, the Lord has answered my prayers. I wondered why it took so long. However, it is not mine to question the Almighty; I must just be thankful. I am also thankful that you could join us at our celebration get-together. Greetings and peace to you, Zacharias," she said, turning to Elizabeth's husband.

"Yes, greetings to you both, Elizabeth and Zacharias," said Joachim. "How wonderful to see you. We are grateful that you made the journey to see us and to share our happiness."

"It is our pleasure to be with you at such a joyful moment. It is our hope that you will return the favour when we are equally blessed," replied Zacharias.

The women then split from the men to enjoy their own gender talk.

"Like you, Anna, I am wondering what is taking so long. It is so disheartening when the moon time comes again."

Anna nodded in understanding. "For all the frustration and disappointment, it is all forgotten when it actually happens. Our tears were turned into dancing. Joachim and I both know that this child is very special. She has been worth waiting for," related Anna.

"How are you so sure that this baby will be a girl?" asked Elizabeth.

"Both Joachim and I learned it in a moment of deep prayer.

How can I explain such a thing? How do I explain it? The whole world stood still and glowed in a pink hue when I received the message. There was a presence there—a peace and an ecstasy. I was both afraid and overjoyed at the same time. This was followed by a complete calm and then a clearness of thought as though the thought had come directly from the heart. With this serenity came a great knowing."

"Did it feel like being overcome by wisdom and once overcome, there was no unknowing it? Was it followed by great joy or rapture?" asked Elizabeth.

"Yes, yes! You have experienced this also?" asked Anna.

"I have had short glimpses of this experience when solutions or answers have come to me in a moment like this—like the mist has cleared and there it is. You are right; it is both awesome and joyful," explained Elizabeth.

"Can I tell you something in complete confidence? You can tell Zacharias, but only him." When Elizabeth nodded her assent, Anna responded in a whisper.

"I felt all that you described but I was also visited by an angel. His name was Gabriel and he said that he was a messenger from God. Joachim got a visit too," explained Anna.

"Well, I never got a visit like that before. That must have been amazing and also fearsome. What did he look like, this Gabriel?" asked Elizabeth.

"He was splendour in wings! Amazing! The world was still, as though life were held in suspension. He was an unformed body, flowing like a liquid and continuously changing shape and colour. It was breathtaking! I was in a moment of complete despair. I was so down in spirit in my misery that I was empty, and I completely yielded myself to the Lord."

"I am also getting close to that point in my desperation to have a child."

"Be not afraid, and have hope in the Almighty, Elizabeth. You are a good and righteous woman; perhaps it will happen to you as well, my dear cousin. Come and refresh yourself, as we have much to talk about."

Elizabeth no longer found it strange that the couple was so sure that the baby was going to be a girl. The expectant parents also felt that this miracle girl-child would be especially blessed, not only in Israel but in all the nations. They had already decided to call her Mary. Now, there was an explanation for their confidence. Miracle of miracles, Anna was pregnant and that was evidence in itself. Who was she to question the mind and intentions of the Good Lord? She resolved to keep praying and to enjoy the feast before them, and to rejoice in Adonai's gift to her dear cousin.

Joachim and Zacharias were enjoying a cup of wine and were deep in a more private discussion on the side. Joachim was relating his humiliating experience with Reuben, the High Priest, before his decision to remove himself in shame and penitence in the wilderness.

"No, he didn't say that! For truth?" exclaimed Zacharias.

"Truly, he did. He told me that my offering would not be accepted because I had not begotten a son for Israel," explained Joachim.

"Well, that was a very unkind thing to say and certainly went beyond his role. Who is he to judge the will of the Lord? I am sorry that you had to hear that, my friend. I feel the shame was his and not yours," claimed Zachariah.

"Zachariah, I was very troubled by that judgement, and felt that as I had offended the Lord; I needed to seclude myself in reparation for my sin. I contemplated a long time in the desert in repentance."

"You are not the one at fault, Joachim. I think that Reuben must have been in complete shock to hear your news. It would serve him right to be humbled and reminded of who is the Master in this world. He really was mean-spirited and had no call to insult such a generous, righteous, and faithful man."

"Truth be told, he has admitted to me that the other priests had scolded him for risking the loss of a generous tithe for his stupidity and arrogance. How insensitive!"

"I will pray for him and for your growing family. Tomorrow, I will be green with envy, but today, I am happy for you and Anna and will celebrate this great blessing that the Good Lord has bestowed upon you. 'L'Chaim', to life!" The two men struck their mugs together in an easy and happy friendship.

It was a balmy day for Shevat and the company took advantage of the warm, sunny weather to celebrate outdoors on the roof. Lanterns were placed around the roof space and a large banquet table had been set up, laden with the riches of food and drink provided by the sale of Joachim's herd. The invited guests had also contributed to the celebration banquet. The wine was liberally poured from urns into pitchers, and pottery bowls displayed a bountiful spread of olives, nuts, dates, figs, boiled eggs, cheese, little fishes, lamb and goat meat, and bread dipped in copious amounts of olive oil. There were honey cakes and dried apricots for the sweet tooth. The children were especially fond of the honey cakes washed down with goat's milk.

As the evening wore on and the libations were having their happy effect, they all danced and sang. The men told old fish stories. Everyone enjoyed Joachim retelling the story of the adventure with his bold and feisty goat which had saved them from the bandits. They laughed even harder when Joachim explained that he had punished the bandits with the gift of the reckless little felon. They talked about crops and herds, and the political unrest in their land, and how the Roman occupation was altering the way they could worship. They recounted the many ways that the Roman soldiers had fouled their sacred places and how some sacred holidays and temples had been desecrated by the Roman authorities. Herod, their supposed king, was no friend of the Hebrews as he spent most of his time appeasing the foreign prefect and the Caesar. Herod had grown to love his position and all the riches and privileges that came with it.

"The talk all over the villages is that they used to be able to sell their crops and have a surplus of grain for their own use, but not now," reported Joachim.

"I have heard a lot of talk that the demands on their goods are getting excessive to feed the city centres and the Roman troops. The cities don't grow much of anything, and they commandeer greater and greater quantities of goods for their needs, leaving the growers and farmers starving," said Joachim's brother-in-law.

"It's not like we are having a choice in the matter. What the Romans want, the Romans get!" exclaimed a neighbour.

"And they keep raising the taxes to pay for all their efforts to keep us from our independence and authority over our own lives! We see it all the time in Jerusalem under the thumb of these foreign brutes—in the synagogues and certainly in the Temple. These heathens and their Jupiter, Apollo, and Athena gods don't understand our worship of the one Almighty God and his commandments and laws," added Reuben.

Another neighbour spoke up. "Don't even speak to me about our priests who are supposed to be guiding their people in the laws of Elohim and observing leadership in all matters of faith. Many have become as corrupt as the Roman officials and are only interested in benefitting their position and enriching themselves."

"Oy vey! If Moses and King David could see what has become of the Temple and of his people," added Anna's father, Stolanus.

"May all the Romans be trampled by the pigs they eat! And may they fall face-first into the excrement of those profane and blasphemous beasts!"

At the very same moment, the men all put their cups to their lips and drew in the wine.

"They are greedy, and they demand more and more of the people's basic food supply to enhance their filthy and unholy habits!" said another, shaking his head in complete disgust.

"The practice of our faith according to Adonai is growing more and more difficult. They are using their ill-gotten gains from the rural labourers to finance the Temple to their gods that are so offensive to us," said Joachim.

"And Herod is the worst! He struts among the Roman authorities seeking favours. He is hungry for power, wealth, and position. He does not care for his people; instead, he sides with the enemy. He is weak, corrupt, and wicked. And he is not even a real Jew!" added another.

"Our people are in misery, and they take advantage of our King's lack of support. The Romans are growing bolder and bolder in their abuses of our people. If ever we needed a Messiah, it would be now!" averred Stolanus.

The moon rose high in the sky when all the joyful and wobbly guests finally went home or to bed to sleep and face the new day on the morrow.

Joachim and Anna had decided that it was probably best for them to remain in Bethlehem until Nissan so that they could attend the Passover in Jerusalem. Anna was not sure that she would be able to make the trip back the following year with a young baby. They would enjoy their family and Joachim would work on his trade markets while Anna and her female relatives worked the loom and the fabrications of cloth and clothes for the expected little Mary.

At the same time, they made another important family decision. Anna's older sister, Maraha, was facing a family difficulty and hardship. Maraha's daughter, Cocharia, herself now an ailing widow, was struggling with the upbringing of her child. The extended family she was living with was bursting at the seams, whereas the six-year-old might be of great help to Anna, a first-time expecting mother. As a result, Joachim and Anna made the decision to adopt Cocharia's young daughter. They certainly had the means and space to accommodate this child. Unfortunately, her name was Mary. This would cause a problem when Anna gave birth to her own daughter, who was directed to be called Mary by the angel. To distinguish the two 'daughters', both Anna and Joachim agreed that they would call their adoptive daughter, Mary Salome. She was a sweet girl, and she would have a comfortable childhood with the older couple and would be great company and help to Anna in the absence of Joachim during her pregnancy. All in all, this would accommodate everybody beautifully.

After the Passover was over, the newly formed family said goodbye to Anna's parents and the other relatives and neighbours and set out on their way back to Cana. Thankfully, they did not run into Assault, the plucky little goat, en route.

Chapter 7
Birth of Mary

"Mary, Mary Salome, come here!" called Anna. "I think that my time has come!"

"I am here, Auntie. How do you know it is your time? What can I do? "

"I have just felt a gush of water and the pain has come soon after. Send Judith up to my room and please run for the midwife. Judith will begin the preparations for the birth."

"It will be done, Auntie, and I will say a little prayer for your well-being and for the safe arrival of the infant."

"Oh, see if you can find Daniel in the stock yard and ask him to send a message to Joachim. Daniel will know where to find him."

"As you wish, Auntie. May you have an easy delivery." Mary Salome donned her cloak and hood. "Mizpah, Auntie. May the Lord watch between me and thee while we are absent one from the other. Now I'm off."

Anna took advantage of the fact that she was alone and said a quiet prayer for the safe delivery of this baby. She knew that the girl-baby would be well, but there had been no prophecy about it being easy or of her own survival. She was glad that the time had come because she was as big as a house and moving about was getting more and more difficult as she could no longer bend easily or even see her feet. She often had to laugh at knocking things off shelves and tables simply by turning around. She frequently had to use the chamber pot and it was getting harder and harder to manage the task. She was glad that her trials would soon be over. She was fully aware that the travail would be long, and it would be long because she was not a young woman, and her pelvic bones would not be so supple or forgiving of the struggle. Nevertheless, this is how babies had been introduced into the world for ages and she just needed to brace herself and face the pain and the exhaustion.

Judith arrived clucking like a mother hen. This was not the first birth she had attended, and Anna had often sent her to her neighbour's birthing to do the leg work of heating water and finding linens for both mother and newborn.

"This is not going to be an easy 'un, my lady, as you are older than most by much."

"No need to remind me, Judith."

"Well, you're not the first and won't be the last, I'm thinkin'," replied the occupied servant. "Thank the Lord, it is the fall season and the weather is cooler, and even if it's rainin', it's not too hot. You'll be sweating enough with your effort, to be sure."

The rain had stopped and so had the time, as Anna endured her contractions.

"Where is the midwife? Where is Joachim?" yelled Anna.

"My lady, the midwife is on her way. You must be patient, for it hasn't been that long since Mary Salome left. Give the poor girl time to get to her and for them both to return. The midwife is not young herself, as you well know."

As the forthright Judith continued her work getting the room ready for the birth, she added, "Mam, you don't want the likes of a man anywhere near the birthin'. They don't have the stomach for it. I have seen them hit the floor with a thud just for hearing the sounds coming out of the birthin' room.

Useless, they are! Master Joachim can wait outside with the goats and the donkeys."

In the end, the birth occurred minutes after the midwife arrived. It was an easy delivery and Anna did not experience a prolonged labour, and little Mary was born in a sunbeam as a shaft of sunlight brightened the room. Joachim had burst into the room to see his offspring. He heard the baby cry when he had been at the washstand cleaning his body for the introduction to his new daughter. He had no doubts that she would be beautiful. Why would she not be? She was the fruit of his beautiful wife. She was a gift from the Creator. She was announced by an angel; what else could he expect but perfection? She was a miracle! He took the stairs two at a time and his heart was bursting with joy when he laid eyes on the vision before him. Anna was cradling Mary in her arms, beaming with pride, and Mary was wide awake, staring at her mother with wonder and delight. The ever-present beam of sunlight shone on them both and dust particles and motes danced in the light, animating the scene. Joachim knew that the angel Gabriel was there. He couldn't see him, but he felt his presence.

"Come meet your daughter, Joachim. She is a beauty and perfect in every way."

"Praise the Lord, my soul! Welcome, little one," said Joachim as he beamed with pride and joy.

Chapter 8
Young Mary

"Come to Abba, Mary," called Joachim to his 10-month-old toddler.

"Look, look, she has taken a step, and another and another. She is walking, Jo!" exclaimed Anna.

Mary called out "Abba" as she wobbled unsteadily on her bare feet. She reached her father's arms and made a delightful noise of joy at reaching her abba and wrapping her arms around his neck. He picked her up and hugged her, laughing and tossing her in the air. "What a clever girl you are!" he extolled.

"She is a clever girl," repeated Mary Salome. She has astounded all the village, who thought that she would be simple-minded as she is the fruit of late-life pregnancy. You should have heard them in the market.

"You know that Anna was well past her prime when she had this baby," one of the village gossips said.

"Naomi had one late in life and she is not normal. But you would never know it by the way her parents love her," said another.

"Joachim was no spring chicken either," commented her husband who was selling his fish.

"I heard Mary had an easy birth, slept through the night after one month and has the most knowing eyes," said the first. "And such a beauty!"

"Oy vey! How did that happen with Joachim as the father?" retorted the fishmonger.

Mary Salome shrugged and summarized. "It goes on and on like this. They pay me no notice and do not bother to check their gossip. Most of the time, it is just talk, but sometimes it can be vicious. I know who to stay clear of at the well and at the synagogue."

"Well, we have been blessed with little Mary's sweetness. What does the psalm say? 'Take delight in the Lord, and he will give you the desires of your heart.'[9]"

As the months went by, Anna continued to be amazed. Little Mary was growing beautifully. Now two and half years old, she was bright and picked things up quickly. She had walked early and talked early. Anna knew her daughter was special because the angel had told her so; however, it was remarkable how much she really was exceptional. Anna taught Mary how to pray. Anna was astonished at how bright and what a quick learner the child was. Her eyes would light up as she sat on her mother's knee and gave her full attention to the words that were spoken to her.

Early on, Mary was perceptive to the feelings of others and showed great presence of mind in social situations. Moreover, she seemed to be uniquely aware of God. She learned her prayers and spent much time in prayers. Anna had little experience with small children, but she had not seen or heard of a child who was so keen to learn things. Mary was very active in exploring her world. She loved to play hand and finger games, skip, and dance. She enjoyed helping her mother while she worked at baking bread or spinning and weaving cloth. She was showing an early aptitude for the fiber-twisting spindle. Mary seemed to love the outdoors. She stopped to look at plants, she gently touched flowers, and she pointed gleefully at birds in the air. Working in the garden and in nature was Mary's favourite activity because she always felt the presence of God and angels there.

---

[9] Psalm: 37-4

One day, unbeknownst to little Mary, she found the nest of little sparrows that had inspired her mother's appeals to the Lord on that fateful day when the angel had appeared. When Anna saw that, she lifted her eyes and once again made a quick prayer of gratitude to her Creator Father in heaven.

"Judith says that she has never seen a child who is so lovely. She says that something in her face feels like she is surrounded by angels. I know what she means. I want to be with her and hold her all the time," said Mary Salome.

"My mother says that she is full of grace," added Anna.

"Well, Mary is beautiful and thoughtful, like my Anna, her 'Imma'. I love them both because they are loving, and so endearingly close to my heart. Now, I must hurry to the pastures. I must deal with all the lambs, and their parents need shearing," explained Joachim. He then made a great show of preparing for his departure by dressing in an exaggerated manner, putting his kettiyeh scarf over his head and tying it fast with his woven leather thongs. He made Anna laugh and blow him a kiss.

"Bring back the fleeces, so we can begin our weaving again," reminded Anna. "And please bring them back washed; I don't want those stinking cling-on bits of dung all over the place when I start to work on them. And Kashmir fleece, please," called Anna out the door.

Anna turned to Mary. "Yalla, yalla, let's go, little lady! How sweet and dear you are. No wonder you are the apple of your father's eye. And you are my miracle. Let's get you changed and say your prayers."

Anna and Mary Salome each took one of Mary's hands and walked her tenderly to her room. Anna had insisted that they set aside a room that was just for Mary. This was also a room of prayer and devotion to Elohim. In the quiet of this sanctuary, Anna sat on a carpet with Mary and told stories from the Torah—stories of Adam and Eve, Abraham, and Moses. Mary

Salome would often join in and add a serving of youthful enthusiasm to the lessons.

"Jo, Mary is almost three years old now. We promised her to the Lord." She knew the consequences of what was to happen.

"I know, my dear. I dread the day. I will really miss this little girl. She is the beat of my heart. I didn't know that I could love a child so much. My heart bursts every time she puts her little arms around my neck and plants a kiss on my cheek."

"Truly, I say to you, she is the most endearing child I have ever met. She continues to learn at an astonishing rate. She is bright, sweet, and kind. She is so obedient! She has never caused me a moment of grief or concern in these past three years."

"Her soul is pure, and she does radiate goodness. The angels protect her, and she is, as Gabriel said, 'very special for all the nations'. Still, I know it will be a huge sacrifice to let her go, since we have waited so long to become parents and now, we are passing her on to others to raise. I hurt deeply. But a promise is a promise."

"We will offer her, but we are not sure that the Temple will accept her as only a few girls are selected to be Daughters of Israel in the Temple."

"I have every confidence because of how dutiful and intelligent she is. She radiates purity and holiness. She surely is a sacred gift from the Lord!"

Anna opened the door and called out to the courtyard. "Mary, come in and help me set the table for supper." Outside, Mary patted the little goat she was playing with, washed her hands at the washing stand, and skipped to the house to do as she was told with a light and happy heart.

Chapter 9
Honouring the Oath

"She's so little," cried Anna.

"She is very smart. You must be strong," responded Joachim.

"She cannot look after herself; she is just a child. She has only seen three spring seasons," continued Anna in complete anguish.

"The holy women will look after her. That's their job, Anna. And most of them are your friends. Come, chin up. We have made this promise before the Lord. We need to honour our oath to present her to the Temple."

"Ohhhhh, I'm not ready. I have not been a mother for very long. I need her near me, Jo!" she whimpered.

Joachim turned his beloved wife to face him, and he gently held her. He backed up a little and continued to caress her by rubbing his hand down her arms in a consoling fashion. Anna placed her head on his shoulder to grieve the anticipated loss of her flesh and blood.

"She may not be chosen. You know that she needs to be commissioned by the council. It is not ours to determine," comforted her husband.

"She will, Jo. You see what I see. We have a special child, a sacred child," bemoaned Anna.

"We will do the will of the Almighty. If He wants to have her consecrated to the Temple, He, who hung the sun and the stars, will make it happen."

"I don't want Him to, Jo. Am I wrong to feel that?" A tear rolled off her cheek and Anna swiped it off with her sleeve.

"I will miss her also, Anna. I, too, have been too recently a father. I just love her little face and her smile lightens my heart and brightens my day. I will miss the sweet smell of her, her petting my face, her tender eyelash kisses. I will even miss the whisps of curly hair that fly in my face when I hold her close."

"Come on, Jo. We must both be strong and remember that we knew that this was coming. We made a vow to Adonai. If he gave her to us, we would give her back."

"You are right, Anna. Now it is I who is blubbering. I can't help but see the visions of her. She is so good with the animals. They all come toward her in the barnyard. They make their happy noises to greet her and gently sniff her hand. They won't leave until she does. I declare that even the flowers in the field turn their faces to meet her and seemed to perk up when she holds them. I love that little angel and do not want her to leave us—ever!"

The couple squeezed each other again and then set down the garden path back to their house.

"Let us keep her for the summer, Jo. Let us take her later in the year when the season is saddened by the rains and the gloom."

"I agree. Let us plan a big party and invite the Temple priests and your Daughters of Israel friends, Cael, Abegia, Rebecca, Sephora, Suzannah, and other Temple sisters."

"We will make our case for her consecration then. Until then, I hope to enjoy every minute of our dear and beloved daughter."

"Hmm," they both sighed simultaneously. At that moment, Mary came running with her arms out to greet her parents and hugged them around the knees and thighs.

God bless this little girl, they each thought.

Rays of sunshine beamed into the early morning room. Dust motes danced in the streams of light and hinted at an invisible presence that populated the room in watchfulness. Mary was awakened from her sleep by a symphony of bird song outside the open window. She rubbed her eyes and stretched her arms above her head and then spread them out to the sides as if to embrace not only the day, but the great, almighty power that was her Creator. She felt a nurturing care and guardianship deep within her and her soul leapt for joy and energy as she looked out the window and met the new day full of wonder and mystery.

The Lord's presence overwhelmed her being. The world would blur around her, and she would see only an empty space filled with something that she thought was grace. She could almost touch the spirit that overpowered her senses and brought her to a place inside of a different consciousness. She could not yet put the feeling into words, but the sacred space in her heart and mind were filled with wisdom, serenity, and joyful peace. This feeling followed her all day but was felt most intensely during prayer.

She heard footsteps and a noise at the door, and her mother entered the room.

"Shalom, my little Mary. Shall we pray together?"

"Of course, mother. I would also love to sing a psalm. And I would love to hear about Abraham and Sarah."

"Mary, you know that story by heart," replied her mother with a chuckle.

"I know, but I understand something more every time I hear it. It's a marvelous story and I love it!"

Mother and daughter spent time in Mary's special bedroom singing praises and gratitude to God and then went out to break their fast with milk, bread, cheese, and pomegranate seeds. Mary Salome was already there enjoying her morning meal and her eyes sparkled with excitement at seeing Mary and her aunt, Anna. She wished them a good morning and was absolutely sure that Mary would be accepted at the Temple and that Anna and Joachim were not going to be the only ones to miss her.

"The whole village will miss you, Mary! "You know that your father is preparing a big feast for you. It is to see if they will take you to the Temple to be one of the special little girls that study and work there," explained Anna.

"Oh, she is a sure thing, Auntie. Everyone can see that!"

"Yes, Mother. I want to go, but I will miss you so much." Mary skipped away to play with her spindle on the other side of the room.

"I will miss her terribly," cried Anna to Mary Salome. "The selfish part of me would like to keep her here by my hearth and heart forever, but I promised that we would do this because I believe that this is where her destiny leads. Woe is me."

At that moment, Joachim came in from the barnyard and pretended to trip on the door threshold before greeting his family. He made them laugh as he always did, their dear Jo. Judith rushed into place a plate of food before him.

"How are my lovely ladies today?" he asked.

"We are full of excitement for the party!" exclaimed Anna.

"Good, because I have invited many important people. Besides your relatives and the rest of our family, there will be the local rabbis, scribes from the synagogues in Nazareth, Sepphoris, Tiberias and Capernaum. I have invited family friends from Magdala, and Simon and Naomi from Bethany. I have requested the presence of the Temple priests and the High Priest. You will be pleased, Anna, that your sisters of the Temple, Susannah, Naomi, Joanna, and Maya are also coming to celebrate with us."

"I know those holy women and I feel so much better knowing that my precious daughter will be in their care and tutelage," Anna replied.

"Have you arranged the food and music, Anna?" Anna nodded.

"Mary Salome, how are the decorations coming?" asked Anna.

"They are going well. I will hang everything with the help of Judith and Daniel on the morning of the festivity. I will drape the grape vines, the veil swags around the roof standards. The bouquets of wild summer flowers freshly picked from the hillsides will adorn the stone fence and several lanterns are ready for the evening fun."

"Have you placed a special chair for the High Priest?" asked Joachim.

"Yes, and Daniel is building the dais for the chair with a large canopy to shade the honourable priest, a platform for the musicians and several large trestle tables under the awning for the food and banquet," reported Mary Salome.

"I have been working on a magnificent table cover. I hope that it will be long enough. It has taken me many hours to embroider the edges with white lilies. The white on white is so exquisite, so pure," added the lady of the house.

"You were always so skillful with any form of cloth and needlework, my Dove," complimented Joachim.

"I think that this may be my best work, my Love."

"I will be so proud of you all. May the Lord forgive my exuberance and lack of humility on this occasion," Joachim said with hands together and looking up to heaven. "Now I will go check on the wine, milk, and cheese in the cool room." He headed downstairs to the cellar.

Chapter 10
Celebrating Mary

The guests started to arrive at various times in different sizes of groups. Some came from the nearby villages and others came all the way from Jerusalem and Hebron. It was good that they did not come all at once because the servants were having a hard time keeping up with the fresh water and towels as it was.

It was customary that visitors washed the dust off before entering a home. All of them refreshed themselves at the washing stand. Many of the invited guests were gathered in small bunches and conversing, laughing, and enjoying the glorious day. A big fuss was made when the holy contingent arrived from Jerusalem. The milling crowds split to make a passage for the High Priest and his Temple entourage, like the Red Sea for Moses. The convoy of Temple officials had taken several days to arrive in Cana because they had lodged at the various synagogues on route. It helped them to keep in touch with the Hebrews who resided outside the busy metropolis of Jerusalem.

"Peace to this house, Joachim," greeted the priest in a loud voice designed to make the people listen. The High Priest was not wearing the full trappings of his high official status, but he was nonetheless very majestic in his large, flat-topped turban and tallit prayer shawl bearing four long tassels called tzitzit—a very imposing and colourful man, indeed.

"Shalom, Rabbi. You do us great honour and we welcome you to our banquet," answered Joachim, bending his head humbly. Joachim welcomed the other honourable guests and proceeded to introduce them to other invitees. Once the formalities were out of the way, the libations were distributed, and the musicians began to play. The happy conversations, the banter and the friendly encounters were mingled with the sounds of flute, lute, lyre, and tambourines.

About an hour after the party had begun, Anna arrived. The music stopped. She climbed to the rooftop celebration to join the others. She was resplendent in her red and green embroidered tunic and veil. Even her humble demeanor could not disguise the elegance and the beauty of the woman. Her face shone with welcoming joy. At the end of her arm, trailing behind a bit, was a little girl. Her mother pulled her forward gently and placed her in front of her and rested her two hands on the child's shoulders.

"This is Mary," she announced when all the guests had turned around to see what had caused the mysterious silence. Joachim, beaming with a smile of unbridled pride, stepped forward and spoke.

"Mary is here to determine if she can be a 'Daughter of the Hebrews'. We have invited the Temple authorities for this trial of worthiness. We hope that our pious, pure, and devoted daughter will be accepted as a Temple virgin. Her mother and I offer her willingly to our Lord." Anna moved aside and Joachim moved closer and placed his hand on the shoulder that had been vacated by her mother's.

All eyes sought the little child in the happy, hopeful hold of her parents. And what a vision they witnessed!

Mary was taller than most three-and-a-half-year-olds. She held herself demurely and displayed a beautiful head of brown, bronze-streaked hair that flowed in gentle curls to her shoulders. She had hazel eyes that shaded to green depending on the angle of the light. They sparkled and danced as she sheepishly faced the crowd of spectators. She had a heart-shaped face with blossom lips. When she smiled her greeting, her smile lit her face and two dimples appeared in her rosy cheeks. This girl had been gifted with undeniable beauty. She was wearing an ankle-length, white silk gown. Anna had embroidered the hem and collar edges with white lilies. The cloth for this gown had been purchased by Joachim when a caravan hailing from the east had come by. The fabric had cost a fortune, but its fine, flowing, and graceful texture had been worth every denarius. Mary, with her hands folded in front of her, showed an elegance and poise that was natural and plainly visible.

Although Mary displayed a glorious carriage, what was most noticeable, by inexplicable vision beyond understanding—sensed more than seen—was the aura that encircled her entire person. It was bright and moved through many pastel colours, and there seemed to be some unexplainable energy and sparkle in the air that surrounded her. Even the High Priest was amazed at the countenance of this young girl. He had never seen anything like it. She seemed full of grace.

The High Priest, followed by the other Temple authorities, moved toward the dais and sat down. The other priests, scribes and Temple women surrounded him.

"Come, my little one. Let me have a closer look at you. Be not afraid," spoke the priest quietly.

Mary approached the chair under the canopy and kept her head bowed but held her shoulders high. Everyone gathered around and formed a semi-circle of support and anticipation around their darling candidate.

"Hmm, Hmm. Let us begin, shall we? What do you know of our Lord, Adonai?" inquired Rabbi Simon.

"I know that He created the world and all the animals and things that are in it, but He loves us best of all," answered Mary in a confident voice.

"And what does He want of us in exchange, my dear girl?" continued Simon.

"He wants us to love Him back with all our hearts. To love only Him and have no other Gods. He said to our great prophet Jeremiah: 'Obey my voice, and I will be your God, and you shall be my people, and walk in all the way that I command you, and it may be well with you.'"[10]

"Well done, young lady. There are boys much older than you who would not have that understanding," applauded the High Priest rabbi. "What story is your favourite in the Torah?" he asked.

"I like many stories of the Torah, Rabbi. I like the one about Adam and Eve."

"Go on."

"Well, when Adam and Eve had disobeyed the Lord, He sent them out of the garden as punishment, but then He made them a promise to send them a Saviour," she explained.

"How would that happen?" asked the Rabbi.

"Adonai would send them a Saviour to bring the people back to His good graces."

"That is very perceptive of you. I can tell that your mother has taught you well. While most students would quote directly from the Scriptures and not know what they are really saying, you have a simple wisdom in your understanding. I am impressed. What is your favourite part of the Book of Prophets?" he asked.

Mary hesitated for a moment as her brain scanned through the many stories in the writings. "Today, I will say that it is the story about how Daniel faced the lions. He refused to dishonour his God by breaking His commands, so he faced hungry lions instead," replied Mary.

"Why is that important, Mary?"

"Daniel was not afraid. The lions were hungry and ferocious. He should have been fainting with fear, but he put his faith in the Almighty and the lions did not harm him."

"And what does that tell you?" asked Simon.

"That we don't need to be afraid. If we do the Father's will, He will take care of us. We need to trust in His love and His might."

"What do you want, Mary?"

"I want to love and serve him and serve with all my heart and to be with Him always in prayer and obedience."

"Would you do His will even if it was not easy?"

"Yes, I hope so, Rabbi."

"You are a very pretty girl, Mary," noted the High Priest. "Would you not want to get married and have children?"

"If that is the will of Adonai, it is what I will do," answered Mary confidently.

"Can you sing, Mary?"

"Yes, if it please you."

"Let us hear a hymn from the 'sefer t'hillim'—a psalm then. Lyre, can you accompany her?" The musician nodded.

"What psalm would you like to sing?"

"I would like to sing from Psalm 91 if it please you, Rabbi." The Rabbi nodded to the orchestra and the lyre player strummed his chords and Mary began to sing with a voice that was so sweet; everyone there placed their hand on their heart, and many were brought to tears.

She sang:

For he will give his angels charge of you

To guard you in all your ways.

On their hands, they will bear you up,

Lest you dash your foot against a stone.

You will tread on the lion and the adder,

The young lion and the serpent you will trample underfoot.

Because he clings to me in love,

I will deliver him;

I will protect him, because he knows my name.

When he calls to me, I will answer him;

I will be with him in trouble,

I will rescue him and honor him.

With long life I will satisfy him,

And show him my salvation.[11]

"Oh my, you have a good memory for long songs. That was beautiful." The High Priest dried the tears from his face. He looked up to find many people stirring in their efforts to suppress their tears.

At that moment, a heavy black cloud covered the dwelling and cast a foreboding shadow on the party. A wicked wind picked up fiercely and people ran for cover as trees bent and awnings flapped, and clothing clung to their legs. The crowd cringed in fright and made a collective intake of breath.

"It is the shadow of the Evil One," called one person.

"He wants to hurt that dear child and keep her for himself," called another.

---

[11] Psalm 91

Mary looked up towards heaven, pressed her hands together in prayer, touched her fingertips to her forehead and raised her arms skyward and began to sway gently. She moved like honey, and she danced with poetic motion. The musicians picked up on the rhythm and the bewildered guests watched the three-year-old dance to the melody in rhapsody. Her little silk dress twirled and flowed with her graceful and lyrical movements. There seemed to be a positive current about her that flowed with her. Leaves and petals of end-of-summer blossoms eddied around her like an aura of colour and light. Heartened by the beauty and peace that the dance emanated, the crowd started to sway as well, and they joined the tempo and the cloud lightened and sunbeams returned, radiating on Mary and the group of guests. The gale lost its fury and was tamed to a whimpering breeze. The whirl of leaves and petals settled down at Mary's feet and her dance came to a silky end. The storm had passed. Nobody mentioned it, but they knew that there had been power in that event. They did not know what had happened, but something great and mighty had occurred, and they were in awe. It had become clear to them that Mary was not an ordinary child. She was blessed. God favoured her and the Devil hated her. Oh, what Lucifer would do to bring her over to the dark side.

The Temple authorities had witnessed this entire event and were immediately convinced that Mary would make a wonderful, special addition to the holy consecrated acolytes of the Court of Temple Women. The High Priest, Simon, approached Mary's parents and they started to make arrangements for Mary to join the school of consecrated virgins. The scrutiny was over, and the decision was made. Mary was chosen.

Seeing the transaction being concluded, the people, full of joy and mirth, came back to the moment and once again began to laugh, talk, and joke. They organized dances where the women danced together and then the men, in turn, danced ecstatically. They finished the night with a banquet resplendent with rich food and copious drink. The table was lavishly arrayed with all the fresh fruits of the season: melons, pomegranates, apricots and oranges, along with fresh meat and plenty of bread to soak up the sauces of the many special dishes prepared by the people of the village. Joachim and Anna had done well, and the Lord had indeed blessed them.

After the sun went down and the day was late, Mary went to bed to a peaceful sleep. Before she got under the covers of her cot, she fell to her knees and gave thanks for a beautiful party and a successful outcome. Her mother hugged and kissed her goodnight. Anna rejoined her husband on the stairs heading to the rooftop activities.

"Alleluia! We were successful, Anna. Mary will leave for the Temple in the autumn, during Kislev," exclaimed Joachim.

"Truly we were successful, you Old Goat," responded Anna as her eyes filled with tears. "You realize what this means to our life now?"

"I was putting off that thought, Anna."

"Today I am happy, but tomorrow I will be miserable."

"Let us make the most of the time that we have left during the month of Tishri. Mary doesn't leave until near winter. We will be able to celebrate the Festival of Trumpets, Atonement and Tabernacles with her. We will visit friends along our journey and call upon your elderly parents. We will dance praises to our Lord in thanksgiving for the harvest and for our precious daughter."

"What are we waiting for, you big oaf? Let us dance now!" demanded Anna. Joachim grabbed his beloved. He brought her close to his chest, twirled her until they had joined the exuberant revelers, and danced late into the night.

Chapter 11
The Journey

Mary's home was abuzz with preparation activities. The servants were getting ready the food, water gourds and skins and travel clothes. Anna, Mary Salome, and Judith were putting the final touches on Mary's dowry. They had been working on this endeavour for a while because Anna had always known that Mary was destined to be a Temple Virgin. Nevertheless, there were a few new things that needed to be placed into several chests bound for Jerusalem. Mary's dowry would consist of the animals that Joachim and Daniel were rounding up, as well as the many bundles of fabrics that the women were compiling. Some of the material was homespun wool and linen yard goods that Anna and a group of women from the synagogue had spun and woven using the fleeces from Joachim's animals. All of Cana had been engaged in the preparations. Almost all of the local shops and businesses had been patronized in some way or other by the family. Food had been purchased, crates had been ordered, threads had been dyed, washed, and carded. Joachim had paid people handsomely for their efforts and they were grateful. They were all proud that one of their children had been accepted to the Temple. They were all aware of the privilege and honour it was to have a daughter of Galilee favourably received to the Holy Place. They also recognized what a sacrifice Anna and Joachim were making by letting go of their long-awaited, only begotten child. It was quite a tribute, but it was quite a sacrifice, too. How her parents would miss her; how they would all miss her!

It had been a village-wide effort to prepare the beautiful, finely woven textiles. Some were made from the Kashmere and mohair; others were made with the threads of the cocoon fibres of the silkworm from the east, acquired in trade for the local tougher and warmer yarns. The glamorous filaments of silk produced a beautiful, glossy, and smooth fabric fit for royalty. The weaver really needed to know what they were doing when dealing with these more exotic threads. Anna had learned her trade well.

While the women had been working hard at preparing the dowry and the travel fare, the boys had been collecting doves and placing them in cages for transport. There would be a convoy of donkeys loaded with their burdens of goods for the Temple. Herdsmen had already left Nazareth for the long trek because the going would be slower and more cumbersome with the numerous bleating and nervous woolly charges. Joachim had sent a large contingent of men to help protect and deliver the gifted animals to their destination in Jerusalem. The family itself would take a shorter route.

Accompanied by her parents, Mary had been busy in previous days saying goodbye to her friends and other village folk. She visited her favourite cats, dogs and donkeys in the community and gently petted them and bade her farewells. The town talk reported mixed feelings about her placement in the Temple. The whole upsetting situation was lessened somewhat by the fact that Mary was so willing to go. She was excited about it. She skipped and pranced along the streets as she greeted everyone with eagerness and verve. The villagers were both proud and pleased and sorry and sad about her departure. But not all. Two couples were discussing the imminent departure in front of the baker's stall.

"How her parents will miss her," said Deborah.

"Anna was sniffling about it when I last saw her. I don't blame her. I would be inconsolable if I had to let my little Ruth go," admitted Abigail.

"I wonder if we will ever see that child again," complained Samuel.

"Makes one wonder why she is so anxious to leave us. Were Anna and Joachim not treating that little girl well?"

"Don't be ridiculous, Deborah. That cherub is the happiest of children. You must agree that she is the darling of her family and of this village," responded Moshe.

"I have to admit that little girl is special, indeed. She has a spirit and an energy that exude goodness and kindness. I have never seen her do anything naughty. She is obedient, meek, polite, and so caring of others," reported Abigail.

"I think she's too good to be true. Nobody is as sweet as that! I bet she's a little demon in private. And that Anna. She sure puts on airs!" retorted Deborah maliciously.

"That's harsh and unkind, Deborah," rebuked her husband.

"I'm not the only one saying it. I have heard it all over the town. Mary and Anna are no angels!" insisted Deborah.

Moshe quickly changed the subject, "It takes a lot of courage for Joachim to send a three-year-old to the unknown. She is just a baby!

"That experience is not unknown to Anna. She herself attended as a young girl," said Abigail.

"You can say what you want about that clumsy man, but he hasn't got a bad bone in his body. This decision has to have been very difficult to make," commented Samuel.

Abigail concluded the discussion. "Still, it will be hard on her family and on all of us if truth be told. May God continue to bless that girl. Our loss is the Temple's gain, if you ask me."

With all the preparations finally made, Mary, Mary Salome, Anna and Joachim, and an entourage of guards and servants, loaded with tents and other travel cargo, set out for Jerusalem. The way was rough. It was Chesvan, and in the season of rains, the temperature had dropped. The cooler season required warmer clothing, woolen cloaks and mantles and warmer footwear. It was not the best time to travel to Jerusalem, but the couple were happy that they had had the summer to spend their remaining days with their daughter. They had celebrated all the fall feasts, with their family and neighbours. It was worth it, and they would manage the journey well enough. It was slower with a child, but little Mary never complained; often, she wished to walk rather than ride on the donkey. The family would stay overnight in the hospitable homes of friends that Joachim had made along the route over the years.

For the most part, Joachim's party stuck to their country routes, staying away from the King's Highways built by the Romans to serve as trade routes. The network of roads built throughout the Roman Empire was a great engineering achievement of the Romans to facilitate travel to their conquered and occupied territories. They were marked by milestones, and all led back to Rome. The roads were paved with stones and were wide enough to accommodate entire legions and companies of cavalry. The Roman soldiers and slaves had painfully laid down an elaborate highway infrastructure which passed over very rugged, rough, rocky terrain, undergoing several steep grade changes.

The Roman routes were teaming with commercial travellers, including large caravans drawn by oxen, or using camels or donkeys. Hired guards mounted on horses led and supervised the people and the wealth of these desert fleets. The roads were noisy and smelly with herds of animals and cages of fowl heading for market. Foreign tradesmen, their goods-laden carts, both open and canvas-covered, were usually bound for Egypt, and with many stops on route. It was not unusual for one caravan to join another as there was safety in numbers. The merchants and their slaves and servants were often tired and cranky. They were always on the lookout for brigands and political rebels and felt threatened by local bandits and highwaymen. It was risky and treacherous. As a result of their stress and anxiety, they were often unkind and hostile toward the ordinary local voyagers who dared to share the road. As well, the highway was patrolled by Roman legions of soldiers who loved to make mean sport of any humble group making their way to Jerusalem.

On one occasion, when a thunderstorm loomed in the western sky, Joachim's family had decided to spend a night at one of the many inns that served the travellers on the highway. The King's Highway, as well as providing a properly groomed paved road, provided a booming commercial business market by way of inns, blacksmiths, and other providers of food and means of repairing broken equipment. Only the wealthy could afford a stay, so most Galileans would more often opt for the smaller paths and sleep outdoors, in tents, or depend on the hospitality of other Jews. It was during this diversion from their usual rural track that the little family ran into a situation. As they proceeded forward towards their destination, they encountered a patrol of four Roman soldiers on horseback. They were laughing and teasing each other after having over-imbibed in drink the night before. They were spoiling for a fight or at least for some fun at the expense of others.

"Well, what have we got here?" sneered one legionnaire called Antonius.

"Some Jews, I'd say," contributed Aurilius.

"Not my favourite people, Aurilius," Antonius responded as he jumped off his horse.

"These folks seemed to be richer than most, don't you think, Marcus?"

"Maybe they would like to part with some of it," suggested Lucius.

"It might give me an opportunity to practice my gladiator skills," said Antonius as he swung his gladius in large arcs under Joachim's nose.

"And the ladies. Perhaps we could have some fun with these beauties," urged Marcus as he approached and towered over the women who had covered their faces with a cloak and kept their heads low and their eyes down.

Anna, bolder than most women, dared to address the leering soldier.

"Please, dear sirs, we are just a humble party heading for the Temple with our daughter. She is just a child, and I am too old to please you."

"I wasn't referring to the child but that other passenger of yours—the young maiden." He pointed towards Mary Salome. "What you say may be so, but all women are the same where it counts," taunted Lucius.

"Let us pass, brave and honourable soldiers of Rome," urged Joachim, as his protective detail took a defensive stance. "We have nothing to offer but a child's offerings to the Temple."

"Tempting just the same. What do you think, Marcus? Shall we have a go?"

At that moment, their centurion, who had been delayed settling an account, caught up to his men and sized up quickly what had transpired in his absence. He was an astute man, and he knew the behaviours and tendencies of his legionnaires. As he approached the party, he was struck by an aura of light surrounding the group of waylaid journeyers. They were just simple, humble peasant folk on their way to Jerusalem, but there was something unusually singular about this band and his instincts bade him to treat this group with respect and even a touch of reverence.

"What is going on here, boys?" asked the centurion.

"Ah, just a bit of fun, Centurion," Aurilius answered. "We were just having a polite conversation with these nice folks."

"As long as you were not harassing these gentle people. We have no cause to bring them grief. Let us move along.

Sorry for the bother that this halt may have caused you. I bid you a good day and journey." The legionnaire Antonius remounted and the horsemen moved on in the opposite direction, much to the relief of the distressed Galilean family.

Other than this frightening encounter with the Roman soldiers, the passage was rather smooth. They stopped at Anna's parents' house in Bethlehem where they spent several days in teary celebrations to send off their dear Mary and to reunite Mary Salome with her mother and other siblings. Cousins Elizabeth and Zacharius, having travelled from Hebron, were among the group. Elizabeth was still hoping to bear a child. It was important to Hebrew women, but especially to the wife of an aspiring High Priest. The childless couple vacillated between despair and hope, so they prayed.

Later, when all the guests had departed and Joachim and Anna lay spooning on their cot, they talked about the upcoming event and discussed how traumatic it would be for their little family.

"I can't believe that I'm giving up my baby to strangers," cried Anna.

"They're not all strangers, Anna. Many are your friends, and they will look after her well enough. She is very little though, for such a separation from her abba and imma. Poor little mite!" said Joachim in a soothing voice.

"We must not let her see our distress, Jo. It might frighten her and make her refuse to go. Then, where would we be? A mess, I know for sure."

"She wants to go. She says that she is happy to go, but how can we make sure that she doesn't have second thoughts?" asked Joachim.

"Or do we have second thoughts or break out sobbing in the middle of the exchange? I feel that I might lose my self-control and commitment when I see our darling Mary being passed over to the Temple authorities. I can't let that happen," whimpered Anna.

Joachim sighed as he gave it some somber thought. He sat up and said with great enthusiasm, "We can give her a happy parade!"

"What are you talking about, Jo? A parade? Is that dignified enough for the Daughters of the Hebrews?"

"No, no. We can show Mary that we are celebrating her consecration to the Temple. We can change the sadness to festivity—to singing and dancing. The Lord is not opposed to singing 'hallel'[12] psalms. We can make things merry, and we won't think of our sacrifice. What do you think, Anna?"

"Well, it sounds better than sniffles, sobs and snotty noses."

Joachim laughed. Together, they made plans for a joyful voyage to the Temple to disguise their grief and their misery at handing over their beautiful and only daughter.

---

[12] Hebrew word for Praise usually found in Psalms 113 to 118.

Chapter 12
Journey to the Temple

All celebrations and obligations were now fulfilled and the plans for the final stage of the trip to Jerusalem were in place. An even larger party of extended family and neighbours joined the procession to the Temple. They had understood the mood and tone of the march. People had equipped themselves with instruments they could play, like flutes, trumpets and ram's horns, or homemade noise makers like tambourines, cymbals, bells, gourd rattles and hide drums. They carried streamer ribbons on sticks, danced with long veil garlands and grape vines, and waved wheat sheaves and palm branches. Some would say that it resembled David taking the Ark of the Covenant to its new home in Jerusalem.

Joachim had hired a litter to carry his only daughter. The litter was a handsome rig with a silk valance on the top and gold tassels. Mary sat on puffy cushions and was cloaked with a heavily embroidered mantle and hood. Nothing was too good for the princess of the Temple and of their hearts. It was a short distance, but an upward climb to the Temple from Bethlehem. In spite of the exertion, they danced and sang all the way there, striking, blowing, or ringing their instruments. Those who did not have an instrument clapped their hands, snapped their fingers, and made happy noises. It was indeed a merry group that approached the Eastern Gate of the Temple. Crowds of people populating the Court of Prayer split their assemblies to let them through and watch the proceedings. This kind of sight did not happen every day.

The procession stopped and waited while the Temple authorities were called to meet the litter and the group of revellers. Having heard the commotion outside the Nicanor Gate, the priests, who had been forewarned about the incoming pageant, were ready for the ceremony and called on the Daughters of the Hebrews to join them at the top of the stairs. They made an imposing and impressive spectacle of pomp and grandeur with the High Priest, Pharisees, and Sadducees all arrayed in their finest ceremonial vestments. Behind them was a cluster of veiled women dressed in their ceremonial whites.

The High Priest stood at the forefront of the others and waited for silence. Given the great dignity of the authority of his Holy Office, the crowd quieted and stood in awe and reverence for the rare induction. However, this was not new to a regular visitor to the Temple court.

An old woman, a beggar, had entered the Temple as a young woman with no husband or children. Because of her poor and low status, she had not qualified to be a Temple Virgin. Nevertheless, she had devoted herself entirely, body and soul, to the Temple. People said that she was a prophetess. Her name was Anna, daughter of Phanuel of the tribe of Asher.[13] She had been married seven years, but her husband had died, leaving her a penniless widow. Anna was old now, but she had never left the Temple compound and lived on the mercy of others. As a pauper and beggar reliant on alms, she was often cruelly and harshly treated and abused by mean and callous people. She had stopped prophesizing a long time ago because it always resulted in brutal and merciless beatings. Instead, Anna offered up her life to Adonai. She relied solely on the blessings of the Lord and allowed herself to be totally dependent on the goodness of the Almighty. She spent her time in prayer and song. Anna, the prophetess, knew that she was witnessing a special moment in the history of the salvation of the Hebrew people. The Presentation was about to begin.

---

[13] Taken from Luke: 2:36-38

"Shalom, Joachim," the High Priest greeted with open arms, the petitioner before him. It was hard to ignore the Goldplate on the turban and the Breastplate of Judgment worn by the Temple official. The sunlight reflected off the gold, and from the engraved precious stones representing the twelve tribes of Israel prominently displayed on the breastplate.

"Peace be to you," returned Joachim.

"What do you ask of Adonai?"

"To present our daughter to the Temple," replied Joachim.

"What do you ask of the Sanhedrin Council?"

"For our daughter to become a Daughter of the Hebrews," exclaimed Joachim.

"You have asked to have your daughter become a Daughter of the Temple. In doing so, you are accepting that she will be our responsibility to raise her in the practice of the faith. It will be our duty to bring her up to keep the Commandments and the Laws in the tradition of Abraham, Isaac, and Jacob. Do you clearly understand what you are undertaking?"

"I do," responded Joachim.

The High Priest turned to the group of officials behind him and asked, "Are you prepared to welcome this child and take the responsibility for her care and education?"

"We are."

"All who are present here, let us ask the Lord to look lovingly upon this child who is to be received in consecration to the Temple."

At that time, one of the priests came out with a golden censor and waved incense smoke in their direction. It smelled fragrant and sweet as he swung the censor to and fro and proclaimed, "This is our faith that we profess in our Lord's Holy Name."

"What name do you call your child?" asked the High Priest in ritual fashion, as he already knew the child's name.

"Mary."

"Mary, come forward." Mary separated herself from her cortege, descended the steps of the litter and walked forward to stand at the bottom of the steps before the congregation of Temple authorities.

"Mary, daughter of Joachim and Anna of the tribe of Judah, is it your desire to be accepted as a member of this Holy Guild?"

"Yes," answered Mary.

"Do you accept this position willingly?"

"Yes, with all my heart."[14]

"Mary, we accept that you can be ordained in the sisterhood of the Daughters of the Hebrews as a postulant. Let us begin."

"Mary, do you wish to say a farewell to your parents?" asked the High Priest.

"If you will allow me, Rabbi?"

"Joachim and Anna, you may come forward and say your goodbyes."

Joachim came over to their daughter and embraced her. He bent down to her level and Mary wrapped her arms around her father's neck.

---

[14] Inspired by the Baptismal Rite of the Catholic Church

"I love you, Abba." She followed this with a long embrace of her mother.

"I love you, Imma."

The two parents expressed their undying love for their daughter amid hugs, and tears. Joachim and Anna stood up, still holding Mary, as all three embraced as a family. Both mother and father made a heroic effort to hold back their tears, but the witnesses could see both the pride and the sorrow that this sacrifice was costing them.

Mary whispered to them. "All will be well. I want to serve our Lord. Do not be sad. I will miss you and pray for you. I thank you, Abba and Imma. I will miss you."

After a lengthy hesitation, Joachim took Anna's arm and walked back to their place.

The Temple women, bearing lit lanterns, processed down the steps. Anna could see her friends as they approached Mary in two columns. The two rows of women led their new postulant and began to chant the 113th Psalm as they mounted the stairs. With practised and uniform voices, they filled the air with musical prayer.

Praise the Lord!

Praise, O servants of the Lord, Praise the name of the Lord!

Blessed be the name of the Lord

From this time forth and forevermore!

The Lord is high above all nations, and his glory above the heavens!...

They stopped at the top of the stairs and faced the High Priest. While others sang, some women removed Mary's robe and hood. She was wearing her white silk dress with the lilies embroidered on the cloth at the edges of hem, collar, and sleeves. The attending women covered Mary's shoulders with a thick woolen purple cape, heavily embroidered with gold filigree thread which captured the light of the numerous lanterns held by the choir of women. Her mantle danced with the sparkle and energy of the light. Mary stood still and quietly waited with serenity, innocence, and dignity.

The priest received her, and kissed her, and blessed her, saying: "The Lord will manifest His redemption to the sons of Israel." And he set her down upon the third step of the altar, and the Lord God sent grace upon her, and she danced with her feet, and the house of Israel loved her. [15]

A golden cruet was presented to the High Priest. Waiting a moment to give reverence to the ritual, he slowly poured oil, perfumed with Myrrh, on her head and hair. The oil flowed gently down her hair, anointing her into her new role as handmaiden of the Lord. A waiting woman took a linen cloth and wiped the oil from her cheeks and neck. The angels that accompanied Mary swirled and danced around her person. They swirled like a gossamer veil in the scented smoke of the incense. They purified and rose to meet the Almighty in heaven. Nobody saw them, but they could sense that this was no ordinary consecration. At that moment, doves broke out in the sky, and one flew low and cooed his approval of the little virgin being anointed. There was definitely something of the divine present.

"Blessed be the name of our Lord who has created heaven and earth. May the dedication of this child be sweet and acceptable to you. May you bless your handmaiden, Mary, with your grace and favour from this time forth and ever more," proclaimed all the priests in unison.

Four holy ladies, Susannah, Naomi, Joanna, and Maya, processed forward, holding the four corners of a woven

---

[15] Taken from the Protoevangelium of James, Chapter 2

homespun veil and placed the white veil on her head. They placed a miniature Torah scroll in her arms. There was another round of incense and Mary sang the Shema prayer in a pure, childlike voice:

"Hear, O Israel: Adonai is our God, Adonai in One! Blessed is God's name; His glorious kingdom is forever and ever! [16]And you shall love Adonai your God with all your heart, with all your soul, and with all your might. And these words which I command you this day shall be upon your heart; teach them faithfully to your children, speak of them in your home and on your way, when you lie down and when you rise up. Bind them as a sign upon your hand; let them be a symbol before your eyes. Inscribe them on the doorposts of your house and on your gates."

The beauty of her voice brought tears to even the most hardened soul.

All the present Levite officers of the Temple held out their hands towards and over her head and prayed a blessing to her as an undefiled virgin:

"Blessed are You, Adonai, King of the universe, Who has sanctified us with His commandments. Please receive, this our daughter Mary of the family of David, into the realm of our Holy House that she might sing praises to you, serve you and honour You."

After the blessing, two women took Mary by her hands, turned, and faced the door to the inner court. The procession of the High Priest and other priests, followed by Mary and the Temple Women as they entered, singing the rest of the Psalm.

---

[16] Shema Prayer

And all could still hear the lyrics linger as a muffled song behind closed doors.

Anna and Joachim and all who cherished their little girl, felt numb with the emptiness in their hearts that had been filled with Mary's grace. Still, they praised the Lord because they had fulfilled their promise. On the other hand, the heart of Anna, the elderly Prophetess, was elated and filled with grace, thanksgiving, and revelation.

"Now the Ark of the Covenant, the Vessel of the Promise, is entering the Temple," Anna the Prophetess whispered to herself.[17]

---

[17] *The Life of the Blessed Virgin Mary*, From the Visions of Ven. Anne Catherine Emmerich, p. 114

Chapter 13
Growing up in the Temple

Mary was unafraid as she was led into the Court of the Priests. Women were not usually allowed into the inner chambers of the Temple. However, as ritually pure and consecrated members of the liturgical guild, the women were allowed to perform their duties.

The Court of the Priests was where the priests held the sacrificial ceremonies. Here was the bronze altar of burnt offerings for the holocaust, the great bronze laver to provide water and smaller lavers to help with the cleansing. There were eight tables made of marble where the sacrifices were executed. The lofty ceilings towered over a beautifully hewn marble floor. The space smelled of cedar, frankincense, lamp oil and burned offerings. To a child raised in the country the sight of this edifice was overwhelming. It was much larger and grander than the synagogues in Nazareth or Capernaum or Sepphoris. It was enormous, and much richer looking than her abba's house, which was the largest and finest house in Galilee. Her eyes could not take in all that she could see in one view, and they needed to move from side to side, up and down and all around to perceive what was going to be hers to behold during her stay and service in the Temple. As grand as the sacred building was and how massive the outer walls, huge and ornate gates and court plazas were, they were the work of man and not as impressive as the work of the Lord's creation. She compared the Temple structure with the open skies, the trees bearing fruit, the vistas of wheat fields, and the green pastures where the sheep grazed as seen from her Cana home. Where were the birds, and the little creatures that scurried around the garden? She hoped that her new home would still allow her to enjoy the joys of the Lord's artwork.

"What do you think, Mary?" Susannah spoke to her in Hebrew.

"Beautiful, and so big!" responded Mary in the same language.

"So you can speak Hebrew, my dear. Your Imma taught you well and you must be a quick study to learn both Aramaic and Hebrew at your young age," chimed in Naomi.

"I think that she is a bright child, and our work will be easier than with some of our other charges," contributed Joanna.

"Mary, you will be expected to speak Hebrew in the Temple. Do you understand?" added Maya.

"Yes, my Ladies. I understand. I am honoured to speak the language of our Temple and to learn all that you have to teach me."

"What a sweet girl you are, Mary. Truly, I tell you that Anna's loss is our blessing," said Naomi.

The ladies decided that Mary could be introduced to the Sanctuary at a later date. She had had a big day, and she must be very tired. They led her through the Solomon Gate into the residence compound where her regular and routine life would begin.

The formal and lavish garments of the Presentation Ceremony were removed and were replaced by a natural homespun linen floor-length tunic, and a simple cornflower blue robe which was the common habit of the Daughters of the Hebrews. She was allowed to keep her small leather shoes. These would be replaced by leather and hemp sandals in the warm season. Mary would be expected to always cover her head in public but could leave the covering off in the women's private living quarters.

Mary was introduced to her new home. She was toured around the kitchen, the common rooms, and the dormitory rooms. There were workrooms where the tasks of the Temple were conducted: washing rooms, dyeing rooms, spinning and weaving rooms, embroidery and sewing, baking rooms, even rooms for making incense. The Temple required a whole range of industry to function in its activities of finance, school, prayer, and sacrifice. Most importantly, there was a study room where the maidens would become students of Hebrew, Greek, and the Torah and Talmud. There was also training and schooling for young men, albeit in another compound. Mary breathed a sigh of relief when she was taken to the courtyard. There, she would be able to feel freedom from chores and experience nature and the outdoor temple of the Lord, filled with all His beautiful creations. It was truly the work of a genius artist and architect. She knew it in her bones and in her soul. This would be her special place where she could pray on her own and commune with her creator.

Mary was assigned a small cot in a room full of other girls who were in service of the Temple. The girls varied in age from four to fourteen. She was the youngest. The other girls had also been selected but, more often than not, it was seen as a great honour and it was not every girl's desire but sometimes forced upon them by their parents and because their parents could afford the dowry. Not all the girls were sincere in their calling, and many were only putting in time before they would leave to get married. Their position as Daughters of the Hebrews would heighten their status and eligibility to capture a husband of position and means. Thankfully, as Mary was so young, she would work more closely with the older women who would mentor her individually. Not until later would Mary work with the older girls and the more experienced students of the Temple.

The Temple tutors and even the priests treated Mary with special care. The women were treating Mary more particularly because Anna had been their Temple sister and friend, but the men were taken by Mary's particular sweetness, goodness, or something that they could not put their finger on. It was something unique that they could not identify. Perhaps it was grace. Perhaps it was divine favour. They did not know, but they recognized that there was something very special and different about Mary.

And so the work began. At first, the teacher led Mary by the hand. She was shown how to do simple chores like dusting the living quarters. She was allowed to see the baking of the shewbread and the making of the incense. She studied her lessons with one of the senior women and priests. She was given a needle and thread and taught how to embroider. However, the area where Mary seemed to show most aptitude was in the skills of spinning and weaving.

After their charges had been put to bed, the older women gathered in the common room to discuss and fraternize with their Temple sisters.

"How are things going with your students, Maya?"

"They are going very well. As usual, some girls are more gifted than others at the study of languages. Little Mary has taken quite well to her studies. She had a head start, though. Anna had already told her stories from Scripture in Hebrew, and she had exposed her to a rudimentary Greek."

"You can tell that she is like her mother in the skill of weaving and spinning. She already has a fine hand and can turn the raw material into very fine threads. She takes criticism well and she strives for excellence in whatever she attempts," reported Susannah.

"Very precocious indeed! Her knowledge of the Holy books shows a depth of understanding that many of the older girls will never get. And she is very reverent during prayer," said Naomi.

"It is amazing to me when I watch her pray. It is as if she is in another realm. She is oblivious to the noises and silliness of the other girls. There is an aura of piety that I have seldom seen in one so young. She looks like she is in full communion with the Lord. It is quite strange and extraordinary. It's a bit scary sometimes, this depth of her meditative state—almost an ecstatic trance or rapture," offered Esther.

"I wonder what she is destined for?" pondered Joanna out loud. At which point, the others stopped to consider the question.

"I don't know what it will be, but I do know she is destined to be blessed among women. Of that, I am sure." The others nodded in agreement.

Under the attentive care of the Temple sisters, Mary flourished. She excelled at all tasks and showed personal virtues that were without fault. She was obedient, respectful, and appreciative. She was carefully guided and graduated from small tasks to assignments that required more independence and greater responsibility. She was favoured by her teachers, the Pharisees, Sadducees, and the other clerics. While always being reverent and pious, she often imparted her light-heartedness and delight of life on all who were in her presence both inside and outside of the Temple courts.

"Indeed. Her kindness is remarkable—beyond her youth. The other day at the village well, Mary was enjoying an apricot that I gave her for being so helpful at the market," noted Susannah, one of her instructors. "She looked at it and lifted her eyes to heaven and said: 'tawdi Elaha, thank you, Lord.'"

"Just as she was about to put the fruit to her mouth, a little boy came into view. He was very neglected, poor thing. He was unkept, his skin was dust-covered and his hair filthy and his tunic was in tatters and too small for his skinny body. It was obvious that he was an orphan with no one to care for him. He was probably starving. Mary went up to him and gave him her apricot. She spoke to him so gently and then came over and asked her companion for bread to give to him. She is as generous as her Abba and Imma," said Susannah.

Mary found favour with the council of the priests. Because she was pure, without guile and so willing to help and obey, their treatment of her was quite benevolent. Once a week, the shewbread in the Sanctuary had to be eaten and new bread brought to replace the old. The priests would call on Mary to help them with the ritual. This was an extremely unusual precedent. No other girl or woman had ever been asked to do a task that was the exclusive privilege of the high-ranking priests. It was even thought that they had been influenced by the angels that seemed to surround this child. 'And Mary was in the Temple of the Lord as if she were a dove that dwelt there, and she received food from the hand of an angel.'[18]

Mary, having eaten the bread of the angels, took her share of the meals prepared for the citizens of the Temple and shared them with the beggars that hung around the Temple. She was especially reverent to Anna, the elderly prophetess. She would take a moment, at various quiet times of the day, to find her, bring her food and other necessities, and talk to her. She learned much from Anna and felt an empathy and closeness to this wise old soul. They prayed together and shared their love of Scripture together. Anna was an uncelebrated mentor to little Mary, and they were both connected by the Holy Spirit.

Meanwhile, Lucifer fumed at the young chosen female who would be made to make humans better than angels. He wanted her badly. Oh, how he wanted her. If he could get her to turn to his side, it would be his great revenge against the Almighty.

---

[18] Protoevangelium of James, Chapter 8

He bided his time until he found a moment to impact her into sin. It happened in the market when Mary got separated from her chaperone. She got caught by a vendor in a kiosk who bade her to steal a desired item from another vendor.

"Hey, little girl, go get that weight from the booth across, but two over. He promised to give it to me, and he must have forgotten."

"Why don't you ask him again? I'm sure he will oblige you," replied Mary.

"No, no, I can't leave my property, and neither can he. Just go over there and take what I asked. He won't miss it; you can be sure. I will give you a string of pearls. The best there is in the market," as he presented her with a necklace made of polished shells.

At this point, Mary, who had little interest in trinkets, came to believe that she was being set up. She lifted her eyes to heaven and asked for guidance.

"I'm afraid that I will not be able to do that for you. This is an agreement between you and the other dealer. You must complete the deal in person and not by sending a child. I'm sorry, sir, but..." At that moment, Mary was interrupted by Susannah who had finally found her.

"Mary, there you are. I'm so sorry, I lost you. What a fright I had. Were you afraid?"

"No, Mam, I was just having a conversation with this gentleman."

"Well, come along. We have much to do before it gets too hot."

On another occasion, Mary was at prayer by herself in her room. She had just got on her knees and as she entered her meditation, she was distracted by a scurry in the room. It was a scorpion. It was heading toward her, but she managed to scramble away.

"Go away, scorpion. I do not wish to harm you. I wish to pray, so just go away."

But the scorpion was determined to attack her. Mary got up from her knees and stood. She was tempted to stomp on the creature, but her sweet disposition had difficulty with the idea. She took off her veil and dropped it on the pest and it stopped its progression. She reached for a pair of brazier tongs, removed the veil, and gently captured the scorpion in the mid-section between the pincers and carried it outside, away from the compound.

"Run along, little creature and do not interrupt my prayers again." She returned to her room, assumed the prayerful position and engaged in deep and fulfilling communion with her Creator.

The devil was at work again when, on another occasion, Mary had made a mistake in her weaving and the pattern was all distorted. She felt bad because she had spent a lot of time on this piece.

"Just tell Mother Mariah that somebody must have messed with your work. You don't need to take responsibility for this error. Just blame somebody else," said a tempting voice. "Lie, Mary and you won't get into trouble. You have ruined the cloth. Just lie a little lie. No one will be hurt, and no one will ever know."

"No, that would be wrong. I will tell Mother Mariah the truth and accept the consequences."

Upon seeing her work, Mariah asked what had happened. Mary admitted to having been distracted and created the problem. She apologized and claimed to be ready to accept her punishment.

"Oh, Mary, it was a mistake, and mistakes happen. The question is: have you learned from your mistake?"

"Yes, Mam, I will pay attention to the warp and make sure the colour is right."

"Good, now the punishment is that you will unravel the cloth until before the mistake and start again. It is a small setback, that is all. Thank you for taking responsibility for your mistake."

At the age of ten, Mary was released from the constant vigilance and tutelage of the older women and was left on her own to fulfill the duties that had been assigned to her that day. Unable to tempt Mary because she was too incorruptible, the Devil worked instead upon the other Temple maidens. He cast a shadow of malice and evil on some of them. Their hearts had become dark and wicked. Not all the girls were affected, but some of the girls had become jealous of the attention that Mary was given by their counsellors. They resented her goodness and virtues. Behind her back, the wicked girls gossiped in recessed corners and plotted nasty tricks to play on the favoured one.

"Why is she being treated so special all the time?" asked Rebecca.

"Yes, come, sweet Mary," mocked Adina.

"She's not sweet, she's nasty. Thinks that she is better than us. I hate her!" spat Talia.

"Did you see the fuss she made at her presentation?

Absolutely appalling!" retorted Delilah.

"I'm here in this place because my parents did not know what to do with my sharp brain and quick tongue. I didn't just accept everything they told me. They wanted me to know my place. They pleaded for a place for me here because they wanted me out of their hair. I created... what can I say... too much undesirable attention. They're hoping to hold me here until I get married and then I will be my husband's problem," reported Rebecca.

"I'm here because my parents are Levites and need to maintain the holy stature of the family by having an educated daughter. It gives them influence on the Temple Council," said Adina.

"I was flirting with a boy in my village. He was not suitable as far as my parents were concerned. But I love him, and he loves me. My parents had another man in mind for me. He's my father's age and already has three children. Ugh! I hate my life! I'm here on hold until I get of marriageable age. They think that this placement will secure my virginity and my compliance. Oh, the life of a wife!" moaned Delilah.

"I'm here on hold too. I, unlike you three, do not have a pretty face. I'm fat and awkward. Not the best choice for betrothal. My parents are hoping to find a good prospect for marriage for me by increasing my station, because there is nothing they can do about my looks. I'm doomed to an arranged marriage for economic reasons. It's not fair!" lamented Yael.

"We all have different reasons for being here and not one of us is happy about it. But Mary's father is rich, and she is beautiful in face and countenance. She could have anyone she wanted because she is daddy's little girl!" whined Rebecca.

"She wants to be here!" exclaimed Talia.

"Can you believe that girl? She is so go-o-o-od that she takes her prayers and Scripture study seriously. Goody, goody, Mary," wailed Delilah.

"She makes me sick. I can't stand her," Adina declared.

"She has got all the wise women wound around her little finger. She's their precious little baby. I would like to knock her down a peg or two!" opined Yael.

"Let's do it!" said Rebecca enthusiastically.

"What can be done? The little darling is surrounded by her aunties," said Adina in a jeering tone.

"Now that she's ten, they let her work alone more often," replied Talia.

"Let's watch and discover a weak spot in her day," declared Yael.

"Then we'll trap the little brat!" avowed Delilah.

They all put their hands together in a circle and lifted them together. The devil had done his work.

Amidst the constant harassment, teasing and setting up the innocent Mary, she always managed to take responsibility for her apparent misdemeanours without giving away the true cause of her supposed mischief. She never blamed others. Regardless, the malicious and wicked girls tried their best to harm Mary's resolve and reputation. Mary bore the humiliation of the accusations with dignity and meekness. The older women, noting the tricks and machinations and knowing that their interference would only add to the scheming, watched from afar and let Mary handle her problems in her simple and effective way. They admired how Mary's gentle and modest manner managed to make the mean girls feel guilty and regret their actions. Still, the devil was clever and succeeded in corrupting their hearts time and time again.

There was one serious incident that risked Mary being expelled from the Temple School altogether. However, the Holy Spirit and the Angels, in their wisdom, had a purpose and a design for the event. One day, the four mean girls managed to arrange to be on the same assignment as Mary, sweeping, dusting, and scrubbing the sanctuary.

"Mary, go clean the Holy of Holies. It must need doing badly," urged Rebecca.

"Oh, no, Rebecca, it is forbidden to enter the Sacred Room," Mary demurely responded.

"Why not? It's part of our assignment. Women aren't allowed in this space, but here we are slaves to the infernal dirt and dust. The Holy of Holies is just part of our job." Dalilah led Mary to the opening.

"It would be wrong to go in there, Dalilah. I am not worthy of such an honourable task," admitted Mary.

"Are you joking?" remarked Adina. "You are the most prayerful and righteous girl in the school. You are favoured among the girls, the women even," retorted Talia.

"You are blessed, Mary," said Adina sarcastically.

"Go, Mary, don't question, just go," urged Yael.

"I cannot." Mary went to turn around and headed away into the Sanctuary.

"Go!' said the girls in chorus as Rebecca pushed her into the hallowed room. She heard them giggle and run away.

It was not a large room, but it was luxuriously panelled with acacia wood, and it smelled of fragrant incense that had permeated the walls of the chamber over the years. The sound inside the empty space was like a thunderous silence, muted but so present it could be felt in inner parts of her body. The room was empty, but it was frighteningly pregnant. It felt sacred.

Unknown to Mary and the naughty girls, the High Priest, Abiathar, who had replaced Simon as the leader of the Jews in Jerusalem, had just arrived and witnessed the event. After the girls had scrambled out in the glee of their mischief, Abiathar entered the Holy of Holies. He too, had broken the sacred rule of not entering the room but once a year. Yet he felt compelled to do so. He found Mary kneeling in the middle of the floor, right where the Ark of the Covenant would have been placed. She was on her knees with her head very low, weeping and praying. Although the space was empty, there seemed to be energy moving about. He couldn't put his finger on the feeling that they were not alone. He had no reason to doubt this feeling because this was a place of mystery and of the divine.

"Mary, what are you doing in here?" asked Abiathar, who knew exactly how she got there.

"I didn't mean to enter, Rabbi. I know how sacred this place is. It was wrong of me.; Please forgive me." Mary kept her head bowed and her eyes lowered.

"Never mind, Mary, I saw what the girls did to you."

"Please don't get them in trouble, Rabbi."

"I think that they got themselves in trouble, my blessed girl. Can I join in prayer with you?"

"Of course, Rabbi." He kneeled down beside her.

After a few moments of silent prayer, the priest, rocking forward in his supplication, invited her to sit on her heels as he also did.

"Let's have a chat, Mary, daughter of Joachim and Anna."

Before speaking, High Priest Abiathar looked at the sweet young girl in front of him for a long while before he asked her, "What do you know about the Holy of Holies, Mary?"

"It is indeed a very holy place. It is where Moses would meet face-to-face with Adonai in the desert tabernacle tent. It was the Dwelling of the Lord."

"That is correct. Tell me more."

"King David moved the desert tabernacle to the mount called Moriah and wanted to build a permanent place for the Ark of the Covenant. He was very excited about the prospect, but it was King Solomon who built and made it a magnificent and splendid Temple to praise and glorify the Lord. It must have been very grand, Rabbi."

"What happened to that Temple?"

"The Babylonian King Nebuchadnezzar invaded the south of Palestine and destroyed the glorious Temple and took almost all the Chosen People and all the precious things of the Temple away."

"Yes, very true. The Ark of the Covenant is not here. It is empty in here except for you, Mary. What is in the Ark?"

"The Ark held the Tablets of the Commandments, the Rod of Aaron and an Urn of the desert bread, Manna."

"Well done, Mary. You do know your scripture. So, what happened to the Ark of the Covenant?"

"People think that the Prophet Jeremiah had it moved to a safe place in the hills, so that the Babylonian invaders would not take it or bring it to harm."

"After the return to Jerusalem, why is the Ark not restored to its rightful place of honour?"

"I do not know for sure, Rabbi. Perhaps the people involved in concealing it had died and no one could remember the place. They may have searched, but perhaps the sealed niche in the mountains was overgrown with shrubs and trees and other foliage," offered Mary humbly.

"Mary, you are wise beyond your years. What should we do at this time?"

"Await the Messiah, Rabbi. All authority will be given to the Messiah."

"This Messiah can not come too soon. The Romans are horrible, tyrannical landlords who are hell-bent on desecrating our holy places and our Jewish way of life. Come Mary, let us come away. Nobody knows of our presence here, but the Lord and those silly girls. The Lord is just and compassionate, and He will understand. In fact, I think he actually planned it."

They both left respectfully and prayerfully.

On the whole, life for Mary was serene and happy. She fit into the routine life of a Temple sister very well and in spite of her mischievous peers, she enjoyed the study, the work, and the prayers. She grew wiser, more knowledgeable, and more skilled in all her functions. To all who knew her, she grew taller, smarter, and sweeter, much to the chagrin of her bullies. She especially enjoyed communing with the Good Lord in the outdoor private residence quadrangle, under the dome of the sky and the canopy of the world. She was sensitive to the sounds, smells, and activities of nature. There, she appreciated the wonderment of the Lord's creation with awe. She felt humble in the presence of a mighty force and power. God was great! She loved Him and she knew in the depths of her heart that He loved her.

Mary's happiness in her situation was marred in a significant way and only once. It happened when Mary was twelve years old.

"I received a message from our sister Anna today. Her husband, Mary's Father, Joachim, died in a fatal fall while building a barn in Nazareth. There are no details about the death," recounted Naomi.

"He would have been buried by now. It has taken at least three days to deliver the message and, in this heat," said Joanna.

"How shall we tell Mary?" asked Maya.

"The poor thing. She certainly loved her abba. He was as totally devoted to his little girl as he was to our sister, Anna.

Everyone would wish for a husband like Joachim," added Susannah. Not all of us were that fortunate."

"Still, poor Mary will be devastated," cried Naomi.

"And Anna, too. She really loved that man. He made her laugh with his silly and light manner. He made us laugh, too. He was a good and righteous man. I wonder what she will do without him?" asked Joanna.

"Oh, Anna will cry herself empty. She will mourn for sure because there was only one Joachim, and he was the father of her child. Knowing Anna, she will turn to the Lord. Knowing her husband, he will have left her financially secure. She has a great family for support, and she is still very beautiful. A good man would be very fortunate with a catch like our Anna," explained Maya.

"I agree," expressed Susannah, as the women nodded their agreement with her.

"Let's do it together," added Maya.

They called Mary to them under the terebinth tree. They sat on the stone benches and clasped their hands, wondering about the best approach to tell the daughter of their friend the bad news.

Finally, Susannah spoke first.

"We have bad news to tell you, Mary. We received a message from your mother today that announced the death of your father."

Mary was stunned for a moment while she processed the information. A look of deep sorrow crossed her young face. Her first words were concern for her mother.

"Poor Imma. How will she manage without Abba?"

Naomi reached out to gently touch Mary's arm. "Your mother is strong and capable, Mary. She will be very sad, for she deeply loved your father. But she is clever and resourceful; she will manage well enough. Her worry was for you. She is not able to hold you in her arms as you feel the sorrow and suffer the loss of your abba."

"Your father died in a building accident, and according to your mother, he was taken without suffering to our Father in Heaven," contributed Maya.

"Your mother will be visiting you as soon as she can make her way. In the meantime, we will be your imma and bring you comfort as much as we can."

"He is in a wonderful place now, Mary. It is those left on earth that will be full of grief." They waited patiently in silence. "How are you feeling, my girl?"

Mary did not respond right away. Tears rolled down her face and she looked up toward heaven and she mouthed a prayer. This was followed by heart-wrenching weeping. The women all rose together and held their arms up in a circle that surrounded the little girl in sorrow. Each in turn hugged her against their breasts and prayed a prayer over her. The circle of "aunties" surrounded the daughter of their absent friend with love, sympathy, and benevolence.

Finally, Mary looked up at them and said: "He was such a good man, and so good to me. He was always in my heart, even when we were apart from each other. I know that as a heavenly being, he will continue to be in my heart, guiding me, but also making me giggle with his silliness. I will miss his hugs, patting my head, and his tapping the end of my nose when he thought that I had understood something."

"Every time you miss him, remember him in your favourite spot on the farm. Remember how funny he was. Think of how much he loved your mother and you and loves both of you still. Feel him in your heart.

"I'm not sure that Joachim won't be plotting to tease and trick the Lord much like he did to all of us from time to time. He was an endearing man, and all were made to feel special by his loving attention and gestures," Maya recalled.

"We will all miss him, your Abba," declared Susannah. At which point, all the women shared the tears of sorrow while harbouring the little girl who was the one hurting most of all.

Chapter 14
Plans for Mary

Rabbi Samuel looked up from a scroll of work orders as four Temple sisters came into his workplace.

"Shalom, Rabbi. You called for us?" asked Naomi.

"Shalom, Daughters of Israel. Thank you for coming."

"We are here to serve, Rabbi," replied Susannah.

"As you know, I serve the Temple by supervising the physical structure. It has come to my attention that the veil of the Holy of Holies is in need of replacement. Another drape will need to be spun and woven. It will require a fine hand for the work. This is a most important piece in the Temple."

"We have stocked the finest of flax in anticipation of this request, Rabbi," offered Maya.

"Of course, it will need to be broken, combed, spun and dyed, and then woven. We will start right away to collect the purple dye. It will take a great quantity to make such a stretch of cloth. It will be very expensive, Rabbi," reported Joanna.

"Yes, but cheaper than buying it from the Egyptians. After the many rounds of taxes and the cost of shipping, it will be better and purer if we make it here," said Maya.

"I am aware of the expense of those dye colours; however, it must be done. The current veil has served its time, and the Council agrees that it's time for a new one."

"We agree, Rabbi," the women chorused.

"Who have you got in mind to work on this precious task?" asked Rabbi Samuel.

"Well, Rabbi, we have several girls who have honed their skills and have shone in these specialized areas. However, Mary has excelled in all areas of cloth making," averred Susannah.

"Some can do the less skilled tasks like breaking and combing while the more skilled girls do the spinning and weaving. We matrons will embroider the Cherubim with the gold thread," followed Naomi.

"Very well; I will leave the details to you experts."

As they were speaking, the High Priest entered the room.

"I wanted to speak to you about Mary, daughter of Anna and the late Joachim. It must be approaching the time for her departure from the Temple," said Rabbi Samuel.

"Yes, Rabbi. Mary is nearing her woman time, and we should be thinking of finding her a husband," agreed Naomi.

"I have been in contact with her mother, who is aware of the approaching situation. You know that Anna lost her dear Joachim but remarried a couple of years ago. She has employed a matchmaker, and they are searching Galilee for an eligible husband," offered Joanna.

The High Priest considered carefully and responded. "It is my opinion that Mary is a special case. She stands above other girls in innocence and purity. There is absolutely no guile in her. She may even want to remain completely devoted to the Almighty even in marriage. We will need to choose carefully. We will take charge of the search here as well, close to Jerusalem."

The women bowed their Shalom and departed the room. After going over the task at hand, they all agreed that Mary would weave the purple strip of the veil. They then began the enormous undertaking of replacing the drape.

Back in Cana, Anna and her new husband, Cleopas, were also making plans for Mary. They knew they needed to consider a future marriage for Mary. The couple and Shadchan Esther, the local matchmaker, were in conference reviewing all the unmarried men in the area of Galilee. Anna knew how the Temple worked when it came to girls that had experienced their lunar time. They were no longer welcome as Temple girls, and were required to leave, and could only return if they were unmarried and after the change of life. So, they needed to find Mary a husband.

After two years of mourning Joachim, Anna had been approached by Esther with a proposal by Cleopas for her hand. Anna had relied heavily on Daniel, Joachim's first man and friend, to manage the properties and stock left behind by Jo's sudden death. Although Daniel had not been able to prosper the business as well as her husband, he had managed to maintain it well enough. It was time for Anna to share her life again. Cleopas and Anna already knew each other through the marriage of Mary Salome to his son Nathan. They were often at family celebrations, betrothals, weddings, and births. During this time, they had grown to admire and respect each other.

Cleopas had been present during Joachim's funeral. A leader in the synagogue and in the village, he was a widower now with a family of his own. He was a good man, dependable and kind. He was a wealthy man in his own right, and he esteemed and loved the widow, Anna. Anna, for her part, missed her soulmate; however, she was lonely, and it was expected that she would remarry. It was the norm.

"Esther, come and have some mint tea, and tell us what you have found," invited Anna.

Esther responded. "I'm glad that you are both here, so that I can share my information."

"We must do well by our girl Mary," professed Cleopas. "She is not my blood daughter, but she is Anna's, and only the best will do."

"As you know, I have looked high and low in our area. The idea of an educated woman scares some men. They are mostly tradesmen and they do not want to feel inferior to their wife."

"I would have thought that this would have been an asset to pass on this education to their children and improve their status," exclaimed Anna, surprised at Esther's findings.

"Most men want their children to do as their father did and what all the mothers before them did. It is a problem here in the pastures and hills, and in the small villages of Galilee, where most of the men are fishermen, farmers, masons, carpenters, merchants, herdsmen and traders. They think that your Mary will be too clever," explained Esther.

"Mary's desire to remain a virgin devoted to the Lord has also made it nearly impossible. She obviously needs a man who will honour that commitment and not expect to fulfill his conjugal rights, and who already has children—a widower perhaps," noted Anna.

"I was not aware of that, and that will make it very difficult now, because what red-blooded man would want to marry in those circumstances?" asked Esther.

"There must be someone out there! Have you gone further afield? Your increased fee will not matter to us," contributed Cleopas.

"That is what I wanted to tell you. Yes, I heard from a traveller from Bethlehem that there is a widower there who might fit the profile. His name is Joseph, son of Jacob. He is from the line of David, and he is of very good reputation as a religious man and a good and honest carpenter. I will find out more about him and get back to you."

Chapter 15
Zachariah is Struck Mute

Zachariah was a helper at the Temple. On this day, he was working alone, seeing to the sacred maintenance and care of the three tables in the Sanctuary. One task was to replenish the oil in the Menorah. Another was to renew the Bread of the Presence. This was done by eating the bread that was on the Golden table and replacing it with fresh, unleavened bread. This being done, Zachariah was replenishing the incense in the Altar of Incense. As he worked, he recited a prayer of supplication for the positive outcome for finding a suitable husband for his cousin Anna's daughter, Mary.

He continued to go about his tasks when he was suddenly interrupted by a brilliant light. It lit up the whole of the Sanctuary. The happening was quite disturbing and frightful, but eventually, the light took a moving and shimmering shape and eventually, an angel appeared. It was larger than the tallest human he had ever seen. The angel did not stand on the floor but hovered or floated above the ground. He was luminescent. His body was at the same time both sheer and opaque, depending on his movements. Zachariah realized that the celestial being's height was due to the lengthy extensions of his wings, which were large and pointed high toward the heavens. Out of his beautiful mouth, a voice came out and proclaimed:

"Do not be frightened, Zachariah. Your wife Elizabeth shall bear a son and you will call him John. Joy and gladness will be yours, and many will rejoice at his birth, for he will be great in the eyes of the Lord. He will never drink wine or strong drink, and he will be filled with the Holy Spirit in his mother's womb. Many of the sons of Israel will he bring back to the Lord their God. God himself will go before him, in the spirit and the power of Elijah, to turn the hearts of fathers to their children and the rebellious to the wisdom of the just, and to prepare for the Lord a people well-disposed."[19]

"Who are you?" asked Zachariah, trembling with fear.

"I am Gabriel, messenger for the Almighty. I was sent to speak to you and bring you this good news."[20]

Zachariah had not yet overcome his astonishment at the message, and he was disbelieving the apparition in front of his eyes. He was full of reservation and apprehension. His mind and heart were not yet fully opened to the credibility of this godly event. He still had questions. He stood there for a moment, incredulous, with his mouth open wide.

"How am I to know this? I am an old man; my wife, too, is advanced in age[21]" Zachariah shook his head and wiped his eyes. "I'm not sure that you are real, and not just wishful thinking or a product of my hopeful imagination."

"Zachariah, you are not open to the word of God. Your spirit is closed to the elements of life which are not physical and tangible. You doubt."

"I don't know what to believe," retorted Zachariah.

"Do you believe in miracles, Zachariah?" asked Gabriel.

"I guess. I'm not sure."

"That is exactly what I said to you. Your faith is shaky, and you are not fully committed to trusting in your God."

Gabriel then continued: "But now you will be mute--unable to speak--until the day these things take place, because you have not trusted my words. They will come true in due season."

---

[19] Luke 1:13-17, New American Bible
[20] Luke 18, New American Bible
[21] Luke 18, New American Bible

At that moment, the archangel Gabriel, the celestial messenger, vanished from sight.

Zachariah came out of the Sanctuary into the open court, and he was unable to speak to the people who waited for him. He kept making signs to them. They could not understand what had happened to the perfectly healthy Zachariah who had entered the Sanctuary just moments before.

Chapter 16
Mary and Marriage

While Anna, Cleopas and the matchmaker were looking into finding a good husband for Mary, the Sanhedrin Council, headed by High Priest Anainas, had gathered for their regular meeting about the Temple and the state of Judaism in a homeland occupied by Roman legions. Along with the concerning business of the state of Judaism, the council took time to celebrate some good news. Because he was unable to speak, a friend of Zachariah made an informal announcement. The rest of the officials stopped to learn what the spokesperson for Zachariah had to say.

"So, I hear that you are to be congratulated, Zachariah!" exclaimed a council member.

"Yes, praise to the Lord, Rabbi Jose," commented Zachariah's friend, who continued to speak on behalf of the mute rabbi. "Elizabeth is with child! He waited for the cheerful response of the seated rabbis. "Baruk ha-ba. Blessed is the one who comes."

"By having a child, you are closer to becoming the High Priest. You have waited a long time, my friend, and you have certainly earned this position."

His friend admitted that, unfortunately, Zachariah was unable to speak. For some unexplained reason, he had lost his voice shortly after he learned the news of Elizabeth conceiving. Zachariah could only communicate with signs and in writing. "He recognizes what this limitation means."

The members of the council had all been shocked at the sudden loss of vocal ability and how long it was lasting. However, in deference to their colleague, they nodded grimly. They liked Zachariah.

After an uncomfortable silence, Anainas went on. "While it is important that you have been blessed with a child for Israel, your inability to speak will certainly prevent you from being eligible for the position of high priest as expected."

Zachariah nodded somberly. He fully understood the implications of his affliction. He hoped that this further punishment would make amends for his unwise and dismissive reaction to the angel and that his speech would be restored soon.

The High Priest continued. "There is one item that we must discuss involving Rabbi Zachariah more directly. It involves his wife's cousin, Mary. She has come of the age where she will need to leave the Temple household of virgins. This must happen, as you know, before defilement of the Holy Temple. Because she is a Daughter of Israel, it is our duty to ensure a good husband for her."

"She is quite a beauty and has a sweet disposition. She should be a good catch for some man," responded one of the members.

"Is she not working on the Temple veil? The purple colour, I believe."

"That is true, but she can continue to work on that at home. Her mother, Anna, is an excellent spinner and weaver as well. She will be able to guide her."

"Yes, she is a fine girl—a truly special and pious maiden," commented another priest. "However, she has expressed a desire to be forever a virgin and to be totally dedicated to Adonai."

"Nonsense, she is too fair of face to go unmarried. Her duty is to take a husband and make babies," argued Anainas, the High Priest.

"Surely, we can find some widower out there who has had his children and just wants a woman to care for him and his family," suggested another.

"Anainas, as you are the High Priest, perhaps you could go into the tabernacle and make a petition and pray on the subject and we will do as the Lord will show you," said Rabbi James.

"And the High Priest took the vestment with the twelve bells and went into the Holy of Holies* and prayed concerning her. And lo, an angel of the Lord appeared saying to him: go forth and assemble them that are widowers of the people, and let them bring every man a rod, and to whomsoever the Lord shall show a sign, his wife shall she be. And the heralds went forth over all the country round about Judea, and the trumpet of the Lord sounded, and all men ran thereto."[22]

---

[22] Protoevangelium of James, Chapter 8:3 * It is more likely that it was the Sanctuary as the High Priest would enter the Holy of Holies but once a year on the Day of Atonement-- on Yom Kippur

Chapter 17
Joseph, bar Jacob

Joseph was a fine carpenter. He enjoyed working with wood. The texture of the grain, the smell of the different varieties of pine, cypress, olive, and acacia, the sound of the wood saw and the plane all helped to soothe his thoughts and feed his creative urges, as well as his need to create something new. He worked from his woodshop attached to his father's house. He lived there with some of his other brothers. Unlike his brothers, Joseph had shown aptitude for study and so he had been educated and had attended Hebrew school. He could read and was well versed in Holy Scripture and could do figures in his head. He had a fondness for Greek philosophy and spoke Hebrew as well as Aramaic and understood the Greek language and could even speak it a little. He was a pious man who often sought solitude so that he could pray, reflect, and meditate. He was gentle, empathetic, generous of spirit, and kind.

However, he was no longer a young man. He had once been a handsome man in his youth. Taller than most, with curly hair now heavily tinged with silver. His nose was slightly hooked, and his beard had refused to turn grey like his hair but had remained dark brown. His late wife had told him that it was his soft, kind, and sparkly eyes that had drawn her to him. He had been very fortunate in the matchmaker's choice of his wife. He had loved her dearly. He had been devastated when she had died giving birth to their last child. Ever since, he had been dependent on his relatives to provide a house and home for his six children, James, Joses, Simeon, Judah, Salome, and Mary. This was certainly a very common practice in Jewish families. Still, he missed the quiet and serenity of a smaller household. A new wife could be a solution.

Joseph had a secret concern, though. He had not told anyone that he suffered from palpitations of the heart. He avoided lugging large quantities of material, and he kept his walking to a slower pace these days. He relied heavily on his faithful donkey. It had been another reason why his brothers teased and mocked him as a feeble old man. His children were a great responsibility and unfortunately, they required more attention than the extended family could give. Joseph was thankful that he lived in a household of relatives. The wives of his brothers were helpful in bringing up his children, but there were many reasons why he should consider remarriage. One, the house was too crowded with people.

At nighttime, they spread their sleeping carpets all over the place. Adults used dividers for seclusion and intimacy, but the space was inadequate, and if one had a need to fulfil a need of nature, there was no privacy. Joseph yearned for solitude and quiet. He often retreated to a peaceful place in the hillsides where he could pray. There were many caves left there by shepherds. He often sought solace there. The prayer and the meditation often helped him to resolve his anxiety and bring calm to the harried and rowdy life of his family circumstances.

Reason two: his brothers had always been different from him. They were boisterous, teasing, and argumentative. Joseph was a tranquil, quiet and reflective sort. His approach to life was vastly different from theirs and he often sought occasions where he could leave the house and work outside, or on jobs in other towns and villages. Given these conditions, it was definitely time that he considered finding a wife and taking his children to a more peaceful home.

It was at this time that the Temple heralds appeared in his village announcing a declaration of a request for a husband for a worthy young maiden in Jerusalem. He set down his tools and ran to meet them and to inquire about this offer. He was told to bring his rod when he came to the Temple. At the appointed time, Joseph made arrangements for the short journey to Jerusalem, told his family about his mission, took his rod, and set out for the Temple.

He arrived a day early and spent time praying to the Lord for wisdom and prudence with this possible match. Maybe she just wasn't for him. He had been so fortunate with his first wife. This could be a disaster. He realized that he would not be the only one vying for the hand of this woman. He knew nothing about her. What was he thinking? Perhaps she was a harpy, or perhaps she was immature and not capable of being a mother to his children. Nevertheless, he felt compelled to answer the call.

All the eligible men were asked to bring their rods and stand before the High Priest. An official collected all the rods and followed the Priest into the Temple. The two men, led by the Rabbi, prayed together. The Rabbi left to seek counsel in the sanctuary. When he had finished, he re-entered the Court of Israel, the men's court, where all the eligible suitors were lined up awaiting the outcome. The official returned their rods to them. This proved to be an uneventful task until Joseph received his rod. A white dove landed on it and stayed there, cooing away. As the Priest approached Joseph, the dove hopped onto Joseph's head. It became clear to the Priest at that moment. This was the sign that the Priest had been waiting for. He said to Joseph: "Unto thee hath it fallen to take the virgin of the Lord and keep her for thyself."[23]

Thus, Joseph ben Jacob of the line of David, and the tribe of Judah, became the chosen husband for Mary.

Joseph was shocked. His chances had been so slim. He was an older man, and the temple virgin was just a young girl. Wouldn't she want a young, robust man who would be willing to give her many children? Although taking a wife of this age was a very common practice, he could just hear his brothers teasing him and laughing at him. They would accuse him of

---

[23] Protoevangelium of James, Chapter IX-1

robbing the cradle. One of his own children was almost the same age, and she would be their new mother. Impossible. He protested to the High Priest, but the latter rebuked him because he found no problem. After all, the Lord had undoubtedly sent His sign.

"What is her name?" stammered Joseph.

"Mary, daughter of Joachim and Anna and Daughter of the Hebrews, also of the line of David."

Still, Joseph hesitated. "Are her parents aware of this match? Have they not sought the counsel of a Shidduch—a matchmaker?"

"They are aware and will respect the decision of the Temple council."

"Before I accept, I would like to meet with Mary."

"We will make the arrangements. You are from Bethlehem, yes?" Joseph nodded. "Anna has relatives there in the town. They will meet you there at her grandparents' house. We will send word when the parents have arrived, and we will make sure that Mary is present. Although, this is completely unnecessary. It is the custom for young maidens to marry what has been arranged for them, especially maidens from the Temple school."

Joseph politely retorted, "The young maiden does still have the right of refusal and I, an older man, will not marry a woman-child against her will. I await your message."

"In the meantime, you should begin working on the betrothal gifts for her and her parents."

Still in a state of wonder and disbelief, Joseph heeded the leader's command and began to prepare the gifts. Two weeks later, Joseph received a message to make his way to the home of Mary's grandparents, Stolanus and Emerentia. He was met at the door by Anna and Cleopas, Mary's new stepfather, who were courteous and welcoming. They did not show any sign of shock at the older face that greeted them.

"Shalom, Joseph, ben Jacob," chorused the handsome couple.

"Peace to this house," answered Joseph.

"You are most welcome in this house, Joseph. I see that you have washed, as there is no dust on your feet, and your hair and beard are still wet. Come in, and we will introduce you to my parents," invited Anna.

"We have sent all the other members of the family to the market for the afternoon so that you might have a quiet and private moment with Mary," offered Cleopas.

"I hope that you do not think it bold and disrespectful of me to put forth my candidacy for your lovely daughter's hand in marriage," demurred Joseph.

"You need not worry, Joseph, for the matchmaker in Galilee had already heard about you through her sources and your name was on her list of potential candidates," responded Anna.

"Your selection by the Council just served to confirm the choice. Our Mary is a very unusual girl. She is shy and modest but has received a high education as a Temple daughter and is as skilled as her mother with spinning and weaving. She will need a special husband," added Cleopas.

"I hope that she is not anticipating a young and virile husband as I'm sure to be a disappointment."

"The final say will be Mary's. Let us introduce you to her grandparents and then we will leave you alone with Mary who is waiting in the garden."

Mary sat serenely in a grotto, on a bench placed in a hollow of the stone wall. On one side of the grotto was a pomegranate tree, and on the other was a fig tree; neither was bearing fruit at the moment, as it was not their season. It was a crisp, clear golden day so typical of the Mediterranean climate. She was looking up dreamily at the sky and watching the birds making beautiful patterns as they energetically flew into and away from each other. How amazing was the work of the Creator, she thought. The Lord had truly a vivid imagination and had conceived a beautiful world. She put her head down and entered into a state of natural communion with God as she praised and thanked the Almighty. She also petitioned Him for the wisdom that she required. She had questions about the man who was in pursuit of her hand in marriage. What kind of man would he be? What kind of man would she want? What kind of man would want her? She did not want to be a fertile wife. She wanted to be totally dedicated to God, to serve Him and magnify Him. She wanted to remain a virgin, and what man in his right mind would desire that in a spouse? A description of Joseph had been sketched for her, and his merits had been listed. Might he be the right fit for her and her particular needs? In the end, she would just trust the Lord and do His will. She lowered her head and let her supplication float on the wings of angels while she waited for her encounter with Joseph.

Joseph entered the garden, not knowing what to expect as he had not had a description or a list of merits for his prospective bride until meeting her parents. They had just revealed what a remarkable young girl she was. She was shy, pious and hard-working. She could read and write and speak Aramaic, Hebrew and some Greek. She was well-studied and very well versed in Scripture. She was a former Temple virgin who had developed many housekeeping and other skills during her time in the Temple school. Spinning and weaving were her areas of specialty. In fact, she had been commissioned to work on the Temple Holy of Holies veil. She was to continue working on this project at home in Nazareth. Joseph's knowledge of her many attributes made him even more nervous and unsure of himself. As well as being very young, she was a match beyond his humble value! He was just a simple carpenter with no home of his own and six children!

His quiet entrance had not disturbed the young maiden in obvious prayer. He had time to examine the girl seated before him. She was a vision of loveliness. Youthful, but with a surprisingly mature and serene demeanour. She was beautiful. The cool breeze carried a gentle and pleasant perfume that came from her direction. It filled his senses with aromas of fruit and spice. She was wearing a head scarf of blue linen, finely embroidered on the edges with white threads. Escaping from her veil were spiral strands of dark brown hair with some locks kissed by sun. She had fine features and flawless olive skin. Her lips were plump and curved. Her chin was delicate but well-defined. Her neck, partly covered by her veil, appeared to be long and elegant. There was an inner glow about her that could be nothing else but grace. She was a beauty well beyond his humble worth. However, he was smitten by her at his first glance, and he had not even met her yet. He remembered verses from Song of Songs:

"You have ravished my heart with one glance of your eyes,

With one bead of your necklace...

How beautiful is your love, my sister, my bride!

How much more delightful is your love than wine, and the fragrance of your ointment than all spices."

You are a park that puts forth pomegranates, with all choice fruits...[24]

_____

[24] Song of Songs, 9:10-13

111

The murmuring sound that came out of his mouth awoke Mary from her meditation and she looked up to see him. The moment he beheld her eyes, and saw her beautiful smile, he was enchanted. She calmly stood up as he approached her, and their eyes never left each other's. Her alluring eyes were large, shadowed by dark lashes. Their colour was a soft hazel, turning to green in a certain light and ringed with a darker brown circle. They were like inviting pools that drew him into their depths to quench his thirst. He had been besotted by her glow and her shining aura, but it was through those eyes that he was permitted to see her soul.

From her view, Mary was attracted by the soft, kind, and sparkly eyes that looked so adoringly at her. She could also see into his soul and saw goodness, integrity, and courage. His aura was wisdom. Yes, he was old enough to be her father. However, marrying older men was not unusual. Such was often the fate of women. This might, in the end, be a blessing. Joseph might just understand and be complicit in her desired intentions. He might not demand his conjugal rights as a spirited and youthful man would. God had selected well so far, she thought.

"Shalom, Mary, may I approach you?"

"Shalom, Joseph. Yes, of course."

Joseph continued to look into Mary's soul, and he was filled with a joy that he could not explain even to himself. He had to consciously break away from that elated feeling and the trance he was under.

"As for me, I'm delighted with what I see and know. It is my desire to wed you, Mary. You are much more of a catch than I am. You are lovely and all that a man could desire; however, I want you to know that you are not obliged to accept the offer of this old man, with little to offer except six children. You are free to choose, Mary."

For Mary, the birds stopped singing and the insects stopped chirping. The world fell silent except for the kind and reassuring voice of Joseph.

"Joseph, you speak honestly about yourself. Let me assure you that I am not such a great bride choice. Truly, I say to you, it is my wish to remain a virgin. I want to give myself totally to our Lord as I have done in the Temple. This is an unreasonable condition to place on a husband. It would not be fulfilling the requirements of a blessed marriage, and it is not fair to you."

Joseph showed no reaction to this request except relief.

"Thank you for your honesty as well, Mary. It is a blessing that we have been made part of this fortuitous matchmaking, both by your family's matchmaker and that of the trial for a husband at the Temple. This cannot be a coincidence, but the work of our Lord."

"How so?" asked Mary.

"I too, am not interested in the physical communion of marriage. I am old now and suffering some health issues. I have six children and do not require any more progeny. Do not misunderstand me, Mary. I am seeking affection in my relationship with my wife. I desire her to be the love of my heart. I wish to offer myself heart and soul and to be entirely devoted to her protection and care."

"I desire the same, Joseph. I would give you my heart and all the love that is in it. I would be a sister to your family and a mother to your children. I would care for your home, and I would care for you. This is my solemn vow to you."

"Then give me your hand, Mary. We have reached a covenant of the heart, my lovely bride-to-be. May I kiss you to seal the promise?"

"You may." Joseph bent down and placed his hands on both sides of her head. He slowly and softly sought her lips and gently kissed her. Mutual joy! He wrapped his arms around her slender shoulders and held their two bodies together, not as lovers but as soulmates.

"My love and my heart," sighed Joseph.

"Let us pray together," Mary suggested. The couple knelt and looked up to the heavens.

Joseph led with, "O Grateful, Elohim, our father in heaven, thank you for blessing this union. Continue to bless us as we face life and its hardships. May the joy that Mary and I share today continue all life long. Guide us and let us do your will as we continue to serve you on earth."

Mary added:

"Make a joyful noise to the Lord, all the earth.

Worship the Lord with gladness.

Come into his presence with singing.

Enter his gates with thanksgiving,

And his courts with praise.

Give thanks to him, bless his name.

For the Lord is good; his steadfast love endures forever,

And his faithfulness to all generations."[28]

Both ended with an "Amen".

And the birds sang, the sun shone brighter, and the world smiled, as did God. [25]

———————————————

[25] Psalm 100

Chapter 18
Mary and Joseph Betrothed

The proposal and contract would be struck between Joseph and Mary's parents the following day. Joseph arrived at Stolanus and Emerentia's house early. He presented his bride dowry to seal the deal with Anna and Cleopas. This time, the household was full of people. All the resident family and extended members of the family were there to meet the groom-to-be and to celebrate with the happy couple. There was laughing and singing and much food.

Mary had taken care of her dress this day. She had chosen a simple white silk tunic and veil. The cloud-like shift was garnished by a lavish, finely woven sapphire-blue woolen cloak. She looked like a vision from heaven. Her mother and grandmother had woven beautiful flowers around a filigree of gold in a crown to encircle Mary's head. She was splendid in her appearance. Mary gave a wonderful impression of grace and beauty, not only because of her rich clothes but because of the radiance of her face. Joseph was not the only one who was spellbound that day.

Joseph looked handsome and quite youthful in his embroidered brown woolen tunic girdled by a golden sash and an embroidered cap called a kippah. He wore his 'tallit gadol', his prayer shawl, with long tzitzits on the corners. He wore new knee-high sandals, and his hunter-green Kashmir robe flowed like palms around him. He looked younger than his forty-three years and he shone with the pride of a lion as was befitting a man from the tribe of Judah, and of the line of David. He held his lucky staff in his right hand as a reminder of the miracle that had brought him to this moment.

Even though Joseph was not a rich man, he was a talented and a skillful one. He had made many of the gifts for the dowry himself, and for the rest, he had traded his skill or the product of his woodshop for more exotic merchandise. He presented the bride's family with an ox yoke, a water-carrying yoke, and a small cart with a pregnant donkey. He had fashioned a weaving frame ready for assembly in Mary's home. He had made a large chest of expensive acacia wood and two smaller ones to hang on the donkey's sides when Mary travelled.

Inside the larger trunk, Joseph had included a leather-bound package. It was tradition that the groom should gift the bride-to-be with a piece of her bridal clothing. Coming from Bethlehem, Joseph had access to a unique piece of outerwear. In his hometown, there were weavers who had developed and perfected the fine skills of assembling fibres into a striped over-tunic called a "malak". The malak often sported many colours in its elaborate design of stripes. It was a long, heavy gown with a split opening in a beautiful panel at the breast-front bodice that allowed the head to pass through. It was a wide and long garment with pointed sleeves. The malik was the pride of his hometown and his family had purchased the valued and coveted piece for the bride's attire.

In addition, Joseph had presented Mary's parents with a small wooden chest that held a variety of salt, spices, frankincense, and myrrh. Joseph had traded some wooden items and labour to the caravan travellers that were on their way to Egypt. He had also traded for silk threads and cloth dyes. He brought in a large jug of olive oil and a jug of good wine. He kept one more gift for Mary for later. The family opened the jug of wine and drank to a marriage bond. Although the gifts were presented to the father of the bride, it was generally understood that many of the gifts would be held or given to support their daughter.

Joseph presented his children to their new family. All were present except for the baby, Mary, who was too young to travel with the others. The children were introduced to their father's new wife-to-be. They had all been nicely groomed for the occasion. There was a small resentment on their part because this woman was hardly older than they were. How could Joseph replace their lovely mother so soon? Yet, they knew that their father needed a person to care for him and all of them. They hoped that she was a sweet person at least and not a nasty stepmother about which they had heard others tell stories.

"Mary, may I present you my dear children?" Mary smiled and nodded eagerly. "This is James, the oldest. He is thirteen, Joses is eleven, Simeon is nine and Salome is four, and little Mary is back home with my family as she is only two years old."

Mary looked directly at them when she greeted them.

"Welcome, my new family. What beautiful offspring, Joseph. The boys look so handsome and strong." At that point, the boys visibly stood straighter and smiled at Mary. "And the girls, what beauties. I bet they already know how to run a household. I shall count on their guidance as I learn all about the running of your home." At that point, a funny noise came forth from the direction of the boys. Joses bore a sheepish look. Mary laughed.

"Joses, I bet there is a frog in your pocket." Joses lowered his head and put his hand in his pocket and pulled out a croaking green creature. Everybody laughed.

"I was going to put this on your chair if I didn't like you. I'll put it back in my pocket now." Everyone burst into another fit of laughter.

"At least it wasn't a snake or a scorpion. Whew! Why don't you release the poor thing and sit close to me at the table and that way, I can watch that you have no more tricks in your hat." Mary gave him a very exaggerated wink and a smile.

The girls came forward and presented Mary with a cloth-wrapped package.

"This is a gift for you from all of us," chorused the girls.

Mary took the bundle and placed it on the table and opened it. The outer wrapping was a homespun linen apron. Within the apron was a whole set of eating implements: a fired clay plate and bowl, metal spoons, and a beautifully carved and oiled goblet.

"These are yours. Welcome to our family. Will you be our Imma?" asked Salome on behalf of the others.

Mary looked at them with tears in her eyes. She had a look of pure appreciation for their kind and welcoming gesture. "Tawdi, tawdi, thank you. Thank you for such a wonderful acceptance into your beautiful family. I will try to be good to you and love you with all my heart. You can call me Imma or you can call me Mary if you are more comfortable with that."

Mary had also thought of offering gifts to her new family. She went to get a stack of woven, woolen blankets.

"My mother and I made these from sheep to shawl. The weave is yours. I hope these coverlets will keep you warm wherever you are." Mary handed them to each person by name, including Joseph. The children put their new blankets to their faces and sighed and moaned.

"Oooh. They are so soft."

Joseph stood back to watch the little drama and was amazed at the affection and tenderness for his betrothed. He sighed contentedly. God was good.

Mary put her arms out wide. "Is it too soon for a family hug?"

"No!" was chorused, as the younger ones ran forward to be wrapped together in a family embrace. The older boys hung back a little, somewhat hesitant and feeling too big and proud to take part in such an intimate affair. Joseph noticed their reluctance and called them over to the huddle as he also joined the merging family in the group hug. They all sighed, smiled, and snuggled together in a loving circle.

All evening, Mary was warm and welcoming. She made them laugh and they fell in love with her as had their abba.

As tradition would have it, the bride would usually move back with her parents while her husband built her accommodation. This living space was often an addition to the father of the groom's house. However, that home was already at full capacity. Rather than have Joseph build an addition to his family home, and now that his older brother's house was just outside the village of Bethlehem, Anna and her husband had offered their place in Nazareth as a gift to the couple. Cleopas had taken over Joachim's herding business and still carried out his affairs in that village. Mary Salome and her husband, Nathan Cleopas, lived there now with their children and there was plenty of room to build a large addition. Joseph could convert part of the stables for his woodshop and there were plenty of jobs in the area. Construction in the nearby town of Sepphoris was growing wildly with the Roman occupation. There would be much work there. There would be many caravans from the east going by. They would always be in need of wheels, spokes, cart repairs, litters and the multiple tasks that would fall into Joseph's area of skills.

The next day, the party of Mary's family and Joseph's children travelled to the Temple. They made for a merry parade of newly formed relatives as they approached Jerusalem, not more than five miles away. A tone of solemnity fell upon the crowd as they approached the steps in the women's quarter. Many of the women and girls who knew Mary from her time at the Temple school were present, and they were delighted that Mary looked so happy with her betrothal. As usual, Mary was glowing with an inner light and her beautiful smile reflected her satisfaction with the present situation.

The couple presented themselves before the new High Priest, the Rabbi Abiathar, who recited prayers of thanksgiving and blessing on the betrothal and who reminded everyone that this was a binding covenant between two people as designed by the Almighty from the beginning of time and Adam and Eve. Joseph spoke of his promise to care for and love his new wife. He fumbled a little and found the ring in his pocket and placed it gently on Mary's finger. She placed her hands together in front of her chest and bowed her head low in thanksgiving for his generous gift. The registration scrolls were signed by both parties and the betrothal was made legal as well as spiritual.

At that moment, a dovecote nearby was opened, and the skies were filled with swooping doves creating streamers of flight. All things seemed to applaud the young maiden and her fatherly spouse-to-be. God-signs were everywhere for those who believed, and to those who were open to them.

Chapter 19
Mary and a Celestial Visit

The news of the impending marriage of one of their cherished citizens had arrived in Cana, and the town talk was flourishing. Four women were gathered at the village well, and they were exchanging information on the rumours that were circulating.

"I hear that Mary is back from the Temple," offered Eva as she dipped her bucket into the well and heard it plop in the water.

"Yes, and I hear that she got engaged to a fellow called Joseph ben Jacob, of the tribe of Judah, from the line of David," added Leah as she helped Eva turn the winch that brought up the full bucket.

"Too bad, because I was hoping to get a match with my son, Issac," bemoaned Leah who wiped her forehead of perspiration, for she had already filled her two buckets.

"You are joking. My Levi is much more suitable for Mary than your Isaac. He is stronger and much better looking than your son," declared Kelilah.

"Many would disagree. Besides, Isaac has a better trade as a blacksmith. There will always be a need for nails, hinges, and metalwork. This is a more solid and important work than tent making."

"I don't know. His father has done very well over the years."

"Dai, enough, you two. This is a useless discussion. A husband has been chosen for Mary by both the local shadchan and by the Temple council. It is done. Joseph will be her husband," scolded Eva.

"You're right, Eva. I was told that he is a carpenter from Bethlehem," added Leah, as she awaited her turn for the water bucket.

"Not only that, but he is an old man, and he already has six children! Has Anna lost her mind? Her daughter will be nothing more than a nurse and housemaid for that household!" cried Eva.

All the women had finished their tasks, but still stood together gossiping about Mary and her new circumstance. "Mary is in Nazareth now. Her parents have gifted them a place in their holding there. Joseph will be setting up shop in that village and I hear he will be working in the surrounding towns and villages," continued Eva.

"Mary is lucky to have such wealthy parents and such a loving and generous stepfather. They have even given her some servants help to prepare the home and do the chores. Mary Salome and her husband, Nathan Cleopas, are there as well. Joseph, Mary, and his brood will live in the main portion of the house and Mary Salome and her husband will live in the addition as they only have one daughter," opined Kelilah.

"I understand that she is still working at weaving the purple cloth for the Temple veil. This is quite an honour for her and for the village," offered Shira.

"I'm not sure that this honour will compensate for a young maiden married to an old man, though," questioned Eva.

"Poor Mary. There will be little hope for excitement under the blankets," laughed Leah. The other women joined her laughter.

"So true! She will be too exhausted caring for the home even if this Joseph is interested," contributed Shira.

"I don't understand the benefits of this match. Mary would have been better off with your Issac or my Levi," said Kelilah. "What is the world coming to?"

"Look, Eva, you just slopped a lot of water on my feet. They will be caked with mud by the time I get home," admonished Leah.

"Wash dust, or wash mud. It's all a wash," rebuked Shira.

They all laughed and headed for their houses.

"Yalla, yalla! Let's go!" cried Eva.

Mary was aware of the town talk because the servants informed her of the gossip and conversations that they overheard. Mary did not pay much attention. There would always be town talk. It passed the time and how else was information to be shared among the citizens of an illiterate village? She only wished that people made a better effort to pass on accurate information. On the whole, it was well-meaning and only occasionally mean-spirited.

Today, she was working on weaving another length of the purple cloth. She finally sat down at the loom that Joseph had constructed for her. There were so many morning chores! The servants were an immense help, but bed mats had to be aired and rolled, bread made, breakfast set out, house tidied, dishes cleaned, and chickens and other animals fed, just to name a few of the tasks. It was important to get the hard labour jobs done while the day was cool. Weeding the garden and harvesting were done as early as possible to avoid the harsh rays and the heat of the sun.

It was early afternoon when she finally got to sit in her shaded and cool loom room and let her fingers and hands lovingly work toward the completion of her sacred assignment. The wooden frame was strung with warp and weft and the fine woolen fabric awaited her talent. A basket at her side was heaped high with finely spun skeins of a deep Tyrian purple yarn, dyed from the secretions of a sea snail called the murex.

It was a very expensive yarn, only used on rare and special occasions. It only awaited her animated shuttle.

Mary loved this work. It had lovely rhythmic movements and soothing, harmonious sounds. She was very skilled at it, and it felt good to see the progress of her hands. The sun shone through the window and the air was full of her happy mood as she quietly hummed psalms of gratitude while she worked.

Mary was deep in her peaceful, harmonious rhythm when there came a sudden flash of bright and colourful light. It was as though a rainbow had entered the room! She closed her eyes and covered her face with her arm to protect her from the intensity of the brightness that overtook the space around her. Not understanding the phenomenon that was overwhelming her, Mary shook with fright. The light then took shape and a winged being of great splendour appeared before her, and shimmered as its brightness dimmed to a lesser intensity that could be gazed upon. The light was reflected onto Mary, and she shone in a heavenly glow.

"Rejoice, O highly favoured daughter. The Lord is with you. Blessed are you among women."

Mary looked upon the floating diaphanous form with its robes moving and fluctuating. She was unsure what she was seeing, and she was again both alarmed and confused.

"Mary, do not be afraid. The Lord looks upon you with favour,"[26] said the angel in a soothing musical voice. I have glad tidings." Mary gazed at the angel and nodded meekly, still in a state of shock and confusion.

The angel continued, "Mary, you shall conceive and bear a son and give him the name Jesus. Great will be his dignity and he will be called Son of the Most High. The Lord will give him

---

[26] Luke 1:30

the throne of David, his father. He will rule over the house of Jacob forever and his reign will be without end."

Bewilderment crossed the face of the amazed Mary. She was still unsure as to what was happening. Her mind was trying to truly comprehend what was being said. Finally, she asked the angel, "How can this be? I have not been with a man."

The angel answered her, "The Holy Spirit will come upon you and the power of the Most High will overshadow you; hence, the holy offspring to be born will be called Son of God."

Mary responded quietly and reverently: "I am the servant of the Lord. Let it be done to me as you say."[27]

The angel left her, but the room was not as it was before the appearance of the celestial being. Mary was overwhelmed with a bright light different from that of the angel and it entered her being. She consumed the light, and she knew that she had been overcome by the Holy Spirit—a true communion with the Almighty. Something heavenly had happened to her in that moment and she radiated with the glow of the divine grace.

The room returned to normal. However, in the aftermath, she was still shaken by the enormity of the occurrence and yet she felt both a deep joy and a sense of peace. She lowered her head, prayed to the Adonai, and thanked him for having chosen her to be his handmaid, and again accepted the duty to serve her Lord and do His will. She was in a deep meditation of praise and gratitude when her mind suddenly came to a realization. She gasped as she saw the consequences that would arise from this situation.

"Joseph! What will I tell Joseph? Or my mother and stepfather?" She started to shake and feel very clammy. Panic overtook her. "They won't understand. They will say that I'm

---

[27] Taken from Luke 1:28-38

lying and that I have been unfaithful. Or they will be angry at Joseph for not waiting until the wedding day according to the law. Oh dear, God. Help me tell them. Help them understand. Give me the words to convince them that I am doing your will, oh dear Hashim." Immediately, her panic settled down to a calmness, and then joy and elation overwhelmed her once again.

Mary sat at her loom and restarted her weaving. Her apprehensive and troubled mind felt calmer and soothed by doing a routine and familiar task. She trusted completely that the Lord would help her to deliver the news to her betrothed and her family.

A month went by. This was enough time to confirm her pregnancy. When Anna came down to Nazareth from Cana, Mary told her that she needed to speak to her privately. They made their way to the garden courtyard and sat down on a bench under the olive tree. The day was overcast, and the clouds shaded the two women in the garden.

"What news have you for me, Mary?" asked Anna.

"It is very difficult for me to tell you this, Mother, but with the help of our Lord, I will tell you honesty. I hope that you will listen with an open heart," responded Mary.

"This sounds grave."

"It is life, and world-changing, Imma."

"Oh," whispered Anna.

"I am with child."

"You are what?"

Mary didn't respond, but let Anna absorb the information. She knew it would be a shock for her mother.

"How do you know? You're just a child in such matters. Who have you been with? How can this have happened as I assume you have not been with Joseph? Has somebody taken advantage of you here in the house in Nazareth? Have you been unfaithful? Oh Mary..."

"I know, because an angel announced it to me about a month ago. I was by myself weaving the Temple veil cloth when suddenly he appeared in the room."

"What did he look like?" asked Anna. Mary described Gabriel to her, and Anna nodded. She recognized the angel because he had once appeared to her to tell her about the conception of Mary.

"I know the angel that you are talking about, because he visited me too about fifteen years ago. What did he tell you?"

"That I was blessed among women and that I would bear a child. I was to name him Jesus. When I asked how this could be so as I had known no man, he told me that the Spirit of the Lord would overshadow me and that the fruit of my womb would be a King like David and reign over the people and the world."

"Truly?"

"Yes, Mother, and he also told me that Elizabeth is pregnant too."

Anna was silent for a long while as she reflected on the miracle and the trouble they would face. Pregnancy at this time was a serious matter. Mary would be blamed. Joseph would be first surprised, then angry. This was a grave problem. She believed her daughter, but would others?

"Praise be to Adonai! I believe you, Mary." She took her daughter in her arms and embraced her. "This is earth-shattering, Mary, but it will cause a problem for you and for us. You know the town talk. They will say that you were unfaithful.

They know that you are not yet married, and Joseph has been away all this time."

"I know," said Mary demurely.

"I am happy to learn that Elizabeth is with child; she has waited such a long time," responded Anna, gently changing the subject.

But Mary still needed to discuss her own situation. "I know that this will be a great calamity and I don't know what to do about that; however, I feel sure that the Lord will look after it. I am here to be His servant and do His will. I must place all my trust in Him and let Him manage the situation."

"Oh, dear. What will Joseph say? He will know that he is not the father."

"I must trust in his goodness."

"Let us hope. What do you think all this means? Why did He choose you? What did He mean by 'he will reign over all the people and all the land?'"

The two women spent a lot of time discussing the information and how it would impact them, without finding any resolution.

Chapter 20
Mary and Joseph Face Trials

Mary was three months pregnant when Joseph arrived back in Nazareth to see her. He had finished his contracts and was free to travel north to Galilee. He was looking forward to seeing his betrothed. There was definitely something very alluring about this young woman. It was as though she was surrounded by angels, and one needed to be a part of her grace. As he approached the house in Nazareth, he noticed her in the vegetable garden. She was weeding a patch of earth around the eggplants. She didn't notice him as she sang away in a sweet, quiet voice. He did not wish to disturb her communion with nature and stood and watched her for a time.

Mary eventually looked up and saw Joseph there watching. "Shalom, Joseph," she said with a wide smile that displayed her dimples.

"Shalom, my dear Mary." She rose from her place and ran to him. "It is wonderful to see you again."

Joseph took her in his arms and breathed in her fresh air smell. She was so small and delicate in his embrace. He would do everything in his power to care and protect her. "How are you, Mary? You have been well and busy with your Temple assignment?"

"It is finished now and officials from the Temple have already collected it," answered his betrothed.

"Have the servants been kind to you and have the children been obedient?"

Mary nodded happily in affirmation, "Yes, Joseph. I have been well, and the servants have been most kind and the children have been darlings. I do have something important to tell you, so why don't you refresh yourself from your travel and I will await you on the garden bench."

Joseph happily went to the laver and cleaned the dust from his body. He beat his clothes and shook out his mantle. He took a cloth and wiped off his arms, legs, and feet. He threw water on his face and beard to remove the dirt and let the water cool him. He now felt refreshed and respectable. He moved towards the garden to meet his beloved.

"Does that feel better?" asked Mary.

"I am much restored, my dove. What is this news of such great importance?"

"It is difficult for me to tell you this, Joseph, because you may be shocked and think that I have been untrue to you."

Joseph looked bewildered and just stared at her with a questioning look. His head at first tilted left, and then he looked beyond his beloved into the distance. His eyes finally came back to face her.

"I'm with child Joseph." Mary could not help but observe the pain in his face as he comprehended the information, and the various thoughts crossed his mind.

"How can this be, Mary? We have not been together."

"I have been with no other, Joseph. Let me explain."

"Mary, I know that you are young and innocent of all the facts, but I know that you know that women do not become pregnant if they don't lie with a man." His face became clouded with anger. "This is too much for me right now. I must go and pray and decide what I am to do."

"It wasn't like that, Joseph," pleaded Mary desperately.

He got up in a jolt and quickly walked away. Mary got up to follow him and could see him leave the premises and head for the fields. She understood his distress. Again, she would need to trust the Lord and hope that He would relieve Joseph's pain and help him understand. She loved him.

Joseph walked for a long while. Conflicting thoughts and feelings invaded his spirit. This was certainly not what he expected to hear. Not from his Mary!

Many questions tumbled out of his brain. Who was she with? There was only one way to conceive babies and his betrothed was with child, and not by him. He had been deceived. Even if he was the father, how could he explain his own indiscretion? If he concealed her indiscretion, he would be found guilty by the laws of the Lord. He was not supposed to have marital relations with her until they were married. And if he revealed her to the children of Israel, he feared the consequences of that declaration. So now, what was he supposed to do? [28]

He could reject her on the grounds of infidelity. What would that do to Mary? The community would surely stone her for reasons of adultery. It was done all the time. He did not want that. He could not let that happen to his Mary. It was a brutal way to die. He could just quietly divorce her. No one would be the wiser. But he would. He would have abandoned her in her greatest need. How could he live with that? But how could he do otherwise? He fell to his knees beside a large rock outcrop, and in agony, he cried out in his anguish and pain. He completely emptied himself of all emotions. He was done in. He was powerless and so he cried aloud:

"Father in heaven, help me know what to do. Help me to understand." He fell to the ground and slipped into a trance-

---

like sleep. In this dream state and complete emotional weakness, Joseph encountered a magnificent angel.

"Joseph, son of David, have no fear about taking Mary as your wife. It is by the Holy Spirit that she has conceived this child. She is to have a son and you are to name him Jesus because he will save his people from their sins. All this has happened to fulfill what the Lord had said through the prophet: 'The virgin shall be with child and give birth to a son, and they shall call him Emmanuel', a name which means God is with us."[29]

When Joseph awoke, he was clear-headed and knew what he must do. He must stand by his wife and protect her at all costs. He was familiar with Scripture, and he understood what was to happen. Why him? This was a huge responsibility. He was not certain that he was up to this heavy burden. Mary was to be the mother of the Messiah sent to earth to save the world! The unbelievable extent of this obligation rested heavily on him. He was not completely clear as to what this child would be, but he knew he was sent by God and the rest would evolve as he needed to understand. For now, he needed to find Mary and make arrangements for the wedding. It should happen soon, for everyone's sake.

It was late in the evening when Joseph knocked on Mary's house door. The sun was low in the sky, fanning beautiful hues of saffron, coral and purple into the sky while a large orange orb sat on the horizon. The hills were lit and shadowed by the descending light.

---

[29] Taken from the Protoevangelium of James, Chapter 9: 14-16

One of the servants answered the door and bade him come in while she went to fetch Mary who was at prayer. Mary arrived a few minutes and greeted and welcomed Joseph quietly and with some trepidation.

"I apologize for leaving you so abruptly this afternoon, Mary. I was in shock and needed to process the information and its implications for us."

Mary displayed a reserved smile, nodded, and said: "I understand Joseph. I have had more time than you to take in this astounding revelation."

"I'm listening, Mary."

Mary spoke quietly and simply to Joseph. She claimed the innocence of her actions and recounted her story much as she had to her mother. Joseph listened attentively. His eyes never once left Mary's. At the end of her account, Joseph asked questions that helped to clarify and compare her experience with his. "Can you describe the angel? Did he give you a name for this child? What happened to you with the Holy Spirit? What did the angel tell you about the destiny of this child? Were you frightened about what will become of you and your child? Are you ready for this?"

Mary smiled at this litany of questions, many of which she had already asked herself. She answered all his questions calmly and nodded at the state of her readiness. She answered, "Yes, I am his handmaid. I am prepared to do the will of the Lord with your help, Joseph."

"Are you still willing to have me as your husband?" asked Joseph.

Mary responded with an enthusiastic nod and said: "Yes, of course. More than ever!" She asked, "But, more importantly, are you still willing to take me as your wife, Joseph?"

"Yes," was his response.

The town talk was charged with rumours and gossip.

"Did you hear, did you hear? Mary is getting married early."

"She need not wait because Joseph was given the house in Nazareth and doesn't need to build an addition to his father's house. There is nothing to prevent them from getting married earlier than announced."

"I suspect that they have engaged in relations, and she is pregnant. Wouldn't put it past them. Holier than thou is that Mary and her rich family."

"Now, you know that many have benefited from that family's generosity to the Temple and the community. Let us not be vicious in our chatter. We do not know for sure, and Mary does not deserve the nasty rumours based on hearsay. Such unfounded gossip could be very hurtful to her. We really do not know."

"Yes, yes, but it all seems a little quick and unexplained, don't you think?"

"You are incorrigible. Do not continue this line of thought."

But the rumours still spread wildly. All the possible stories were wondered at and shared. Something had to be done because the falsehoods had reached the ears of the synagogue before the date of the wedding could be set. The scribe Annas said to Joseph, "Why have you not come to see us since your return?"

"We have been sorting things out, making plans. We wish to advance the wedding," replied Joseph.

"People are saying that Mary is pregnant. Is this true? Have you privately married Mary, not revealing it to the elders of Israel?" reproached the priest.

Joseph swore that he had never touched her at all. However, they did not believe him and sat in accusation and judgment of him. Joseph vowed that he was innocent and asked the rabbis for a Trial by Bitter Waters. This was a legitimate but rarely used test to determine the fidelity and voracity of the accused. The authorities ordered the trial to determine if his guilt would appear on his face. However, they determined that Mary would have to submit to the trial as well.

Upon the official order, both Mary and Joseph were brought to their trial before the priests, and the chief priest said to her, "Mary, have you done this? Why have you debased your soul and forgotten your God, seeing you were brought up in the Holy of Holies[30], and received your food from the hands of angels, and heard their songs? Why have you done this?"

To which, with a flood of tears, she answered, "As the Lord my God lives, I am innocent in the sight of God. I have known no man."

Then, Kohen, the priest, replied, "Then let us put you both to the test. Even though this trial is usually just for women, I will cause both of you to drink the water of the Lord, which is for trial, and so your iniquity or your innocence will be laid open before you."[31]

The priest went over the procedure for the Trial by Bitter Waters. According to Scripture,[32] this was a divine ordeal to verify the fidelity of women to their husbands when two witnesses accused her of adultery. The Sotah water was equally effective for guilt or innocence as the Lord would intervene for

---

[30] Here again to the Holy of Holies probably refers to the Temple Sanctuary.
[31] Trial by Bitter Waters appears in both the Protoevangelium of James and the Gospel of Pseudo-Matthew
[32] Numbers 5:16-31

the innocent. He explained that running water, dirt from holy ground, and the bitter herb wormwood, and a small piece of paper with the name of God on it was crushed and mixed in a clay vessel. The accused was ordered to drink of the Sotah water. If the woman was guilty, her thighs would fall away, and her belly to swell. Their sin would be evident if they got sick. While the ingredients were not fatal, they could have a psychological effect on the guilty. They could experience symptoms because they were afraid of the wrath of God because they had sinned.

And so, Mary and Joseph both submitted to the Trial of Bitter Waters.

'When, therefore, Joseph had drunk the bitter waters, and had walked round the altar seven times, no sign of sin appeared in him. Then all the priests and the officials, and the people justified him, saying: Blessed are you, seeing that no charge has been found good against you. And they summoned Mary, and said: And what excuse can you have?

'Or what greater sign can appear in you than the conception of your womb, which betrays you? This only we require of you, that since Joseph is pure regarding you, you confess who it is that has beguiled you. For it is better that your confession should betray you, than that the wrath of God should set a mark on your face and expose you in the midst of the people.

Then Mary said, steadfastly and with trembling: "O Lord God, King over all, who knows all secrets, if there be any pollution in me, or any sin, or any evil desires, or unchastity, expose me in the sight of all the people, and make me an example of punishment to all." Thus saying, she went up to the altar of the Lord boldly, and drank the Sotah water of drinking, and walked round the altar seven times, and no spot was found in her.'[33]

And when all the people were in the utmost astonishment, seeing that she was with child, and that no sign had appeared in her face, they began to be disturbed among themselves, making conflicting statements: some said that she was holy and unblemished, others that she was wicked and defiled. It was always the way with town talk.

---

[33] The Gospel of Pseudo-Matthew, Chapter 12 and Proto Evangelium of James, Chapter 11

Chapter 21
Mary and Joseph Wed

The wedding day was finally here. During the period of preparation, Joseph had gone back to Bethlehem to finish up some work with his brother. Upon his return to Galilee, he had taken up residence in the house in Nazareth with his brood. Mary Salome and her husband, Nathan, would help him settle in and assist with the care of the home and family. His betrothed, Mary, had moved back to Cana to live with her mother until the marriage. The move had lessened the glares and the whispers and diminished the hearsay. But not entirely. Mary was still the subject of rumour and gossip. However, Mary and Joseph had passed the test before God and what more could people say? Besides, there was no time for that nonsense; there were many preparations to make before the big day.

The marriage between Mary and Joseph did not follow all the usual traditions. Instead of joining the groom's household at his father's command and instructions, Joseph was going to his wife's home. His father had passed away, and he was not a young man. Anna and Cleopas were happy to give their extensive and prosperous property in Nazareth to Mary and her husband. Joachim would have liked that. As well, there was plenty of work in Sepphoris. The city, not four miles from Nazareth, was wealthy and booming with construction due to the Roman occupation and its status as Galilee's administrative centre. Herod's son, Antipas, the Jewish client king of the Roman Empire, had made it the first capital of Galilee. Many Jewish families had relocated there, and a new elaborate synagogue was being constructed, and they would need many skillful builders to accomplish the task of building a city worthy of the king and the emperor. Joseph's eldest son, James, having just completed Hebrew school in Bethlehem, was now of an age to apprentice with his father and learn his craft. He was already showing skills and ability at the trade. He had a good head for numbers like measurements, angles, and weight bearing. Joseph was proud of his son, who was of his own heart. He had been an excellent scholar, and he would be a great help in his building and carpenter business. However, at the present moment, building was the farthest thing from Joseph's mind. He had to make himself and his family presentable for the wedding.

He and his boys would cleanse and sanctify themselves in the family mikvah. Joachim had had the pool built on his property. It was a large freshwater reservoir with stone steps to the bottom where it was possible to fully submerge the body. Joachim had built stone benches around the mikvah, so users could sit and be completely covered in water to the neck. The pool was able to capture the water from a spring on the site, allow it to pass through the mikvah and then very slowly drain and irrigate the garden. They had been fortunate to enjoy the benefits of an intimate purifying ritual in the privacy of their own home. At present the male family members were sharing prayers and songs together.

For this happy celebration, the boys would wear their finest garments. Joseph himself had purchased new clothes for the occasion—all but his prayer shawl. He had worn this prayer shawl for as long as he could remember and much of his past was wrapped in its prayers over his lifetime. He would don a long natural homespun linen tunic and an ankle-length gold woolen outer tunic with sleeves. He would cinch his waist with a wide blue brocade belt. His treasured prayer shawl would be proudly worn during the ceremony. Later, if it was chilly, the whole apparel would be topped with a heavier royal blue woolen mantle and a gold brocade kippah. James would wear his prayer shawl. The boys would don similar garments. Joseph and his boys would indeed cut fine figures for the occasion.

Meanwhile, the bridal party was enjoying a similar ritual in Cana. The women, including Mary, Anna, Mary Salome, and other cousins were also taking part in the ritual pre-wedding cleansing and purification. They wore light linen shifts to enter the water, sang psalms and said prayers of praise and gratitude to their Adonai.

As Mary was Anna's only child and Joachim had been a wealthy man, and so, with the full support of her equally rich second husband, Cleopas, Anna had spared no expense. Mary, on the other hand, who was close to nature and preferred simplicity and humility, had opted to do away with some of the jewelry and the headdress that often adorned brides. After some negotiations, Anna and Mary had agreed to a less elaborate set of apparel. While it was a more modest attire, Anna had still opted for rich, superior, and valued fabrics.

Mary would wear a white linen undergarment; it would be topped with the Bethlehem 'malak' dress that had been given to his bride-to-be by Joseph at the betrothal. Anna, an accomplished weaver, could only admire the garment. The craft and technique had been skillfully fashioned by the finest spinners and weavers in Bethlehem. The malak had been woven in a series of aqua, light blue, dark blue and purple stripes. The sleeves were straight, wide and long, and finished in a point at the wrist. Joseph, or more than likely one of his relatives, had shown great taste in selecting the elegant but sturdy garment. This gown was of great value.

Mary's head veil was made from the very rare and expensive sea silk. The silk was harvested from the sea. It was the product of a Mediterranean giant sea mollusk. Few people had the ability to weave this pricy and rare fibre which was finer than human hair. It was silky soft and shone with flashes of gold in the sunlight. Anna had ordered and purchased the expensive cloth from a trader when she was last in Jerusalem at the time of Mary's betrothal. The gossamer textile was crowned with a diadem garland of almond blossoms twisted with olive leaves.

Mary would not wear sandals today; she would wear jewelled Arab slippers that Anna had also purchased from the trading caravans that often visited the Galilee region on the route to Egypt. Mary would be dressed simply, but richly and elegantly. Joachim would have wanted it no other way and he would have been so proud of his little girl. Mary was truly an awesome sight to behold. Her grace and beauty shone from her inner loveliness, and it glowed in celestial splendour as though angels surrounded and lauded her. How captivating she was!

The 'nisuin'--the wedding--, would take place outdoors. Joseph, the 'hatan'- the groom--and his party of men would parade merrily to Cana to fetch the 'kallah'--the bride--Mary. She would be carried in a litter, followed by her bridal party who would either walk or ride. The donkeys were laden with some of the prepared food and dishes. However, much of the banquet food would be purchased and prepared in Nazareth by Mary Salome and the people of the village who were all invited to the festivities after the holy and solemn vows taken before the rabbis. Everyone loved a wedding, and the excitement filled the air with joy and singing. There would be much dancing and merriment to celebrate the newlyweds. Even disappointed mothers who would have liked to celebrate a marriage of Mary with one of their sons would gladly be there to witness the matrimonial revelries.

The huppah—the canopy--made of a white silk sheet, was set up in front of the synagogue. It was set up on poles decorated with the vines of the grapes, with bands of white silk billowing in the breeze. A nearby bougainvillea bush in bright fuchsia colours draped from the sides and corners of the canopy. The sun shone only slightly through the silk canopy, affording both shade and a golden glow to the ceremony, investing the entire scene with glory and majesty.

In ancient days, after Laban had tricked Jacob into marrying Leah instead of his true love, Rachel, the Hebrews had adopted a tradition that the bride would not wear a veil which obscured her face from the groom. The couple would meet outside the wedding location and the groom would remove the veil himself before he married the woman, thereby ensuring that it was indeed his intended and not a substitute. Joseph approached a veiled Mary just before the ceremony under the canopy and lifted the delicate and diaphanous veil from Mary's face. He looked upon his beloved and gazed into her eyes. He saw the purity of her soul. There was no guile or guilt in those soft and gleaming orbs. Only his Mary, his to love and protect. He smiled at her, and she smiled back. No words were exchanged, but the powerful and mystic radiance was felt by both of them. This was surely a marriage made in heaven. Joseph and Mary walked together towards the canopy and the waiting official, and solemnly made their vows before God.

The high-spirited banquet, celebrations and dancing went on for three days. Wine and oil were poured, and happiness and good cheer spread through all the celebrants. At one point on the first night, the couple was allowed to spend some time together without people around. Mary and Joseph quietly left the jollity for a few moments of peace. "How are you, my beautiful dove?" asked Joseph.

"Tired, Joseph."

"Well, I'm not surprised, seeing as you are carrying another person inside you," said her husband sympathetically. "Come, sit with me on this bed and I will calm you and hold you until you are rested."

Joseph sat down cross-legged and invited Mary to lean back onto his chest. She gathered up her clothes in order to climb onto the bed and rested herself snuggly between his crossed legs. She comfortably rested her back on his warm body and her head on his neck. Joseph let her relax and hummed a soothing song into her ear. He caressed her tense shoulders and arms. He stroked her head until her breathing calmed, and serenity and tranquility settled into both of their bodies and hearts. He placed his hand on her abdomen and acknowledged and caressed the precious fruit of that womb. Mary fell asleep in perfect peace and joy. Joseph sighed and gave thanks to the Lord.

After a while, they re-entered the garden and mingled with the revellers. The group of men met them with subtle, bawdy comments and tastefully expressed teasing references. They were more reverent than usual as, after all, Mary had been a temple virgin. The couple smiled demurely, linked arms and joined the singing and dancing.

Chapter 22
Mary and Joseph

Life had settled down since the three hectic days of wedding celebrations. Mary and Joseph had moved into their new home in Nazareth. Joseph engaged his son James to help him organize the woodshop and begin the process of setting up a business in the community. The first thing to do was to provide James with his own proper tools. They could share some larger workshop tools like adzes, saws and wood vices; however, every carpenter would need small tools that could be carried in a leather pouch. Tools such as files, sharpening stones, chisels, small blades, and a variety of hammers were part of the kit required to do jobs. Constructing farming tools like yokes, plough handles and rakes topped the list of their commissioned work. Repairs to litters, wagons, and wheels brought in work from the caravans travelling through the region. However, Joseph was hoping to seek larger contracts in Sepphoris, where many builders were required to work on location and satisfy the demand for lintels, doors, windows and framed wooden structures and the like. The Romans seemed to be in no short supply of wood from Lebanon, and, as they travelled frequently back and forth to Rome, they could furnish the materials that were scarcer in Palestine. The work possibilities were encouraging.

Joseph entered the wood-fragrant workshop. There was comfort in seeing the layers of wood chips on the floor and the tools hanging on the wall above the workbench that had been left by Joachim and to which Nathan had added when he arrived with Mary Salome. Nathan's trade was that of a stone mason. As he carved in stone, his tools were hammers, plumb bobs, chisels and calipers. He would shape the stones to fit archways, wells, or window lintels. Sometimes, Nathan was asked to build an entire structure, such as a building or wall.

Naturally, many of his jobs were off-site, so he would not be using the shop much. Joseph liked his brother-in-law. He could easily see sharing this workspace with him. There was affability, kindness, and jolliness to his nature. They had discussed the idea of working together on building projects and contracts. Nathan would work the stone and Joseph the wood and the work agreements. Joseph's son, James, would work as required, learning the trade and helping with the calculations and figuring.

Joseph sighed and smiled. He gave the Lord thanks for his new working environment. It was already work-ready and well-equipped. It was larger than the space he had shared with his brother in Bethlehem. Even though the two brothers worked together, they were not close in personality or temperament. Joseph's older brother never fully appreciated his more quiet, sensitive, and reflective nature. Reuben and his other brothers were loud, boisterous, and constantly harassing, teasing, and joking. Joseph made the best of the situation but was happier to have his own business apart from his rowdy and unruly brothers. He would enjoy working with the smart and pious James and Nathan.

Mary was also busy setting up the house. She now had the care of Joseph's little ones, Salome and baby Mary. Joses and Simeon were helping out in the shop with their father and older brother, James. There were many little tasks, like sweeping, fetching, sorting and carrying smaller things, that the younger boys could easily manage. It was the first step to learning the chores of construction work. As for Mary, there were many tasks to finish before the day was done. She was very thankful that her mother had left two servants, one for the household chores and the other for the outdoor barn and field chores. She also had her stepsister, Mary Salome, to work alongside her. They had all agreed that there were altogether too many Marys and Salomes in the house. It was decided that from now on, Mary Salome, wife of Nathan ben Cleopas, would be called

Mary Cleopas to distinguish her from Joseph's wife, Mary, and from Joseph's two little daughters, Salome and little Mary.

It was early morning and at the moment, Mary's hands were knuckle deep in bread dough, kneading it into loaves that could be placed in the ovens before the highest heat of the day. She would need to harvest vegetables from the garden to make the evening meal. While she was there picking eggplant, leeks, and artichokes, she would do some weeding. The weeds had taken over while they were preparing and celebrating the wedding. There were many tasks to do now that the real work of living had begun. She didn't mind the labour because she prayed and sang while she toiled. She was never far from the Lord and knew that the angels watched over her. She hoped to get to her spindle and work on fine woolen yarns and textiles that Joseph could trade in the towns and to incoming merchants on caravans. Of all the tasks of the day, she loved the spinning and weaving the most. Tomorrow was washing clothes and bedding, and that was her least favourite chore.

After the evening meal and the sun had just set, she found herself alone with Joseph.

"How are you feeling, my love?" Joseph asked, concerned.

"Fat. I believe my waistline has thickened. It won't be long before I show."

"It is just that subject that I want to talk to you about."

"What do you mean? I am surely not the only woman who has born children and who has a family to care for. I will not be a princess, Joseph."

Joseph laughed. "No, you are not. I have seen the progress in the garden, and I have seen my children happy and well cared for. Laziness is certainly not in your nature. I would hate to be a weed around here!" he teased.

"I will begin school for the children soon if that is acceptable to you?" Mary asked.

"That is something they did not get at my brother's home. I will be thankful if they can take advantage of your fine education at the Temple. Wonderful, Mary. Not everybody gets that opportunity. We are truly blessed."

There was a long, poignant moment of silence when each soul reflected on the situation and wondered how to move forward in the conversation.

Mary was first to speak. "I am thinking that you are suggesting the town talk is about to notice the advanced state of my belly and start the rumours and innuendos again?"

"Yes, Mary. They will count the moons. You know how the town loves to talk and many times the talk is not kind. I'm afraid that town talk will turn into nasty talk."

"Hmm." Mary bowed her head as she considered how the consequences of the earlier onset of her pregnancy would appear on the people of the village and the consequences this would have on her family's reputation and good standing in the community. Although people already knew, it would just stir up the gossip again.

"I have an idea. Tell me what you think," said Joseph. "Why don't we go and visit your cousin Elizabeth? You told me that the angel told you that she was also with child. Is that not right?"

"Yes, it is. She thought that she was sterile, and she is quite advanced in age, and pregnancies later in life are often difficult. It would be a tragedy if she lost this baby after many prayers and such a long wait. Perhaps I could be of help with her waiting period, and she can help me with mine."

"I've thought about it some and think that I could take the boys with us, leaving only the two girls with Mary Cleopas. That shouldn't be too burdensome for her. Before seeing you to your cousin's house in Hebron, I will take the boys back to my brother's shop and continue my business there. I hope to be more involved in contracts of house building and therefore I will frequently be away from the shop itself. James can continue his apprenticeship and the other boys can help or play with their relatives. It will be very familiar to them, and my brothers' wives are used to having them around and caring for them."

Mary let that sink into her mind for a minute and said, "Perhaps, the timing of the birth might be overlooked, or at least confused with a period of absence. I shall go where you go Joseph, and I would very much like to see Elizabeth once again."

"The road will be hard. We will walk over hill and dale, but I will bring a couple of donkeys and a tent, and the boys will be a help on the journey."

"Joseph, you are so good to me. I have been blessed with you as my husband."

"No regrets, then?" asked Joseph, smiling gently.

Mary shook her head and looked at him with such loving eyes that Joseph could not help but take her in her arms. He kissed her on the forehead and squeezed her to himself and petted her head, down her neck and to her shoulder. In that moment of intimacy, both Joseph and Mary felt the intercourse of tenderness, love, care, and sacrifice for the other—a union of hearts. Although, they were not able to see it, angels danced, glowed and gloried in the hallowed grace of souls.

Chapter 23
Mary and Elizabeth

The journey to Hebron had been long and hard; however, the people of the north land were quite used to travel and to the hardships and exposure to the elements of living outdoors in rough and diverse terrain. Travellers often relied upon the kindness of people along the route and on the hospitality of relatives. One happy stop they made was in Bethany, at the home of their good family friends Simon and Naomi. Naomi was pregnant with her third child, who would soon join brother Lazarus and sister Mary. Naomi had hardly had time to breathe between babies before another was in her belly! It had been lovely for Mary and Joseph to share a supper and a safe place to sleep for the night with that family. The boys had spread their rugs on the roof of the building, happy to watch the stars and wonder at their creator.

Joseph also made a stop to visit his relatives in Bethlehem, as well as to see Mary's elderly grandparents and cousins and other members of their extended family. The boys were happy to be reunited with their cousins.

Finally, Joseph and Mary arrived in the town of Hebron in the late afternoon. This location was considered a sacred place. It was known as the burial place of Abraham, and was situated in the Judean hills, less than twenty miles south-west of Jerusalem. It was a three-day walk from Bethlehem, with quite a climb over hills, so Joseph did not push it. His wife was with child and that was reason enough to slow the pace.

Joseph stopped the heavily laden donkey in the yard before Zachariah's house.

"You must be exhausted, Mary. Refresh yourself and then go inside to see your cousin. I will see to the donkey; I'll make sure he is fed and watered and has a rub down. I'll follow with the items you need for the stay."

Taking a pitcher of clean water and pouring it into a basin, Mary ran water over her glowing face and washed her hands and then took off her sandals to wash her feet. At least she could still see her feet. She fondly remembered the women saying that they could hardly bend to undo their sandals and wash their feet as their growing bellies got in the way. It would come soon enough, but for right now she could manage it just fine. She quietly entered the house. It took a moment for her eyes to adjust to the darker room. It was much cooler inside as well. She sighed softly, as many travellers do when they finally reach their destination. She was filled with happiness.

"Shalom, Elizabeth," Mary called. "It's your cousin, Mary."

Elizabeth came into the room and saw Mary at the door. At that moment, her baby boy quickened and made a great leaping movement in her womb. At that moment, Elizabeth just knew! She was overcome with the knowledge that could only come from the Spirit.

"Mary," cried Elizabeth with a loud and happy voice. "Blessed are you among women and blessed is the fruit of your womb!" she proclaimed, as she placed her hands on Mary's abdomen.

Mary looked at her with surprise. "You already know I am with child?"

"'Yes, but who am I that the mother of my Lord should come to me? For the moment your greeting sounded in my ears, the baby leapt for joy in my womb'."

"And you know that Joseph is not the father?" Elizabeth nodded.

"Mary, you are twice blessed. Once, because Adonai has chosen you to be the mother of our Lord, and twice because he has blessed you with such a caring and gentle soul as Joseph as a husband." Elizabeth, with tears in her eyes, crossed her arms over her breasts in thanksgiving and then spread them out wide to receive Mary in a sisterly embrace.

"Welcome, my dear. Come and sit, Mary, and I will make some mint tea. Tell me about the journey. Have you been worried about what is happening to you? And, oh my, you are so young!"

Mary smiled and replied, "My soul magnifies the Lord, and my spirit rejoices in God my Savior, for He has regarded the low estate of His handmaiden."[34]

"Mary, for someone so young, you are unbelievably strong and wise and full of grace! I am so pleased that you have come to visit Zachariah and me."

Zachariah met Joseph outside and helped him stable the tired donkey and collect the baggage. He did this in complete silence and body gestures. Joseph had heard from family that Zachariah had lost his voice at about the same time as Elizabeth conceived, but he did not have any details. When the men settled in Zachariah's office space, he took his writing implements and answered Joseph's questions.

"I have sinned, Joseph," confessed Zachariah.

"How does a holy man like yourself sin to such a degree?

"I was visited by an angel who told me about Elizabeth's condition."

"Was this the angel Gabriel?" asked Joseph.

"The very one. You have encountered him too, I imagine. The problem was that I didn't believe my eyes and ears. I had

---

[34] Luke 1:46-55, Excerpt from The Magnificat

doubts as to what I was experiencing. I challenged the magnificent messenger from God. Elizabeth and I had given up on being parents. Elizabeth was beyond her time for childbearing. So, when the angel told me what to call my son, I did not trust his word and thereby the word of our Lord."

"Will this affect your prospects for the position of High Priest?

"Yes, I have been taken out of contention, for now anyway."

Joseph nodded in sympathy and understanding. They sat there in silence for a while and then stood up to join the women in the main room.

Joseph stayed for a couple of days and then made his way back to Bethlehem to join his brothers and children to work. But his thoughts were never very far from Mary. Mary spent some beautiful time with Elizabeth. They genuinely liked each other and spent much time praying, talking, and sharing their pregnancy experiences. They prepared baby clothes, swaddle wraps and blankets. Mary's visit lasted for about three months, and then, when Joseph had finished his contract, he came to take her back home to Nazareth.

Shortly after the departure of her cousin, Elizabeth was delivered of a robust and hardy baby boy who came into the world with loud howling and conviction. The whole village rejoiced with the couple. On the eighth day, the family assembled for the circumcision, assuming that the baby would be named Zachariah after his father. However, Elizabeth told them that they were going to call their son, John. Everyone was shocked because it was common to call your firstborn son after his father, but when they looked to Zachariah for an answer, Zachariah wrote on his tablet, "His name is John." At that moment, his voice was restored. The people were at first stunned, and then afraid. It was not very long before the town talk had spread the miraculous news throughout the hill country. People wondered what force had intervened to bring about this child, John, and what would become of him. [35] Zachariah seemed to be enlightened with prophecy at the birth of his son and his newly found voice. He began to recite a Canticle to answer their questions and fears.

The canticle started with 'Blessed be the Lord the God of Israel because He has visited and ransomed His people.' It ended with, 'And you, O child, shall be called prophet of the Most High; for you go before the Lord to prepare straight paths for Him. Giving his people a knowledge of salvation in freedom from their sins. All this is the work of the kindness of God; he, the Dayspring, shall visit us in his mercy to shine on those who sit in darkness and in the shadow of death, to guide our feet into the way of peace.'[36]

Thus it was that John, later called the Baptist, was born and named.

---

[35] Taken and quoted from Luke 1 57-65

[36] Shortened from Luke 1: 67-79

Chapter 24
The Advent

"Well, the Romans are at it again!" exclaimed Nathan as he entered the workshop.

"What have they done now?" asked Joseph.

"There are notices on the synagogue and there was a Roman messenger in town crying out that Cyrinus, governor of Syria, is responding to Caesar Augustus and demanding that all the world be enrolled for census and tax purposes."

"How is this to be done?" Joseph probed.

"Every head of family is to go to the town of their birth and register their spouse and their children with the authorities there. At least I only need to travel to Cana."

"Travel will be difficult for Mary. We've just returned to Nazareth a couple of months ago. She is now in her ninth month. It will be too uncomfortable and too risky."

"I'm sure that they will make an exception for pregnant women."

"Perhaps I might be able to register everyone without hauling a pregnant woman and little children to Bethlehem."

At that moment, Mary entered the shop with a pitcher of lemon water and cups. Nathan left the shop and returned to the house to give the couple a moment to discuss the upcoming challenges.

"Have you heard the news, Mary?" asked Joseph.

"Yes, I was there in the village when the messenger called out the edict."

"You don't need to go, Mary. Stay here, and I will register us all."

"I don't mind going with you, Joseph. I'm young and strong and I feel very well. I have done the trip to Jerusalem many times. It is not new to me. I will manage. Besides, I want you to be with me when the baby is born."

"Oh, Mary. This may be too much for you in your condition."

"Pregnant women go about their lives all the time, Joseph. We are made of resilient constitutions and I know that the Lord will watch over us."

"I don't know, my dear. It will be difficult, and you know the road is fraught with danger," pleaded Joseph.

"It has never stopped people before," replied Mary, unperturbed.

"Yes, but you are nearing the advent of your delivery and that makes quite a difference."

"We can take the she-ass and I will ride her. She is stout, sturdy and sure of foot. She is very protective of me. We can stop at our usual places on route and be safe for the nights."

"Mary, you are too clever by half. You have a stout heart. I find it hard to go against your will, for I know that a strong force of wisdom guides you and that angels seem to protect you."

"You're right, Joseph. This knowledge comes from a compelling urge."

"Then, I yield to that urge and that wisdom."

Joseph and Mary decided to make the trip alone. They left their children in the care of Mary Cleopas, and Anna stayed a few days after her visit with her daughter. She hoped to be nearby when Mary had her baby. She understood the need for

Joseph to go to his hometown but tried to persuade Mary to stay behind.

"What if the baby comes, Mary? One cannot always tell if it will be early, on time or late, you know," cried Anna.

"All will be well, Imma. You need not worry," responded Mary, in a voice full of certainty.

"Although Joseph has had six children, I don't know that he is a skilled midwife."

"I place myself fully in the hands of the Lord. I trust in Him and will do His will. He guides my decisions even now. His will and my will are in harmony."

"I will pray for your safe travel and your quick return. You know that I'm dying to see and hold my grandchild. I also want to be part of your birthing experience and get firsthand care of our darling baby."

"You can call him grandson, Imma. The angel told me I would give birth to a son. He even told me his name. Jesus."

"Good, that makes it easier to prepare clothes for him. Oh, Mary, I await his coming with such impatience. You will need to forgive your mother, and Jesus' 'savta', grandmother. Cleopas is just as impatient.

The weather conditions were usually not the best at this time of the year. They were nearing the period of Tevet which finds itself in the cooler and rainier winter season. The roads could get muddy and slippery. Their she-ass was sure and steady, which helped them navigate the poor road conditions. However, the angels had looked down favourably on them and they had managed to experience warmer and drier days as they journeyed closer to Bethlehem. They imposed upon the hospitality of Naomi and Simon once more.

Simon had been happy to see them and share news from Galilee and to whine and complain about these new and continual demands of the Roman Empire. The Jews just wanted to be left in peace to worship their God and practice their faith without constant edicts and impositions, some of which went against their beliefs and defiled their synagogues and Temple. The Romans did not respect the Hebrew people and seemed bent on making their lives miserable paying taxes and more taxes. This was, by and large, another decree to do just that.

Naomi was just days away from being delivered of her third child and was happy for adult company. The two women shared their pregnancies, their trials and delights. Mary took advantage of her conversations with Naomi to discuss what she could expect at the delivery of the baby, nursing and caring for such a helpless little person. They laughed when their tunics were being disrupted by the unborn kicking and jabbing their mothers internally.

"Simon says that the baby is dancing in there."

Mary laughed and agreed with Naomi's husband's assessment of the situation.

"Yes, sometimes the foot sticks out so far that I think I could grab it and hold it," chuckled Mary.

At night, when Mary lay down with Joseph, he would whisper soothing things in her ears. He would hold her back to his front, caress her body, kiss her shoulders, and wrap his hands lovingly around her belly and sing songs to the infant. Joseph was besotted with the two people in his arms.

After leaving their home in Bethany, they did not have too far to go before they arrived in Bethlehem. Just before they arrived at their destination, Mary started to show signs that the birth was near. Joseph was very concerned, almost on the verge of panic because everywhere was full. The traffic into the town was dense. It seemed that everyone was responding to the decree and had made their way to their hometown for the census. The talk among the travellers was that there would be very few places to stay. This was confirmed by the voyagers coming out of the town because they could find no available shelter. They had all said to forget about finding lodging because the town was overflowing with visitors.

Joseph was counting on staying at an inn because he knew that his family's homes would be teeming with many relatives who had come for the enrolment. The first few places he approached bore out the information he had received. No rooms were available. This was getting urgent. Although Mary did not make even the slightest moan or complaint, he knew he had to find a place very soon. So, he turned the donkey around and headed for a small cave just on the outskirts of town where he had often retreated to pray and get away from his brothers. It wasn't far. Because it was sometimes used by shepherds when they came into town to sell their stock, it had a few amenities that would be useful for their stay. He was anxious but hopeful. He repeated, "The Lord will provide" when Mary asked where they were heading, and when his heart was palpitating as panic arose. The donkey seemed to sense the urgency and picked up the pace.

"How are you, Mary?"

"I am well, Joseph. I'm not worried. I trust in the Lord. What is happening is the natural way of things."

"Well, not having a place to birth this baby is not a natural thing! It is a frightening thing!"

In a soothing voice, Mary said, "I trust the Lord and I trust you, Joseph, so slow down your breathing and be at peace. All will be well."

Joseph calmed himself, looked up to the heavens and muttered a plea and continued toward his out-of-the-way, spiritual place.

They soon arrived at the spot, where there were pine and terebinth trees around the hillside standing guard. However, it was the large jujube tree at the forefront that dominated the landscape. Because of the season, the jujube tree bore no leaves and no fruit. All that was visible were the long, pointy, menacing thorns. The tree was known by healers to have many beneficial properties. It was large and, in summer, provided ample shade. Its fruit was edible and had medicinal healing value. It was rooted in the hillside and hung over the cave entrance like a canopy. Unbeknownst to everyone, the tree would later provide the crown of thorns for Jesus' head at Golgotha.

The opening of the cave was set into the rocky hill and was inconspicuous to the occasional passerby. Besides being well hidden and unnoticeable, the cave provided a small spring near the tree. Unless you had knowledge of the location, the little spring that gently bubbled was disguised by the tall grasses and wildflowers that grew around it, and so it too was essentially unseen. Itinerant shepherds had known of the site for centuries and occasionally made use of it when they moved their flocks from pastures to market, but as there wasn't enough grass pasture around to sustain the flocks, it remained a location only for temporary housing when required.

Over the years the shepherds had built a few amenities to make the lodging more comfortable. Well hidden behind the tree, the former users had built an overhang covered in grass. Under the overhang, there was a wooden bench made from branches and woven into a lattice seat. There was a heavy sackcloth curtain that covered the entrance. Joseph cleared the debris around the entrance and urged Mary to sit on the bench while he readied the place and saw to the donkey. Mary declined the invitation to sit and claimed it was easier if she kept herself busy. She assisted Joseph in removing the packs from the donkey. They had travelled lightly, but Mary had taken care to pack some baby things, including a gift of a kippah for the baby given to her by Naomi. These items were so small that they took up no room at all in the packs.

There were three different 'rooms' in the cave. Two rooms were connected, and the other was behind and had its own entrance. It was separated from the main room by a waist-high stone wall. It was obviously where the beasts of burden were kept and fed. It was useful to stable animals such as oxen, donkeys, or other animals in need of cover. It would do so again. Joseph entered the cave holding a torch he had made with the rags and grasses that had cluttered the entrance. Joseph needed to bend to enter the cave chamber, but the low doorway gave way to a vaulted room. He had used this place before and he knew there was a place for a fire below an open fissure that seemed to draw the smoke out of the cavern very well. He entered the cavity and found the space, at first glance, to be in good condition. He burned off a few spider webs and circled the space to clear out any crawling creatures that may have nested or dwelt there. Inside, in the dim light, he could see the attached room. He made the same inspection in it and any unwanted creatures scurried out of the cave. This space was obviously used for the sleeping quarters as there were homemade bunks made of a wicker base covered with thick sheep skins. Joseph would put their sleeping rugs on these, and Mary would be able to rest her weary head before her labour began.

Mary entered the grotto and looked around the sparse and meagre surroundings. She smiled because she would at least have a roof over her head to bring this baby into the world. She was not afraid or worried. She even felt a peace in her innermost spirit. It was a humble place, but it was the will of the Almighty, Creator of all worldly things. She knew that her time had come, but she wasn't feeling the pain that had been described to her by other women who had experienced labour. She only hoped that the birth would be easy, even if the setting was not.

The couple made a number of trips to the pack-donkey and relieved her of the rest of her baggage. With the help of additional torches that Joseph had found inside, they had the things they needed for a least an overnight stay. Joseph was not certain that this was the best place to have a baby, but they had no further options at this point. Like many expecting fathers, Joseph was nervous, afraid, and almost weepy. He kept asking himself what he had brought his pregnant wife into. The panic was driven by his feeling of helplessness. It was all up to Mary and Adonai now. Thankfully, he did have jobs to do. He needed to ready a decent place for the birth and find a midwife. Work would calm his spirit.

Mary placed her bundle on the broad stone shelf by the wall. She opened it out and took out a linen sheet and swaddling clothes and the little cap given to her by Naomi. Joseph, who had laid out their sleeping rugs on the cots, guided her with his torch to the little room and suggested that he would place the sheet on the sheep skins and that she should lie down to rest. He reached for the sheet, but Mary was already in motion to do so. He had little choice but to watch her do this. He smiled and shook his head at her strength and determination. She finished and insisted that she was well and feeling little pain at the moment. She reminded him that there was more work to do and that she was quite capable of helping to set things up for the night.

Looking around, they found a bucket and a few rudimentary implements for cooking, and workable oil lamps. There was straw on the floor for warmth under the feet. There was a small manger which was probably left for feeding small animals. It was lower to the ground and was full of straw. Joseph removed the old straw and replaced it with a layer of rushes, and then topped the rushes with sweet, fragrant grasses, and finally, covered the grasses with the down and feathers that the doves had shed nearby. He examined the makeshift bed and ultimately fitted it with a beautiful piece of tan rabbit fur. Joseph then used the bucket to bring in water and lit a fire with grass debris and the stack of wood found beside the fire pit. He set a pot of water on the trivet over the reduced flames and lit the lamps. The room was now bright and warm.

Joseph stepped up to Mary and stood before her, holding her shoulders. He looked her in the eyes and asked, "How are you doing, my little mother?"

"I have some discomfort, enough to know that the baby is on the way, but I am not suffering any great pain."

"It might take a while, so why don't you lie down?"

"Before we do that, Joseph, shall we pray together?" Joseph agreed and led the prayer for a safe and easy delivery.

"Amen," said Mary. "Things seem to have progressed further, my love, and I think that it is time to go to fetch a midwife from the town."

"Are you sure, my sweet, because you will be all alone here."

"I have my Lord and my angels. But do make haste. I know it won't be long now."

Joseph did not waste any more time. He quickly removed the blankets on the she-ass and tethered her to a tree in a grassy area and left on foot towards Bethlehem. He was an older man with a weakened heart and so he could not run, but the Lord had given him strength and stamina and he walked at a pace that would have surprised younger men. He was on a mission, and he needed to be quick about it.

Chapter 25
The Birth of Jesus

Joseph was gone now, and Mary was alone. She continued to tidy their makeshift and provisional home. It was surprising what the herdsmen who had inhabited this grotto had left behind. She stepped outside to watch the sunset. The sky was crimson and radiated gold rays that made the clouds pink and purple. She watched until the brilliant light was replaced by a demure full moon and a smattering of stars. She watched the artwork of the Creator and couldn't help but be grateful for all her blessings. She quietly sang a psalm of thanksgiving. Fortunately, she still felt no real pain, only fullness and a charged movement that wished to radiate outwards. She was feeling a sense of great and intense expectation and at the same time, great peace and serenity.

She re-entered the cavern and noticed that the ceiling fissure must have encountered a down draft and black smoke was billowing into the room. She started to cough. The donkey outside brayed like it was in frantic danger. She needed to look after the animal. Bending over to get a cloth, she noticed that a serpent had secretly and slyly slithered into the room. It was heading for the manger and Mary was filled with dread at the threat that this venomous snake could cause if not caught. She looked around her surroundings and found a staff on the wall. The staff was probably used to prod animals along their treks. The bottom of the stick was divided in two, forming a prong. She slowly moved to it and equally slowly moved towards the viper. It was leering at her, and its forked tongue was sliding in and out of its mouth. Twice, it raised its head off the ground and charged forward. It hissed and bared its pointy and deadly teeth at the woman in its sights. Mary patiently waited as she returned its gaze. Suddenly, in one quick motion, Mary caught the staring, hissing and slippery serpent's head between the prongs and held it to the floor. She was not sure what to do next. The snake's body was twisting and writhing, making large loops with its body in hope to seize Mary's arm. It was getting harder and harder to keep the traitorous, twisting, turning snake pinned to the ground. She secretly prayed for a solution that would save her. The smoke was clearing out and she spied a pair of tongs near the firepit and she bent down and reached for them, but they were just out of her range. Mary kept her eyes on the writhing creature and stretched for the instrument. Her belly had grown large, and it impeded her efforts. The serpent, after many fruitless tries, finally managed to get loose and escape its prison. Alarmingly, in this last desperate attempt to rid itself of its accursed captor, it moved closer to Mary. Mary had to dodge its rising head in its aggressive attack position. With the help of the stick, she again caught the snake by the throat and held it until she overpowered it and pinned it to the earth once again. Alas, for the snake, its machinations had placed Mary closer to the tongs. She grabbed the tool and pinched its head into an incapacitated and stupefied position. By nature, Mary was a lover of animals, even the odious and repulsive ones; however, her motherly instincts and nature were stronger, and she would not allow this creature to remain and return to hurt her family. At that moment, her belly glowed internally, and the snake, still in Mary's tight grip, suddenly stopped moving and stared blankly at Mary and her glowing middle. Its eyes slowly clouded over. At that moment, she knew it was dead. She took a deep breath of relief and walked outside with the tongs and snake at arm's length and deposited the creature a fair distance away, on the other side of the craggy cave, into a stoney pit.

The need to place her hands on her roundness was very strong. She caressed her middle, the womb that held such a precious and sacred bundle. The agitated donkey was still in a fright. She had not stopped braying since the snake had arrived. Mary made her way to the she-ass and petted her mane and nose and soothed her panicky heart.

"We are alright now. The evil is gone. We don't want evil here and he was overtaken. Rest, my loyal friend." She untethered the animal and led her to the stable cave. She would be able to see and be near Mary and that would no doubt calm her excited condition. Mary wandered back to the cave and wondered if she should share this incident with her beloved. The smoke was gone, and the cave was warm and smelt like sweet grass again, and she smiled.

A little breathless, Joseph arrived at the hard beaten road to Bethlehem, where he encountered a group of people heading out of the town. He stopped them and asked if anyone knew of a Hebrew midwife. They pointed to a woman, but she claimed that she wasn't as experienced as another woman, Salome. Joseph asked how he could find her, and the woman gave him directions to Salome's home.

"My name is Ruth," said the first woman. "I will wait for you here, and I will go with you to the birthing. I need to better learn the craft. Where are we going? Which house?" asked the woman.

"My name is Joseph and if you wait here, I will return with the midwife, Salome. I will lead you to the place because it is not a house. It is a cave on the outskirts of town. As you know, there is no room in town anywhere. I have tried," explained Joseph.

Joseph ran ahead quickly to find the midwife. He had no trouble finding her because he knew this town very well. Salome was not the midwife that helped bring his own children to the world; however, she was old, and suffered from a crooked spine stance. If her age was any indication, she indeed was experienced. She responded to Joseph's request immediately but admitted that she would need to ride her ox cart because she was not able to walk that distance. She brought a little leather pouch with rudimentary instruments

166

and healing herbs and oils. She told Joseph to help her harness the ox and guide it through the throng in the busy streets. He picked up the woman, Ruth, on the way.

The pace was slow, and Joseph was anxious to move quicker. A large star lit the midnight-blue skies and also lit their path and so, in that way, they were blessed. As he walked along, tired but full of energy, the world went still. He heard no sounds and saw no movements. Everything seemed to have frozen in place; even the ox was in mid-step and the conversation between the two women had stopped in midsentence. Was this happening? Was it a result of his fatigue and his anxieties? Was it a manifestation of a divine intervention? He had no idea how long it had lasted— perhaps minutes or was in seconds? Then, the universe resumed its life's rhythm and they continued.

Mary was feeling more urgency in the activity within her body. The pulsing had increased. She hoped that Joseph fared well and would soon be there with the midwife. She missed his comforting fussing. To distract herself, she went about making the place homier. As she continued to keep herself busy at this task and that job, she noticed that the fire was getting low and so she added some thick sticks to the coals. The water in the pot that Joseph had set up was getting low as well, so she found a clay pot and went outside to the spring to fill it.

The night was tinged with an unusual bluish hue. The sky was black, and the stars sparkled, but the moon was imbued with a beautiful shade of azure. There was a great silence. No cricket sang, no bird chirped, no creature scurried, and no branch moved. The world was perfectly still. The universe seemed to have come to a sudden and complete halt. She carefully filled her pitcher and stared again at the night sky. The image filled her with a sense of awe. She gazed reverently at the wonder and splendour of the sight before her. Her spirit was suddenly filled with an energy and verve that completely consumed her. She was in full communion with nature, her person, and the divine.

After Mary had finished collecting the fresh water, she re-entered the cavern and poured it into the iron pot over the embers. She turned and put the clay pot away. As she did so, her abdomen began to glow and to gently and continuously pulse. The room around her changed. It was filled with a shimmering blue light. The light gradually transformed into the shapes of several angels. She recognized that Gabriel was among them.

"Hail, Mary, full of grace. Blessed are you. Your time has come to deliver," he announced.

"I am the Lord's handmaiden. May it be done to me according to his word."[37]

At that moment, an even brighter white light appeared. It was so brilliant that she could not look upon it, but rather bowed her head. The splendid and shimmering white light came forth towards her and enwrapped her with its dazzling aura. Now she too was shimmering and shining. She felt warm, cherished, and in a state of complete peace and ecstasy. Time did not exist. It was a moment of eternity. Mary felt the relief of a weight. There was a lightness and an emptiness in her body. There was no pain, just a sublime joy. Rapture. She opened her eyes and slowly raised her head, and the white light was gone but the angels in their blue light were holding a beautiful and hearty infant radiating a soft white light like an aura around his body. Wonder of wonders, Jesus was born as he was conceived. Godly and miraculous conception, and godly and miraculous birth! Gabriel held the baby in his extended arms, extended the infant forward in divine presentation, and firmly and gloriously pronounced: "Alleluia,

---

[37] Luke 1:38,

alleluia!' The other angels chorused the words in heavenly melody.

"Behold, the Son of the Most High," announced Gabriel. "He will be the sacrificial lamb who will save His people and the whole world. He is God's promise that our prophets proclaimed."

At that moment, a chorus of the most beautiful music ever heard by humankind filled the cavern as the celestial beings sang 'Glory to God in the highest' in a most blissful harmony. Then, all the angels bowed down in homage to Jesus. Mary looked upon the fruit of her womb with euphoria and worship. [38]

Mary repeated her canticle:

"My being proclaims the greatness of the Lord,

My spirit finds joy in God my saviour,

For he has looked upon his servant in her lowliness;

All ages to come shall call me blessed.

God who is mighty, has done great things for me,

Holy is his name..."[39]

Mary fell on her knees and looked upon Gabriel, holding the young infant, and said:

"I know that he is not mine. He is my Lord and my deliverer. I am filled to the brim with love for him and, with God's will and might, I will humbly serve Him by caring for his Son."

––––––––––––––––––

[38] See also: Ven. Mary of Agreda, *The Divine Life of the Most Holy Virgin, pp. 79-82*
[39] Luke 1:46-49

Gabriel then reached out and placed the infant into Mary's waiting arms.

"Oh, my sweet Jesus."

She caressed his little face, kissed his little head, and embraced his little body to her breasts. The newborn squirmed and stretched and twisted his body slightly, throwing his little arms as he yawned. He fluttered his eyes a couple of times, pouted his mouth, and then fell into a deep sleep. Mary did not know how long she sat there holding her baby and looking at his beauty and his wonder. She did not notice that the angels had left with their blue light, leaving instead the gentle, warm red glow from the fire. Mary rocked the sleeping baby and gave thanks to the Lord for having been so blessed.

Joseph and the two midwives approached the cave, the ox plodding along far too slowly for Joseph's liking.

"I see lights of different colours coming out over there!" shouted Ruth.

"That is where the cave is located," replied Joseph, concerned, and growing more fearful by the minute.

The younger woman did not wait for permission but ran ahead to the grotto. By the time she arrived there was only a red light that filled the space. She pushed the curtains aside and entered the cavern.

She was stunned. There, sitting on the floor on a blanket, was Mary, holding her newborn. There was no evidence of trauma, blood, or afterbirth. She could not believe her eyes. Even in her experience, this was not the way of things. This was totally unnatural. What had just happened here—a miracle?

By this time, Joseph had come jogging into the cave. He saw that Mary and the baby were fine, even calm, and serene. He took a deep breath and blew it out in a great sigh of relief.

"How are you, my dove? And the baby?"

"We are both well, Joseph. Do not fret. It was an easy birth."

"I'm glad to hear that, my love. I was so afraid for you."

By this time, the profile of a hunched-back old woman leaning on a stick appeared at the entrance. She, too, was stunned and amazed at the domestic scene before her.

"I have never seen anything like this," exclaimed the younger woman, lifting her arms in the air.

Shaking her head, the old midwife said: "Nor I. This is a very unusual birthing, indeed. It is all too clean and neat."

"Does the new mother usually look fresh, calm and immaculate?"

"Not in all my years! It is completely contrary to nature. This looks like a miraculous birth," noted Salome, the old midwife.

"There should be afterbirth, a cord, body fluids. Where is the afterbirth?"

Joseph, finally coming out of his shock and stupor, bent down before his wife and had his first look at the boy. He gently removed the covering that Mary had placed over her son in her arms. The cherubic infant was naked and sleeping peacefully. Joseph took the soft, tiny hand in his large, rough one and gazed at him with adoring eyes. He picked up his little foot and placed a tender kiss on his toes. "He is absolutely beautiful, Mary. He is perfect! And you, Mary, my love, look so lovely. You are radiant and magnificent. You have done well. How are you feeling?"

"I am very happy, Joseph. We have a beautiful boy, my love."

"Mary, did you deliver on your own?" asked the younger midwife.

Mary nodded but added: "I had help from on high."

"Did you deliver the afterbirth?" questioned Salome.

"No, midwife," responded Mary.

"My name is Salome, and this is Ruth. Mary, is it possible to examine you? It is important because the afterbirth must be delivered, or you will get sick and could die."

"If you feel it is important, you may examine me," Mary said.

Joseph looked at his wife, and the women, and without being asked, he left the cave and went to deal with the ox.

"I will take the child from you, if I may?" offered the second midwife. She carefully shifted the infant to her arms. She laid him on the shelf, expecting to give him a bath. She discovered that the baby was already spotless, and his fine dark hair was already dry and needed no attention. She covered the baby again and held him in her arms and rocked him gently. There was something about this child. For some inexplicable reason, she did not want to put him down.

In the meantime, Salome had placed Mary on her cot and in position for an intimate examination.

"I don't see an afterbirth anywhere and I need proof that you delivered this baby by natural means." And she saw that Mary was still a virgin. This was not possible. Was she imagining this scene? What was going on? She was confused and doubtful. Was this baby brought to the cave? How could this happen? It did not make sense.

Upon removing her hand, she noticed that her hand had gone limp. She no longer could straighten her fingers. They just hung there useless. A midwife needed both her hands to do the work of a midwife. She groaned and became terrified. If her hand was useless, she was useless. "Oh, Lord, what have I done, what shall I do? I was wrong to doubt to question your power, Lord." Salome, now in an attitude of humility and contrition, expressed her sorrow for having tempted the living God, and prayed that He not blame her, and to remember the poor children of Israel, and she pleaded to the Creator of the universe that she did much good for expectant mothers and newborn children in His name. After making her supplication, her mind inexplicably sensed that the Lord had heard her prayer and urged her to reach for the infant and carry him. Upon touching the baby in loving contact, her hand was restored, and she held the baby close to her heart and gave thanks for the miraculous blessings she had just experienced.

"This is no ordinary child," announced Salome. "I will defend and protect this child for the rest of my days."

Then, she made a pot of mint tea for Mary, and she and Ruth prepared a small supper with the provisions that Joseph had purchased in Bethlehem.

The two midwives coached Mary on how to nurse and care for the infant. They cooed and reassured the new mother and calmed the new father. Later, when they left to go back to town, they vowed to Mary and Joseph that they would keep this birth a secret and make certain that no evil would be directed their way.

Chapter 26
The Visits

According to the book of Leviticus, a mother who had just given birth to a male was considered unclean for seven days. Although Mary had not experienced the usual form of birth, she nevertheless respected the Jewish law. She also held to the requirement of a forty-day confinement. She took advantage of this time to keep house and pray, but mostly to admire and care for her baby. The donkey and the ox, when the older midwife came to check in on Mary, looked into the room where the infant had been laid in the manger. They never made a noise when he was sleeping but seemed strangely interested in the newborn child.

After the first couple of days, Joseph went into town to announce the news to his family, and to purchase supplies for Mary and the baby. He officially registered himself, his children and Jesus, as prescribed by the law. He sent a messenger to Cana to alert Anna that she was a grandmother. She would be thrilled with the announcement, but disappointed that she could not have been with Mary during her hour of delivery. No doubt, she would make her way to Bethlehem to visit.

During his stay at the cave, Joseph built a table and some stools for sitting. He carved out eating bowls and a platter. He also picked up a few small jobs in town that provided him a small earning. He bought food, wine, and other provisions that they needed in their new home. He tried to pay the midwife, but she refused because she said she had done nothing to earn that pay. Joseph left gifts of nuts, vegetables, dates, and figs at her door anyway. He was thankful for her discretion. The last thing he wanted was for stories to spread and be amplified into wild rumours in the community. He was also thankful that she visited Mary, especially when he was working in town. She was a righteous woman, that Salome.

On the eighth day, Joseph and Mary took their baby to the synagogue to be circumcised. They gave their infant the name of Jesus as they had been instructed by the angel Gabriel. Jesus recovered well from the surgical ritual that marked him as a son of the Hebrews. Only Mary and Joseph knew that he was also the Son of God. They kept that knowledge in their hearts and understood the breadth of the sacred responsibility that had been given to them.

Mary continued enjoying the quiet and the natural beauty of her surroundings. Joseph had fashioned a canvas sling for her to carry Jesus on the front and a wooden carrier to transport Jesus on her back. She went for walks and talked to God and admired his creation and handwork. She gave thanks for the great honour he had bestowed on her with the gift of Jesus. She asked for the graces needed to care for her precious gift from God and asked for his protection to ensure his well-being and safety.

Late one afternoon, Mary and Joseph both heard a commotion outside. As they listened more carefully, they heard the bleating of sheep and the commands of shepherds.

"It sounds like shepherds and their flocks," said Joseph.

"Oh, dear. I wonder if we are in their spot, and if they were planning on staying here for the night?" wondered Mary out loud.

"I'll go and greet them and offer hospitality." Joseph went outside, and Mary, who had just wrapped her baby in swaddling, placed Jesus in his manger crib.

"Shalom," hailed Joseph. There were three shepherds, and a flock of about a hundred sheep with them. The shepherds were a pretty shaggy lot, wearing short sheepskin tunics with no sleeves. They kept themselves warm with large, coarse woolen cloaks. They were heavily bearded and wore old and dusty sandals strapped up their calves. Each held a crook in his hand as they walked slowly toward the cave.

"Shalom," the shepherds returned in unison, bowing their heads.

"I hope that we are not occupying the lodging you were hoping to use tonight," inquired Joseph.

"No, no. We didn't know about this shelter. A few nights ago, we were in fields not far away, minding our sheep as usual. The night sky was very clear, and we were curious about an unusual star marking the heavens," explained one of the shepherds.

Another took over the story. "And something wonderful happened. The sky flashed with a beautiful blue light. It was frightening, and we were afraid," told the shepherd. The third man was too shy to speak but he nodded firmly and demonstrated how they were fearful upon witnessing the display in the sky.

"The bright light took the shape of angels, and they began to sing the most beautiful music we have ever heard. I know that we are just poor, humble sheepherders, and we are dirty, and we smell, but the angels were glorious! Far too beautiful for folks like us."

"We fell immediately to our knees and covered our heads with our cloaks. We were shaking with fear," exclaimed the other.

"They were singing the most lovely refrain: 'Glory to God in the highest and peace on earth to men of goodwill.' It was the most amazing sight we have ever witnessed. We may be poor, humble, dirty, and smelly, but we are good men."

"One of the angels said to us: 'Be not afraid.' We slowly took our covers off and looked at the magnificent splendour of the glorious angels."

"'You need not fear,' they said. 'We bring you good tidings. Tidings of great joy! For unto the world is born a saviour. In the town of David, you will find him. You will know him by these signs: he is wrapped in swaddling clothes and lying in a manger.'" The third, shy shepherd continued to nod and applaud the news.

Again, the other shepherd took over the story and said, "Behold, they started singing the refrain again. Music so sweet and glorious that all the world seemed to stop. We left the fields and led our sheep towards Bethlehem, and on our way, we found ourselves here with you. We apologize for talking so much, but we shepherds don't usually have much to talk about, and when we have news like this, we just can't stop talking."

"Is the Saviour in there?" finally asked the shy shepherd.

"Yes. You can come and visit the baby. His name is Jesus and my wife's name is Mary."

The three shepherds walked quietly and humbly into the grotto, and in the glow of the fire and lamps were able to lay eyes on the most radiant child, wrapped in swaddling clothes and lying in a manger just as the angels had described. Their hearts were filled with a worshipful spirit and great joy. They nodded to acknowledge the young, beautiful mother. She welcomed them graciously. They fell on their knees. They knew that this was not an ordinary boy-child. Might this really be the promised Messiah? The angels had told them that this, indeed was the Saviour. They were beside themselves with awe and adoration. They stayed in that position for a long moment. They did not want to leave. There was such a pull towards this infant. Mother Mary was also surrounded by a gentle, shimmering light that seemed to glow from within her. The entire scene was just too awesome to describe.

After a while, Joseph spoke up and said, "Let me offer you water for you and your sheep. There are troughs over there and I will fill my buckets from the spring. You can fill your cups in the spring, too. I can offer you some bread and some cheese which is left over from our evening meal. When you are finished eating and quenching your thirst, you are welcome to pasture here for the night.

The herdsmen took Joseph up on his offer and slept under the stars as they were accustomed. The next morning, they asked if they could again take a peek at the baby. They each gave a lamb—the best of their flock—perfect and without blemish, as a gift to the family. They then departed for their usual pastures contented, fulfilled, and in peace.

The message had finally arrived, and Anna and Cleopas wasted no time in travelling to Bethlehem. Anna and her second husband would stay in the family home. Anna was impatient to see the newborn infant. Her daughter had given birth to a baby boy! The missive had said that all had gone well and that both mother and baby were hearty. But she had to see for herself. She blew out a long breath and wondered if the distance could shrink or the time speed up so that she could see her precious daughter and grandson. She thought of Joachim and hoped he was experiencing this great joy from the heavens. And she would soon see the child, if only this donkey would move along faster! She knew that she was not being virtuous in her anxiety, so she took some time to pray and sing psalms. That always managed to calm her and return her to more reasonable expectations.

Finally, they arrived in Bethlehem. Anna quickly dismounted the donkey and greeted her family. It was late now, and she would need to wait until tomorrow morning for Joseph's brother to bring her to the site of the birth. A cave! She could not believe that Jesus was born in a shepherd's stable and temporary shelter. What meager accommodations for such an important child! However, Mary was still in her confinement and strangely enough, Joseph, Mary, and Jesus sounded to be comfortable in their private and quiet domicile. At least, so said the other members of the family who had visited, bringing amenities to ensure the new family's comfort. Perhaps being secluded in the countryside so near to Bethlehem was not such a bad idea. This would be better for Mary to recover than in a busy household where there was constant chaos and disruption. Still, such a humble place to begin a childhood! Adonai knew best, she finally admitted, as she asked forgiveness for her questioning the work of the Lord Almighty.

"Oh, Mary, he is perfect and so beautiful!" cried Anna upon seeing her dear grandson.

"He is indeed beautiful. He is awake more now. His eyes are so knowing. They sparkle with an inner flame of the spirit. Sometimes, I am overwhelmed by his beauty and the massive responsibility of care I have as his mother. I am overtaken with elation and then I am filled with the dread of his destiny."

"Do you know his destiny?" asked Anna.

"No. Gabriel only said that 'great would be his dignity and he will be called Son of the Most High. The Lord God will give him the throne of David, his father. He will rule over the house of Jacob forever, and his reign will be without end.'[40] That is a lot to keep in my heart, Imma."

"Mary, my dear daughter. You have certainly been blessed with this duty. But I am sure that you will be given the wisdom that you require to raise this child. God is always in control, and no more than He is with His Son. His destiny is in the hand of the Almighty and you need only obey and listen to His Word."

_____

"You are absolutely correct, Mother. He will provide as He always does, confessed Mary."

"He is awake now. Let me see this little grandson of mine—truly a gift from God—full of hope and promise for our future. Oh look, Mary, he is smiling at me."

Anna examined the baby lying before her. He really was beautiful. He was chubby and he was energetic. His lively little legs and arms moved in a spirited way, and he showed his delight at facing his 'savta'." He had an alluring face with bright, sparkling eyes that were starting to take on their true colour. He looked destined to get soft, green-brown eyes that could hold you captivated as you searched their depths. He had a good thatch of dark brown hair that was already starting to curl like his mother's. He really was perfect.

Anna visited every day and was always disappointed when it was finally time to return to her family's dwelling. What would she do when it was time to go back to Galilee? She would do it, with great regret but with great anticipation of the new family eventually moving back to Nazareth. She was going to miss holding, rocking, and kissing that child. She was smitten with him, and she had to leave as soon as Jesus was presented at the Temple.

Chapter 27
The Presentation of Jesus

At the time of the Presentation of Jesus at the Temple, Simeon was the High-Priest. He felt his many years and could not remember how many Presentations he had witnessed. He was tired now. The years had not been kind to him and he longed to join the angels in a place without distress. The only person who was older was the prophetess, Anna who, in spite of her elderliness, was present at the Temple every day. She was the one who had confirmed Simeon's own revelation that he would experience death only when he had witnessed the Saviour of the world. The Holy Spirit had told him that as well. He hoped that it would be soon because he did not have much leg to stand on anymore. In the end, it was Elohim's will and not his, so enough dawdling. He had a job to do, to consecrate this new son of Joseph ben Jacob. He silently said a prayer that this might be the time when he would see the Anointed of the Lord. He hurried and made his final preparations for the Presentation.

According to the Law of Moses, Presentations occurred forty days after the birth of a firstborn. The family had just arrived and were carrying a small wooden cage containing their sacrificial offer of two pigeons or turtledoves. This time, they were turtledoves. He asked the parents to present their son. As they did, Simeon's heart leapt in his chest. His brain swooned for a moment. He was filled with an overwhelming sensation of joy. This was the Anointed One! He just knew! Reverently, he took the child in his arms and said:

'Now, Master, you can dismiss your servant in peace; You have fulfilled your word, for my eyes have witnessed your saving deed displayed for all the peoples to see: A revealing light to the Gentiles, the glory of your people, Israel.' [41]

All the guests, Anna, Cleopas, Joseph's brothers and all the extended family that had come to participate in the ritual ceremony, were a little confused and bewildered. They did not know what Simeon had meant and excused the behaviour as the mental ramblings of a very old man. Anna suspected something different but was not entirely certain what it could mean.

After completing the ritual, Simeon gazed at the parents. He recognized Mary from her Temple days, and he remembered the contest that had given Joseph to Mary in marriage. He now understood that everything was evolving as it should. He looked at Mary and was saddened by the revelation he had received regarding her destiny.

"Mary, it is wonderful to see you again," acclaimed the High Priest.

"Shalom, Rabbi. We marvel at our blessed son and what you have said about him."

"Yes, but Mary, it will not be easy to suffer the trust you have been given as you are also part of the salvation story."

"I pray that the Lord will give me the wisdom I will need and will make known to me his will."

Simeon looked upon her radiant face and was silent as he composed the words-- the way he would deliver his new enlightenment. Finally, he said: "This child is destined to be the downfall and the rise of many in Israel, a sign that will be

---

[41] Luke 2:29-33

opposed and you yourself shall be pierced with a sword—so that the thoughts of many hearts may be laid bare."[42]

These were troubling words on such a joyful day. Mary understood deep in her heart that this would be her vocation for the rest of her life—a future filled with both joy and sacrifice. She was both elated and afraid at the same time.

Before the little family left the Temple, Mary went to visit her friend and mentor, the elderly prophetess Anna. She presented her with a bundle of food, a new cushion to sit on, a new tunic and a heavily woven cloak for the cold.

"Shalom, dear friend. How are you, Anna?"

"Old and aching, but so happy to see you again, Mary. I see you have a son."

"Let me introduce you to Jesus, my son." She unwrapped the blankets that covered the infant who was excited to kick his way out of his wrappings. Anna looked upon the baby. She placed her hand on his chubby leg and was overwhelmed with delight. She looked to the heavens and gave thanks for the deliverance of Jerusalem. She, too, was now ready to die.

Mary and Anna talked for a short while to catch up on the activities of Temple life. Mary missed Anna and told her so. Anna missed her too and thanked her for the gift of provisions she had brought, but mostly for letting her set eyes upon her precious and holy son.

Mary and Joseph went back to their temporary shelter and began the preparations for the long journey back to Galilee.

---

[42]Luke 2:34-36

Chapter 28
Visit of the Magi

Three distinguished fellows were seated in an inn in Jerusalem. They had come from three different nations but had one common purpose. All three were fascinated by an unusually bright star in the firmament and felt compelled to seek it out. Unknown to each other, they had travelled by camel, horse, and litter to arrive at the same place in Jerusalem, at the same moment. They had met by coincidence in the inn's eating room when they each heard the others inquire about the star and how to contact the king. The three magi shared similar interests in astrology and, in particular, this vivid celestial apparition. They all also felt a calling and a need to discover its meaning. Together, sharing a libation and a meal, they discussed their plans for realizing their story and their goals. They all spoke some Greek and their conversation revolved around what was the nature of the force that had induced them to travel such a great distance. They were curious about the star, but even more about their compulsion to follow and find it. Finally, they were speculating about the outcome of their journey and the mystery of their final destination.

Melchior was the older of the three. He had journeyed from Persia. He was a member of the Parthian Empire royalty. Caspar had travelled by camel from India and was a trained astronomer who was educated in the study of the stars in the night sky. The third man was Balthazar, who had travelled by horse north from Ethiopia through the region of Arabia. He was a chief's son and a healer in his tribe.

"The star seems to have stopped moving here or close by," reported Melchior.

"I have noticed its halt here as well," noted Balthazar, tipping his cup to his mouth.

"How do we discover the specific location of our final destination? I feel sure that it is not here in Jerusalem," added Caspar, shaking his head. "It is a beautiful city, but I do not feel the call here."

"We are strangers here and we need to ask around," suggested Balthazar.

"I have been doing that. There is a story reported by shepherds that came into town to sell their stock, that there was a newborn child nearby that is believed to be destined for great things. He is of the royal line of David and will grow up to lead his people. They also said something to the effect that this child will be called Son of the Most High,"[43] contributed Melchior.

"What does that mean?" asked the bewildered Caspar.

"Regardless, we are foreigners and should present ourselves to King Herod. I understand that he is the sovereign of the Hebrews whilst the Roman Empire occupies the country," said Caspar.

"He is a client king and not too popular among the Jews, so I hear," offered Melchior.

"Well, I have heard that he is collecting taxes for the Romans, and for himself, of course. He aspires to build great palaces to secure his place among the Roman elite and to prove his royalty and power to his countrymen," noted Caspar.

Balthazar nodded, and added, "I have learned a great deal from speaking to the ordinary citizens of Jerusalem. He is like many kings—present royalty excepted. He feels threatened from all sides. He believes that his status as king is precarious. He is not a natural Jew, but a converted one through marriage, and he suspects that the Jews do not feel that he is totally

---

[43]Taken from Luke 1: 3.

legitimate. He was appointed by the Romans and that makes him both suspicious and reviled by most of his subjects, and with one wrong move, he could be ousted by the Roman landlords."

"That is good information to know, Balthazar. It might help us deal with a distrustful king," affirmed Melchior.

After sharing the information about the Jewish King, they left the inn and made their way to his palace, where they succeeded in obtaining an audience with him. They were escorted into Herod's presence, where they offered greetings to the king. When he asked them their purpose in travelling to his land, Melchior responded.

"We are seeking the child who is called the newborn king of the Jews."

"We have observed his star at its rising and have come to pay him homage," explained Caspar. A frown appeared on the king's face.

"I was unaware that there was anybody in line for my throne except my own son, Herod Antipas," returned Herod, obviously perturbed by the statements of the visitors.

Distressed about this news, Herod proceeded to call together the chief priests, scribes, and palace officials, in order to learn just how to find this newborn "leader". A number of his advisors responded that the rumours—and they were just rumours—suggested that the child could be found in Bethlehem. They reminded Herod of what the prophets from the Scriptures had said:

'And you, Bethlehem, land of Judah, are by no means least among the princes of Judah, since from you shall come a ruler who is to shepherd my people, Israel.'[44]

Hearing this, Herod began to feel very threatened. He probed the magi for more information about the star and this royal child and asked them to report back to him about the details of his location in order that he, too could laud him. After the three men had left, he started to make plans to organize the overthrow of this usurper.

"I'm not sure that Herod was totally truthful with us," proposed Caspar from atop his camel.

"I got the same feeling,' said Balthazar as he mounted his steed.

"I agree," commented Melchior. "This news greatly upset him and the last thing on his mind is to pay homage to a would-be replacement to his kingship. I suggest that we do not return by way of Jerusalem but instead seek alternative routes back to our homelands," suggested Melchior as the elderly man was helped into his litter.

Compared to their recent travels, it was not far from Jerusalem to Bethlehem. The star was rising again, and it seemed brightest over a spot just outside the town itself. Arriving at the community, the three scholarly gentlemen made their way into the local market to inquire. Before long, they learned of a family that had set up a temporary home just on the outskirts of the town. The townspeople were very protective of this information because Joseph was one of their own, and they suspected something mysterious and miraculous had happened there. The citizens were afraid for

---

[44] Matthew 2:6-7

the family and were reluctant to give directions to just anybody. However, in the end, the gold coins were too strong an incentive, and, besides, the three scholarly men seemed trustworthy. As a result, some residents provided the whereabouts of the newborn child. It was too late to complete the quest that night, so the three men found an inn and settled in for the night. As they slept, they all dreamed of taking different routes back to their homes. In the morning, with the directions they had acquired the evening before, they set out to the meet this 'miraculous' person.

Joseph was walking toward Bethlehem to look for work when he was met with a caravan of richly dressed and distinguished men riding mounts of evident quality, who were heading in the opposite direction, toward the cave where Mary and Jesus were located. They were foreigners by all appearance, and his protective instincts surfaced as he waited for them to reach him. Joseph looked like an ordinary working man, dressed in a short tunic, sturdy sandals, a leather pouch strapped on his shoulder, a brown homespun cloak, and a walking staff. He was no match, in strength or number, for the strangers on the road before him. Joseph was nervous, and he prayed for the protection of the Lord.

"Shalom," greeted Joseph with a humble bow.

"Shalom," the three men responded in unison.

Melchior spoke passable Aramaic, and so he spoke for the others. "We are seeking the lodging of a family who have just given birth to a royal son. Can you lead us to him?"

"And what business would you have with this family?" responded Joseph carefully.

"We have travelled a great distance from faraway lands of the east, following a star which outshines all the others; it has led us to news of the birth of a special child."

"Yes, I know of what star you speak. It has been high in the sky over us for some time now. Why is this child of interest to you?" asked Joseph, still cautious and suspicious.

"We don't know, really. We felt a strong urge to follow the star to see if our destinies lay in this quest."

"Why do you seek this child?" asked Joseph again.

"We mean him no harm. We wish to pay him homage and we have brought gifts," offered Melchior as he pointed to the full bags on their mounts.

Joseph took a moment to scrutinize them. He looked directly into their faces, and he found no trace of guile or evil there. Finally, an inner voice told him that they were men of their word and innocent of any threat to Joseph or his family.

"I will lead you to them. Follow me. I am the child's father."

On their way, Joseph shared a conversation with Melchior and learned more about who they were and where they came from. He was convinced by the end of the journey that Jesus and Mary were safe.

"Let me go in first to prepare my wife for your visit."

Melchior nodded and the entourage waited outside.

Mary had just finished nursing the baby, who was growing stronger and more healthy every day. She was sitting with Jesus on her lap when Joseph announced the visit of three very noble gentlemen. He gave her a little background about them, and they shared the mystery of a visit by such august visitors from afar. Mary acquiesced. She said, "We must get used to having unusual things happen to us, Joseph, as this child is not an ordinary child." Joseph nodded, then went outside and beckoned the three men of the world to enter and meet the Son of the Most High.

The three travellers slowly stepped into the cave room, and upon laying their eyes on the radiant infant sitting on his mother's knee, they were transformed in their souls, and they all knew immediately that this was indeed an anointed child. They rejoiced, fell to their knees, and paid him homage. After several minutes, they each put forward their gifts. Melchior gave a chest of gold coins. Caspar placed a beautiful jar of frankincense before the child, and Balthazar contributed a container of myrrh. All three items were treasures of great value. Mary and Joseph both gave sincere thanks for these valuable gifts, albeit surprised by this unexpected turn of events.

Shortly thereafter, the three magi made their final bows and left the rustic lodging, then fed and watered their animals. Before they left, Melchior explained to Joseph that Herod was aware of Jesus and that he and his companions suspected that the king might have malicious intentions regarding the child. He explained that stories of the child's royal blood were spreading throughout the region and that Herod felt threatened by this news. Having delivered this warning, the three scholarly men quietly turned away from Joseph and began their journeys to their distant homes.

Joseph was deeply worried and distraught about this report. When he shared it with Mary, she kept it close to her heart.

Later, in his sleep, an angel instructed Joseph to leave his homeland and escape to Egypt and not to return until he received notice, because Herod would soon be actively searching for Jesus.

Chapter 29
Flight to Egypt

When Joseph returned to Bethlehem some days after the visit of the magi, the whole of the population was in a state of alarm. Travellers from Jerusalem were reporting that when Herod heard that the three wise men, whom he had asked to alert him as to the location of the newborn king, had gone back to their homes using different routes, he was in a rage. He went into a fit of anger because he felt that they had mocked and made a fool of him by ignoring his royal request. It was said that his anger was such that he had ordered men to find this would-be-king in Bethlehem immediately. When they returned without having found the child, he went into a further tantrum and ordered his soldiers to kill all male children under two years of age. The mothers of boy babies were in a panic, not knowing what to do with their suckling children. Herod's men would be arriving soon and where could they hide? Would they be spared the brutal loss of their children? There were no secret places for them to hide as the search would no doubt be thorough. Joseph felt the grip of fear as he remembered that he had registered his family at the census roll call. They knew his family existed. He needed to act immediately. With some of the gold coins Melchior had given him, Joseph bought the supplies that they would need for a long and difficult journey. These included a pack-donkey to carry food and clothing for them and the baby, rugs, blankets, a tent, and water gourds and bags of feed for the animals for the passage through the desert. On his way home, he encountered a patrol of Herod's men who rudely questioned him. Joseph was frightened out of his mind. A thousand worries passed through his head as he panicked about the safety of Mary and her baby.

"Who are you? Name?"

"Joseph, bar Jacob."

"Do you have a family? Where is it?" hollered one of the guards.

"At home."

"Do you have a son?"

"Yes, I have four."

"How old are they?"

"They are seven, nine, twelve and fourteen."

"No boys under two years of age?"

"No, not of that age. My sons are older." Here, Joseph was being honest, but not entirely truthful. He was paltering the facts to mislead the soldiers. In reality and honestly, Jesus was not his true son.

"Where is your home?"

"I live in the wilderness on the outskirts of Bethlehem. I am trying to find carpentry work in the town."

"We will be visiting all families soon. It is useless to hide; we will find you!" barked the soldier.

The soldiers continued toward Bethlehem and Joseph hurried back to the cave. He kept looking over his shoulder to see if the soldiers were following him. They were not for now; however, this made the need to flee the area even more vital and imminent. The interrogation could have been much worse, and his mind was somewhat put at ease because Joseph had a sense that these two fellows really did not have the stomach for the butchering task they were expected to undertake. They were probably fathers, too, but they also needed their heads to be able to feed their own children. They would, in the end, follow orders. The incident had put great stress on Joseph's heart, but he needed to make haste and hoped that the angels that seemed to be watching over Mary would do their part.

Mary and Joseph prepared the things that they would need for the journey. Joseph packed the she-ass and his newly acquired donkey. They both tried to catch a little sleep before they left for a nighttime trek. However, their sleep was restless and unsettled. Neither wanted to think about their displacement and frightening new circumstances. They had no friends and no family in Egypt. What had they gotten themselves into?

Before they set off on their perilous journey, Joseph and Mary asked the Almighty to protect them, to keep them safe and to make their journey south and west easy. They asked for the courage to completely put their trust in the Lord as they recited well-known psalms:

'Great peace have those who love your law;

Nothing can make them stumble.'[45]

After sunset, and having given their confidence to Adonai, they left with their pack animals. Mary rode one, with Jesus in a sling close to her breast and heart. The other animal carried their supplies. The air was crisp, the stars were bright, and the moon was luminous. The night was silent as they made their way toward Egypt in hope and prayer.

They headed toward Hebron and would spend their first night at the home of Zachariah and Elizabeth to warn them of what they had learned about Herod's wicked intentions. On the road just outside of Bethlehem, they encountered the place where Rachel, mother of Joseph and Benjamin, had been buried. The sight of the tomb of Rachel filled Mary with distress. Her heart was overflowing with the grief of knowing that innocent babies in Bethlehem were being slaughtered. She felt mortified, and in part to blame for the loss of these innocents. While she and her baby were managing to escape,

---

[45] Psalm 119: 165

many other families would weep with the loss of their children. The cries and shrieks of women and children screamed in her head. She remembered that

Jeremiah had said:

'A cry was heard at Ramah,

Sobbing and loud lamentation:

Rachel bewailing her children:

No comfort for her, since they were no more.'[46]

Her sorrow was heart-wrenching.

The angels of the Lord were indeed with the holy family as they plodded over the hills and through the valleys of their journey. The going was slow, with many rest stops to feed and change Jesus. He was an easy child who rarely made a fuss and only cried when in need of care. Sometimes, Joseph would relieve Mary of the weight of the child in her sling and carry him in the back carrier he had designed for travel. The distance from Bethlehem to Hebron was not far, but it was a challenge for a family with a little one and for a complete exodus of home and hearth. They arrived at their cousin's house in the early afternoon of the next day. Joseph explained to Zachariah and Elizabeth the developing situation in Bethlehem, and that he feared a total massacre of young children of Bethlehem and the surrounding hills.

"You know, Zachariah, that some of the soldiers will not trouble themselves to discover if the child is a boy or a girl. They will treat them all the same and the slaughter will not only be the male children."

---

[46] NAB, Matthew 2:18

"Yes, once the rage of killing gets into their blood, the soldiers will be in a frenzy of indiscriminate and brutal conduct. Some of them seem to feed on the energy and fire of evil," bemoaned Zachariah.

"How horrible! Those poor, poor people," cried Elizabeth.

"We were very fortunate to leave when we did. The three foreign men who came to visit had hinted to Joseph of their fear of Herod's jealous reaction to the stories of a new king having been born," reported Mary.

"But to resort to such brutality and cruelty is so unjust and sinful," lamented Zachariah. "No one deserves this!"

"May the Lord bring peace to the souls of those mothers and fathers," sobbed Elizabeth, wiping her eyes with her veil. She picked up her own baby and held him tightly to her bosom.

"What if it was our John?"

"That is what we wanted to warn you about," injected Mary.

"You have a right to be troubled. The order is to exterminate every male child under two in Bethlehem and in the surrounding hills. John might not be safe, Elizabeth," explained Joseph. "You must leave now. Head for the desert cave where your relatives live. You should be safe there with protection from that community. Only the Essenes know their way around the dry wasteland. Herod's army will not follow you there into the wilderness."

"We will travel with you, dear cousin, until you are in the hands of your kin," offered Mary.

"Yes, yes, but avoid Masada. King Herod's men are swarming that area. It would not be safe to go anywhere near there," said Zachariah.

"Are Mary and Joseph not going in that direction?" asked Elizabeth.

"No, as good as that might sound to me, my instruction is to go to Egypt."

"Zachariah, you must come with me, please," cried Elizabeth.

"Elizabeth, I cannot. I'm the High Priest now and I must do my duty in Jerusalem. I will be safe if you and John are hidden in the desert and not with me. Go, take our son, and hide in the wilderness."

A plan was put into place to travel within a few days. Elizabeth and her servants prepared bread, and stocked baskets with dried fruit and cheese. They filled the water skins and restocked Mary and Joseph's supplies. Soon, the party of five departed for safety in the rocky hills of the Negev drylands.

The arid lands of the Negev consisted of rocky cliffs and stoney terrain rather than the sand dunes of other deserts. The landscape was varied and actually quite beautiful. As they travelled, they saw white chalkstone walls and craggy red eroded craters. The Essenes lived a frugal life there in those desolate, rugged hills, living in caves in the rock faces and overhangs. The road was rough, but the two families followed the many fault lines and wadis towered over by majestic, jagged bluffs pock-marked with caves.

They were able to reach Elizabeth's family within the day, and Mary and Joseph stayed overnight in their tent and enjoyed the supper and company of a hospitable extended family. The men collected around Joseph to discuss the best way for him to travel to his distant destination. As a group, the families told stories around the dung fire and shared their alarm and distress about King Herod and the horrific butchering of innocent children. John and Jesus played together on a blanket. Baby John was quite fascinated by the infant six months younger than he. He kept petting his head and kissing his feet, making baby talk to anyone who would listen.

The next morning, at dawn, the holy family trio set out on their journey. It was always best to travel in the morning and evening, and to rest in the midday. Mary and Joseph were well-provisioned for this part of the trip. They wore scarves over their heads and over their faces to protect them against the dust. Mary kept Jesus well covered in her sling. They were now in the season of spring and the temperature was still cool and the sun was not as brutal on their bodies as it would be later on during the longest and hottest leg of their journey. However, the scarce winter rain had nonetheless left a few waterholes and wells with water to replenish their gourds and enough vegetation to feed the animals. It was always a welcome sight to see greenery that could give them places to stop and rest along the way. Occasionally, there were trees that would provide shade. They witnessed a deer lapping water at a receding puddle, but it ran away at the sight of humans. One evening, a male lion crossed their path a short distance away. He stopped to look at them. He stared at them for what seemed a very long time. The little family was afraid of what he might do. They stood still. Then, the lion seemed to nod to them and moved slowly on.

"That was close, Mary."

"But Joseph, I was not afraid because he didn't seem to be threatening. More like he was checking on us."

"Well, I know the lion is a symbol of the tribe of Judah. It is written in the Scriptures that Jacob said of his son: 'Judah is a lion's whelp'. And we are both from that tribe. Perhaps Jacob's son is watching over us in the wilderness and ensuring us a safe passage."

"Now, if the chatter and laughing of the hyenas could just stop and allow us a good night's sleep, I would be so grateful," lamented Mary.

"That is not their way, but I am sure they won't harm us."

After a modest supper in the late evening, Joseph, Mary and Jesus settled in their tent. Joseph stretched his body, holding on to Mary because the nights were quite cold. Jesus lay between his parents, and he snuggled into Mary for warmth and comfort. Outside, the stars shone brightly, the moon glowed tenderly, and the angels kept watch.

On their second desert night, the winds picked up and the air became unsettled and filled with an ominous energy. Joseph scanned the horizon and then he spotted it—a furious brown wall heading their way. It was a sandstorm! His mind flew through several scenarios as the threatening storm propelled him to action. He immediately put bags over the heads of the donkeys. This would protect their eyes, but more importantly, prevent them from panicking. He helped Mary down from her animal and started pulling out the tent.

"I may need your help, Mary, for speed in setting up our protective barrier," yelled Joseph as the roar of the wind and the whirr of the sand eddies exposed their bodies and senses to the ravages of nature. With Jesus attached to her chest and Joseph working furiously, the tent was soon erected.

"Yalla, yalla, Mary! Enter the tent. I will see to the animals. They will share our space tonight. These storms can last minutes, hours, or days. I can't leave them exposed to the storm."

Mary entered the tent, placed Jesus down on a rug and went back outside to help Joseph pile sand along the base of the tent to anchor it down, and to prevent the wind from blowing the sand into the interior. The wind was fierce now. The light had dimmed, and the gloomy atmosphere made it difficult to work. The wall of the storm, higher than the trees, was approaching, with emerging sand twisters rudely whipping around everything loose. The donkeys, in spite of their eyes being covered, were frantically braying and kicking. The couple's clothes clung and flapped around their frames and their face scarves needed to be tied down more securely to protect their eyes and face from the pelting debris. Fortunately, this early sand invasion provided them with a silty earth that acted as a barrier at the bottom of the tent. They achieved their goal just as the main part of the storm arrived. They led the donkeys into the tent and then quickly secured the entrance. The two parents quickly placed themselves on each side of Jesus. Huffing and puffing from the exertion, both were trying to catch their breath, and urging their hearts to return to a slower pace. Joseph looked at Mary with worry in his eyes. Mary was so small and vulnerable and Jesus...

"The Lord is our refuge and our shelter, Joseph. We will be safe under his wing. Remember: 'Happy is he who has the God of Jacob for his help, whose hope is the Lord his God,'"[47] recited Mary.

"For I know that the thoughts that I think toward you, says the Lord, thoughts of peace and not of evil, to give you a future and a hope,"[48] quoted Joseph.

Even though the tent walls swelled and flapped, and the winds raged outside, the inhabitants of the tent remained safe and calm inside. They were confident and filled their sand-blown shelter with songs of praise and gratitude to their God.

After the massacre of the innocents, Herod was still not satisfied. There was a rumour that a child called John, bar Zachariah, had escaped the purge. Herod was furious. Further investigation pointed to the child's Father, who was High Priest of the Temple. Herod sent his servants to interrogate this Temple official.

---

[47] Psalm 91:4
[48] Jeremiah 29:11

When they rudely entered the priests' court, Zachariah was ministering at the altar.

"Where is your son?" demanded one of Herod's men.

"I am a minister of God and a servant at the altar; how should I know where my son is?" replied Zachariah calmly.

"Where have you hidden your son?" yelled the other servant.

"How should I know? He is with his mother."

Later, when the servants reported their findings to the King, Herod flew into yet another rage and screamed, "Is not this son of his likely to be king in Israel?" The servants gestured that they didn't know the answer to that question.

"Go back and come back with answers!" cried Herod.

The servants went back to the Temple and demanded of Zachariah, "Tell the truth. Where is your son, for you know that your life is in our hands."

But Zachariah answered, "I am a martyr for God, and if you shed my blood, the Lord will receive my soul. But know that you shed innocent blood."

At those words, Zachariah was slain at the entrance of the temple altar. This was discovered by the other priests who had awaited his blessing but who, after a long wait, went in to seek him out. They didn't ever find his body but only found his blood congealed on the floor. They were never able to clean the blood that had hardened to stone, and it became one with the Temple.

All the people who heard about the murder mourned and lamented for Zachariah for three days.[49] He had been well

---

[49] Taken from the Protoevangelium of James, Chapter 16

respected as a man of the law and a man of compassion. His death was a great loss to the community and especially for Elizabeth, who remained in the wilderness and lived her life with John among her people the Essenes.

Unaware of the tragic murder of their cousin's husband, Mary and Joseph woke up to the sun shining into their tent through the fabric. The storm had raged all night but had stopped a couple of hours before, and the sun had taken its place in the sky and suggested a clear new day in the storm's wake.

"Did you manage to sleep well?" asked Joseph.

"Yes, surprisingly well. I was quite secure in your arms, and with our babe in mine. How about you, my beloved?"

Joseph nodded. "Surprisingly well also. I was at peace, if you can believe it. I think that Jesus brought us that comfort. There is something about the child that brings peace and calm to the soul."

"I felt it too, Joseph," added Mary, smiling gently.

"Well, let us break our fast and make our indoor preparations because we may face other challenges outside. The Lord only knows what havoc the sand has created outside the tent. Let us pray."

After eating and completing the preparation chores, Joseph attempted to unseal the tent opening. He managed to open it but was met with a wall of sand. Some of the sand ran into the tent at his feet. As he was scratching his head to find a way to dig out of the pile, he heard noises outside. He heard the grunts of camels and the voices of men speaking a foreign language.

The men were shouting at each other and also seemed to be shouting instructions to the inhabitants of the tent. Joseph could not understand a word they said, but the sounds seemed helpful rather than menacing. Soon, the hill of sand was tumbling away and there was daylight streaming in. Gilded by the morning light were four men wrapped in billowing garments, with long scarves wrapped around their heads, faces and necks. These men were the Bedouin, desert dwellers. They were a nomadic people who raised herds and wandered the desert lands. They often accompanied caravans through the desert and used camels as their main means of transportation. Their society consisted of tribal clans, loyal to tribal traditions, able to survive with sparse resources, and with a strong sense of hospitality. They signalled to the tent dwellers to come out. Both Joseph and Mary took a moment to wrap their clothing over their heads and faces for protection against the lingering wind and sand.

"Shalom," greeted Joseph as he put his hands together and bowed his head slightly in a gesture of humility and peace. Mary held her head down and let Joseph do the greeting.

"Ahlan," returned one of the men as he placed his hand to his eyes and saluted them in the Arabian fashion.

One of the men flagged another who was able to speak a little Aramaic. The man drew a map in the sand. It appeared that they would head to Beer Sheba to meet a caravan and then head west towards Gaza and the city of Rafah. There they would assemble the various interested convoys and commence the hazardous journey through the desert.

By gesture and some spoken words, the two groups were able to communicate. The final outcome of this awkward communication was that the Bedouin people were willing to accompany the little family to Beer Sheba, where they would pick up the caravans and accompany one to Egypt. When Joseph indicated that they could not travel quickly with their child, the men smiled and nodded that they had their herds and families too. They were leaving the wet season, during which time they had pastured their herds in the hills. With the wet season over, they were now heading toward the more populated areas to sell, trade, and escort the caravans. Their expertise in survival in the desert was important to the economy of the merchants. The stream of traders coming from the east needed help to traverse the last difficult stretch through the Sinai desert. Mary and Joseph were welcome to join them.

The trip with the caravan was interesting in itself. It could be an adventure story of its own. During the long trek through the desert, the little family fared well. Mary cared, Jesus thrived, and Joseph prospered.

They met up with Jewish families who were venturing to Egypt to find work or escape persecution. They shared many things in common like their dietary restrictions and their religious practices, but, most of all, their faith in one true God called Adonai. Their observance of the Sabbath was difficult, but the herdsmen leading the convoy needed some time to rest, and thus accommodated their holy day out of respect for them. Jesus had had something to do with that sympathy as the leaders of the pack sensed great power in him. The child radiated a charisma of an unworldly force that they didn't understand, and it awed them. The child was a marvel and a mystery.

Their way was clear of all bad weather: sandstorms, thunderstorms, hail, or locust infestations. Joseph was able to do some work around the caravan train, replacing broken yokes, repairing wheels, and building temporary structures. Mary looked after the needs of little ones, the old and the sick. Jesus was allowed to play with other gentile children from faraway nations. Some fellow travellers were holy; some were desperate. Jesus was being exposed to a symphony of foreign languages and a bevy of people outside of his culture. People would often stop to visit with the little family from Galilee. Jesus was appreciated and admired by folks as the most adorable child on the voyage. As well as working for his keep, Joseph gave the leaders of the caravan, and also those who were in great need, coins from the magi's gift of gold. Joseph and Mary's hearts had opened to how kind these people were, from many different nations. They had become a large extended family. They had been blessed with the company of others, many of whom were different from themselves, and they had felt safe throughout their desert journey.

They eventually arrived in Egypt, where, in due course, they located a community of Jews. With their help, they found a place to live, and Joseph worked alongside a stone mason he had met on the journey. Both men were soon well-known for their skills and righteousness. Together, they contracted work and built homes and civic buildings. They settled into their new village with friendship and opportunity. Jesus grew up during this time in an environment both Jewish and exotic. Mary continued to teach him to sing psalms and enjoy the readings of the Torah. He learned Aramaic at home, and Hebrew at prayer and worship. They continued to live according to their laws but also respected the many different people around them. Mary was a good friend to all who came to her for advice and help with sickness and birthing. In Egypt, she learned about healing herbs and elixirs that brought comfort and reduced pain. She was called upon to pray with the mourning and to join in the celebrations of weddings. She had an open, sympathetic, and wholesome heart. She had a tender approach towards children, and especially the old and the dying. It was Mary's nature to love unconditionally.

One night, when Jesus was two and a half years old, Joseph received a message in a dream. Gabriel appeared before him and told him that it was now safe to return home. Herod had died and was replaced by his son, Herod Antipas. When morning came, Joseph recounted his dream to Mary, and they decided to make the journey home. It was time to go back. Joseph had not seen his own children in all this time, and they wasted no time thinking it over. Joseph was still nervous about the possible threats surrounding Bethlehem, so he suggested they go straight to Nazareth, where they would be farther from the troubles that had plagued his hometown. God have mercy.

They waited for the caravan group to return to their community and as good fortune would have it, the next caravan to arrive had the same leaders that had travelled with them initially. Mary was sure that this was not good luck but a holy intervention. She gave thanks.

The caravan took them through the Sinai, across the Negev, and all the way to Galilee. Jesus was almost three years of age when they finally arrived in their hometown of Nazareth. There was a great party to celebrate their return. Joseph's children had grown. They had missed their father and Mary but were relieved that they had been spared the killings. They all made a fuss over the little brother that they were meeting for the first time. Anna and Cleopas came down from Cana and rejoiced at the return of their dear family. Mary and Joseph spent hours retelling their adventures since leaving Nazareth. The questions were endless, and the laughter was hearty. What joy was in that home now that they were all assembled as a family once again!

Chapter 30
Living the Lessons

Mary looked up from her breadmaking and faced three pairs of eyes looking at her. Salome, Mary, and Jesus were intently watching their mother making dough. The children stood on the opposite side of the table and participated in the task in their own way. Jesus was now five years old and had shown himself to be quite precocious and full of awe for life. He had an insatiable curiosity and was forever asking questions that were beyond his years. He seemed to have inherited his mother's intelligence and wisdom. Salome was ten years old and eager to learn all the knowledge and skills of the domestic crafts. After all, she would be a wife in a few years and needed to learn all manner of housekeeping skills. Little Mary was seven years old and more interested in getting her share of the dough to knead and pat for fun.

Jesus asked, "What are you putting into the dough, Imma?"

The girls eagerly awaited the answer.

"That is the yeast."

"What does the yeast do?"

"Do you remember the bread we ate at the Passover?" The children nodded vigorously. "That bread did not have any yeast in it. It can be made in a hurry because it does not need time to grow, puff up and rise. We sometimes call that flatbread. Flatbread is often used while travelling because it can be made and cooked without an oven."

"How does the yeast work, Imma?" asked Jesus.

"It is like magic. With a small amount of yeast put into the bread dough like this one, the dough will swell and increase the size of the bread, but it needs time to rise. In the end it makes for a nice, fluffy bread that it's delicious to eat. And, by keeping some of the dough for next time, the yeasted dough will spread to another batch and then another batch. It keeps spreading its goodness. I can give a neighbour a bit of the yeast or yeasted dough and they can make their own bread with it."

Jesus contributed to the information given by his mother, "Yeast is like stories. A story spreads and puffs up too, Imma. If I tell a story to a friend, and he tells another friend and so on and so on, soon the story is all around town."

"Just so, Jesus. How clever you are!"

"Now, what are you putting in the bread mixture?" Salome interrupted.

"Salt." Mother Mary placed a little salt in front of them and invited them to taste it and see.

"Why do we put salt in the bread?"

"To make it taste good. It does something to the bread that makes it nicer to eat."

"Can salt lose its taste, Imma?" asked Jesus.

"Not usually, but there are salts that can go stale because they have other things in them that weaken the taste and the saltiness fades."

Less interested in the science of the ingredient, Salome asked, "How much salt do you put in?"

"It depends on the amount of the batch of bread. In this batch, I am putting in a handful."

"When is the dough going to be ready so I can slap it and make loaves?" begged little Mary.

"Mary, I enjoy your enthusiasm for making a loaf, but it will come sooner if you are patient. Can you be patient a while longer?" Little Mary nodded.

Jesus' curiosity about the salt had not quite satisfied his interest in the nature of salt and he asked, "What if the salt lost its taste?"

"Then it would be good for nothing. I would need to throw it out."

"Can the taste be put back into the salt, Imma?"

"Afraid not, Jesus. In some ways, life is like bread. That is why, if life is bread, we must be salt to each other. That way, we can give worth and goodness to all those around us." Jesus became silent as he thought about what his mother had just said. His thoughts were considering what all of this could mean.

Knead, knead, roll, roll, the bread was starting to form. On the dough ball there appeared an unground, fully formed grain of wheat. Salome pulled it off and said, "I guess we don't want this piece in the dough, do we?"

"No, Salome, we don't want that in our bread if we can help it. You were right to pull it out and throw it away." Mary thought for a minute while she continued to prepare the dough. Holding up the grain of wheat, she said, "Now listen, there is a lesson to learn in this little fellow." The children all looked at each other, and then at Mary with questions on their faces.

"The funny thing about a grain of wheat is that if it is not crushed and ground it will not make flour, and then..."

"No bread!" they all chorused. Mary smiled and affirmed their response.

"Also, if it does not fall on fertile ground, it will stay a grain and be no good to the world. The little grain must die, or it remains useless and alone." Salome and Mary shrugged at this while Jesus stored it in his mind to reflect on it later.

The loaves had grown in size, and now little hands could help to make the loaves. Mary gave them each a ball to work with.

Little Mary was happy.

On another day, Jesus was playing in the field with his sisters and brothers. Jesus' cousins, Mary, and the children of Nathan Cleopas had joined the play. Other village children had also joined in the game. Jesus was the youngest. They were kicking a chunk of hard mud around and trying to get past each other to put the chunk between two shrubs. Soon, it became late afternoon and the children needed to get home for the supper chores. Full of laughter and teasing, the children left the field in the direction of their dwellings. On the way home, Jesus saw an array of beautiful wildflowers in the field. At this time of the year, they were mostly lilies, or so Joses had said. This had been confirmed by others.

Jesus stopped and gazed at their beauty. He lowered his nose to smell the fragrance of one of the flowers. He closed his eyes and took in the glory of the moment. The white lilies shone gold in the late afternoon sun and they looked stunning in the grassy field. "I'm going to pick some for Imma," he thought.

Arriving home singing a song, Jesus sought his mother in the weaving room. "Shalom, Imma."

"Shalom, Jesus." He ran to her open arms and received her tender caress. She planted a kiss on his sun-streaked hair and smelled the fresh scent of the outdoors and the pleasant fragrance of the flowers. She held him closely for a few minutes, soaking in his presence and feeling the strong emotions of love that she had for this, her wonderful boy.

"What have you got there, my precious?"

He presented Mother Mary with a bouquet of lilies and the other wildflowers he had found. Together they made a lovely arrangement of varying colours, leaves, and branches.

"Thank you, Jesus. They are beautiful!"

"They are beautiful, like you, Imma." Mary was moved by his expression of love. She looked deeply into his alluring eyes and smiled.

"Where did you find them, Jesus?"

"In the field where we were playing our game."

Mary nodded and displayed her dimples to her son. "Flowers are one of the beautiful things that are gifts from our Creator. They are pretty, and delicate. They are soft, yet strong. They can shine in the hot sun and withstand the powerful wind and mighty thunderstorms. They are there to delight us. Elohim made them beautiful and hardy. He looks after them. The lilies don't work; they don't spin their clothing. They don't worry about how they will live. Not even a princess in the palace of Solomon is arrayed any nicer than this beautiful lily. If the Lord cares so much for a wildflower that can be burned with grass one day, can you imagine what the Lord thinks of you, and me, and all the people who were made in his image? Can you imagine?"

Jesus closed his eyes and said, "I am imagining, Imma. I see all the things in nature, the trees, the birds, and the flowers, in my mind. It is wonderful how well they are made."

"Yes, Jesus and look at us. We, too, are wonderfully made. We can think, learn, play, and pray. The Lord is good and mighty, don't you think?"

Jesus nodded, but somehow, Jesus already knew.

Jesus had grown up healthy, happy, and captivated by life. He had become a tall, slim boy with curly dark brown hair like his mother. People remarked on how he resembled his mama. He had the same green, sometimes hazel, eyes that were alluring because they danced with the sparkle of life. He usually wore a plain homespun knee-length tunic and leather sandals. On cooler days, he had an over tunic with sleeves. His mother and grandmother were spinners and weavers and his grandfather Cleopas had herds of sheep and goats, so he was never short of tunics, coats, and robes. His clothes were often creatively fashioned and sported many colours.

He was an active, athletic boy, who loved to play physical games such as climbing, running, swimming, and participating in games with his siblings and friends. He had a jovial, teasing manner that could never be understood as malicious when it was followed by a beaming smile on his clefted chin. Like his mother had been in Cana, he was a beloved child, admired and cherished by all who encountered him.

Jesus experienced a normal childhood. He cried when he incurred scrapes and cuts from his outdoor activities, but Mary kissed them better. He was occasionally ill with fever, colds, and childhood diseases. His mother walked the floor at night when he was sick with a high temperature. Mary used all the healing tricks and practices that the women in the village knew, plus a few more that she had learned from the women in Egypt and the women she had encountered on the caravan trips. She had a wide knowledge of the herbs that would calm, settle aching tummies, and lower fevers. Her services were often sought by other mothers around the village and beyond, because everyone knew that Mary had a healing hand. However, Mary was a healer who also relied on her prayers to a higher and mightier force. When Jesus or Joseph, or anybody for that matter, was ill, she had faith to petition her creator Lord for healing. She was a great example of faith, hope and love to everyone. She had no favourites among the townspeople, and all around her were treated with equal kindness and compassion.

One night, when Jesus was burning up with fever because of an earache, she paced the room with him, crying into her shoulder:

"I love you, Lord; you are my strength. The Lord is my rock, my fortress, and my savior; my God is my rock, in whom I find protection. He is my shield, the power that saves me, and my place of safety."[50]

"Please take away the pain and the fever from our child for he is your child as well as mine. I am so anxious for him. I suffer in my heart with worry and anguish. Please bring me peace knowing that you love him and will bring him healing and protect him from harm. But not my will, but your will, dear Father in heaven."

At that moment, the fever broke, and Jesus fell asleep on her breast as she rocked him gently. Mary looked up and sighed a great sigh and gave thanks to the Almighty for bringing this agony to an end.

Jesus knew how to recite sections of the Holy Scriptures by heart and asked many questions that deepened his understanding of the law and ordinances of their religion. Mary not only taught him about the words of the Torah and Talmud but also the spirit and compassion that was necessary to interpret them. Before he even attended the synagogue school with rabbis, Jesus was well-versed in prayers, psalms, and scripture. In spite of her busy day with the chores that made a home function, Mary took time to pray with Jesus and the other children of her extended family and teach him scriptures, and the laws of the Lord and of the heart.

---

[50] Psalm 18:1-3

As ever, lessons often occurred while doing other tasks. One day, Jesus and Mary were walking in the garden, inspecting the damage from the last storm.

"What is faith, Imma?" asked Jesus out of nowhere.

Mary smiled, never shocked by her son's profound inquisitiveness. "Faith is difficult to explain and to understand, Jesus. Faith is believing without knowing for sure. Faith is trusting that there is something bigger than us who created and controls the universe. Faith is letting go of earthly things and believing in the Almighty without ever having seen God. It is an inner knowledge deep in your soul."

"What on earth is like faith?" asked Jesus. Mary took a moment to think and figure out a means of explaining to a six-year-old a concept as difficult as faith.

"Faith is like the wind. We can't see it. We can only feel it when it goes by, and see what it does. It bends the branches of a tree. It shakes the leaves. So we know it's there, and so we believe in the wind."

"Hmm". Mary could see the thinking wheels turning in Jesus' brain. She added: "Faith is like love. You can't see love, but you can feel it. You can see what it does, like caring for somebody when they are poor or sick, giving them comfort when someone they love dies, kissing and hugging them just to make them feel good about themselves, giving of yourself and putting your own needs aside, sacrificing for them. Do you understand?"

"I do."

They continued to walk along the paths of the walled garden. The birds were chirping with their new families, flying back and forth with bugs and worms to feed their gaping mouths.

"What is that tree there, Imma?"

"It is the mustard tree and look there is a nest of birds in the branches. Do you see? There, next to the big, big branch."

"It is the largest tree in the garden, Imma. Many birds are flying in and out of it. It gives them shelter and protection."

"You are absolutely right, Jesus. The tree is all of that. Funny thing about the mustard tree. It is the biggest of the trees, but it has the smallest seed. The Lord is good and mighty."

"Is faith like the mustard seed, Imma?"

Mary thought about his question for a while. It had a depth of comprehension that challenged even her experience.

"Why do you ask that, Jesus?"

"If faith is like the smallest seed that can become the largest tree, then even a little grain of faith can have great power and bring about great things."

"I think that you might be right, Jesus. That is very astute of you. I am going to give it more thought to understand its deep meaning. You are getting so clever that I will need to catch up to my own child!"

When Jesus was nine years old, Joseph came into the house grumbling. Jesus was helping his mother by rolling the strands of wool that Mary was spinning into a ball.

"What is the matter, Abba?" inquired the very curious Jesus.

"That fig tree in the field has not produced fruit for two years now. It's taking space where another tree might produce for us."

Mary said: "Joseph, you're right; there is no place for a fig tree that gives no figs. However, let us nurture it for one more year and see if next year it does what it is supposed to do. If it doesn't, we will need to cut it down."

"What do you think, Jesus?" posed Joseph to his adoptive son.

"I agree with Imma. There is no need for a fruitless tree, but let's give it another chance before we chop it down for firewood."

Joseph smiled and nodded.

On another occasion, Mary had just finished gathering vegetables and herbs from the garden for the supper meal. She placed the loaded basket by the door as she went to wash her hands at the well. When she returned, the basket had disappeared. She stood there with her hands on her hips, perplexed, wondering what had happened to the fruit of her efforts. At that moment, Jesus came round the corner of the house from the woodshop where he had been working with Joseph, sweeping all the wood chips to sell at the market for kindling.

"What has happened, Imma? You look like you are deep in a mystery."

"Yes, I am, Jesus. I left a basket of vegetables at the door and now it is gone! I don't know where it went."

"I know, Imma. I just saw Benjamin run away with it down the road."

"That is stealing, Jesus. It is not good for him to get away with that."

"I know it is wrong, Imma, but Benjamin's father has been ill and unable to feed his family. I guess Benjamin was desperate."

"I was not aware of that, Jesus. Let us go to his house. We will bring bread, goat's milk, honey, and eggs with us. I will also see what is causing his sickness and bring some medicine."

With provisions loaded in a cart, Mary and Jesus set out to visit the suffering family. Arriving at the house, they were greeted by Benjamin's mother and a very sheepish Benjamin.

"Shalom, Abigail. I have just learned that Aaron is not well."

"Yes, he has an ailment of the stomach, and he is in such pain that he cannot go to work in the forge."

"I brought you something to hold you over until he is well enough. May I examine him to see if I am able to bring him some comfort? We can pray together for his recovery."

Abigail agreed. After the examination, Mary, Jesus and the family prayed together.

"Lord in heaven, have mercy on our brother Aaron. He needs your healing graces so that the family is not forced to steal to provide for the family. Give us confidence in your goodness and providence. Let the family accept your will and know that you will provide for all those who have faith in your eternal compassion and that we are forgiven for our sins. Despise not the sinner, but the sin. Know that the sinner has a good heart and knows your laws."

"Amen," chorused the group.

Abigail finally understood why a basket of vegetables had mysteriously arrived yesterday and that Benjamin had offered no good answer as to where the goods had come from other than that they had just appeared at the door. Benjamin, too, knew exactly what Mary was referring to. He was ashamed and knew that he should have acted differently. As Benjamin went out to the cart to unload the goods with Jesus and Mary, he stopped Mary and bent his head and confessed.

"I stole the basket of food, Mary. I'm very sorry. I should not have done that."

"You are forgiven, Benjamin. You should have asked me as I could have helped. That is what good friends and neighbours do."

"I know. It was wrong."

Mary, aware of how demeaning it was to ask for charity, said, "Yes, it was, but you have a good heart, Benjamin. I'll tell you what. You come over every day in the early morning before the sun is too hot and help me in the garden and I will send you home with food for your family until your father is back on his feet and earning. That way, you can contribute to your table with the compensation of your work. Does that sound good to you?"

"Yes. You are very kind, Mary. The Lord is with you."

Jesus had witnessed and overheard the exchange and was moved by the love and forgiveness that his mother had displayed.

One warm evening, the extended family gave thanks to the Great Provider and enjoyed a delicious meal of roasted goat with seasonal vegetables on the roof of their home. There was much laughter and sharing of their day's experiences. Mary claimed that she had heard an interesting story in the village.

"Apparently, there was a very wealthy man in Tyre who had two sons." All eyes turned to Mary, and they stopped chewing to listen because Mary was an excellent storyteller. She could spin a story as well as she could spin a yarn. Everybody hung on to her every word.

Mary continued, "Both of his sons worked with him; however, the younger son was wild and restless. He wanted to find himself and seek his fortune elsewhere. He asked his father to get his share of the business right away. What was he thinking thought the father and the older brother. The father and the son had a big argument about this folly. Then, the older brother berated the younger for abandoning the family and pursuing his own selfish interests, and for leaving him alone to do all the work, as their father was ageing and needed extra help, not less. The younger son lost his temper and cursed his brother with all manner of insults and shouted obscenities and injustices to his father. He told him that he never wanted to see him again.

"Did his father give him his share of the family fortune?" asked Jesus.

"Yes, the father gave it to him and blessed him and wished him good fortune. Although the father was very sad to lose his son, he understood his son's need to choose his own destiny. He prayed for his safety and his return to the family before he was totally lost."

"What happened, did all go well for him?" asked James.

"At first, things went well. He had lots of money to spend, and he sought drink, girls, and gambling games. But people took advantage of him. He was robbed and beaten by the very people that he trusted. Eventually, he found himself penniless with no place to live and no money to buy food. He was ragged, hungry, and thirsty, so he sought work. However, there was a drought in the land and the country was suffering from poverty and lack of jobs.

"What did he do?" blurted Salome.

"He finally found work on a farm, feeding pigs."

"Pigs! They are foul animals, and against our laws! Did he eat the forbidden meat, too?" inquired Simeon.

"I don't know for sure, but he probably did. He was starving, and starving people can't be picky."

"I think that I would rather die than eat pig. I think that I would be like Daniel and his friends. I would rather burn in the furnace than eat that unclean food!" burst out Joses.

"Well, we don't know for sure that he didn't eat it or that he did. However, he may have dishonoured our laws, but tell me this. Do you think that what he put in his mouth was a greater sin than the terrible and hurtful words that came out of his mouth when he disrespected his father?" The listeners said nothing, but just looked at each other with uncertain glances.

"Then what happened, Imma?" asked Jesus.

"As I heard it, he was very unhappy. He was filthy, dirty and still hungry and remembering how good his life had been at his father's house. He remembered that even the servants were better treated than he was here in this hole with the pigs. He deeply regretted his actions towards his family and decided that he would beg for forgiveness and work as a servant for his father's estate. Anything had to be better than what he was experiencing. So, he left the pigs and walked home, begging as he went until finally, he reached his former home.

"Did the father take him back, Imma?' inquired all the children.

"Well, the father was always hopeful that his prayers would be answered and that his wayward son would return to the fold, and so he watched from his hilltop estate to see if his lost son would return. One day, he saw him. He saw that he was a diminished version of himself but nonetheless, it was his boy. He was so excited that he ran to him and took him in his arms in a warm embrace. His son fell to his knees and admitted that he had sinned. He begged his father for forgiveness and asked if he could work on the estate as a slave. The father was so happy that his son was sorry and had come back to him that he instructed his servants to give him a bath and provide him with rich new garments and a family ring. He instructed the farm hands to kill a calf to celebrate his son's return with a party.

"How did the older brother take the news?" asked Joseph.

"Apparently, the brother was not so pleased. He was insulted that the father would honour the foolish brother who had wasted his money and done such foul things. He was very angry. He made it very clear to his father that he was the one who had continued to work hard on the estate while his brother squandered their family fortune, and he had not had any such celebration for his constant and faithful service. He did not agree with the merry acceptance of such a sinful son, never mind giving him such a welcome."

"How did the old man react?" inquired James.

"He told his older son that he loved him and was very proud of him. He told him that he was grateful for all the work that he had done for their little kingdom. He reminded his older son that everything he had was his, but that he needed to understand that his younger son had been lost and now he was found. This was indeed a joyous occasion, and he was very happy to have his son back in the family. He asked his eldest to share and celebrate this joy with him."

The family applauded the wonderful outcome of the story and thanked Mary for sharing it with them.

When Jesus was a little older, he had studied with the rabbis in the synagogue school. He was an excellent student, and because he was so intelligent and had had a head start with his Temple-schooled mother, he made great strides in the study of the laws and Scripture. He and the master instructor had lively debates about the meaning of the Hebrew writings. He was quick and enlightened about faith and the world. There were times when the rabbis would assemble their collective skills, knowledge and insights and debate with Jesus, and find themselves shaking their heads at their inability to best him. His abilities were remarkable and unmatched by anyone they knew. His knowledge of the faith was almost frightening. There seemed to be nothing more they could teach him now.

When he wasn't at school, Jesus worked with his father in the woodshop. Under Joseph's tutelage Jesus learned the craft of carpentry and working in construction. Joseph travelled with Jesus and his brothers to the neighbouring cities to build large buildings and structures. By then, Joseph had become a reputable contractor and a respected carpenter. He had many contracts to complete around Galilee. Joseph, James, Simeon, Joses, and Jesus worked as a very efficient team. Jesus often accompanied his brothers to the cities of Sepphoris and Capernaum to sell their farming tools, cabinets, tables, and chairs. Jesus was exposed to people of many nations, and he spoke to them in Greek and learned much of the world from listening to their stories. His exposure to these foreigners gave him an openness and appreciation for the faiths, norms and behaviours of humankind beyond those of the Hebrews.

In Capernaum, they would exchange their wares for fish. The fisherman would take their boats out in the sweet-water lake they called Gennesaret, although most Romans, travellers and strangers coming into town to buy the product of the waters would call it the Sea of Galilee. This large pool of water was an asset to the whole of the Galilean community because it provided a source of water for growing crops in the surrounding area, but it was primarily known for its richness in fish. Joseph had met a man called Zebedee when he had been contracted to repair an old fishing boat. It needed new seats, and a few new boards on the side. The transom needed replacing as well. Over the years, Joseph had done many jobs for this fisherman. He had made chests to store the fish and the equipment and had continued to repair any rotting boards. He had become good friends with Zebedee and his two boys,

John and James. Zebedee was married to Anna's older sister's daughter, Sobe. Sobe's daughter, Mary Salome, was Mary's cousin.

After finishing a job for Zebedee, the day was still young, and the fisherman asked if Jesus and Joseph would like to go see what it was like on the water. The two men and the three boys set out on a little sail to the middle of the lake. Jesus was thrilled about the new adventure. He really liked the boys, especially John. He found in James a jovial nature but in John, he found a sensitive and intuitive man with a kindred spirit. They loved to fish and sail in the evening breeze.

The sun was low in the sky and its gold and coral light reflected on the water's ripples and on the faces of the occupants of the little boat as it headed toward the shore after a good catch.

"It is so peaceful out here, Zebedee."

"It is the best occupation, Joseph. The markets are good right now and the fish are plentiful."

The boys were busy sorting the fish into different buckets.

"Have you ever been caught in a storm, Zeb?"

"Yes, and it is most frightening. The water seems to get angry, and the waves reach as high as the gunnels and often slosh into the boat. So much water enters the boat that you fear that it will sink."

"What do you do when that happens?"

"Head towards shore and pray. Most of the time, I can read the signs of the weather, and if it looks ominous, I stay ashore and repair nets and clean the boat or try to find more markets for future catches. But on a few occasions, I was caught unawares. The signs were good for going out. Once, in the middle of the lake, the winds picked up out of nowhere and tore into our sails and drove us far from our shore. It was very frightening and honestly, I thought that the boys and I were going to see our maker. My wife and daughters would have no breadwinners and no males to look after them. It was an awful thing to realize how easy it is to die."

"Do me a favour, Zeb. Do not tell Mary this when she next comes with me to Capernaum. She would worry about us and wish us to never get into a boat ever again."

However, Jesus would take every opportunity to visit the Zebedee boys and sometimes the boys would be allowed to venture out on their own if they did not go too far out and if the weather looked stable and safe.

Mary was not aware of these little adventures because she was usually at home engaged in her everyday household tasks. That was a good thing.

Sometimes Jesus would help Daniel, the family's longtime herdsman, with the care of the sheep, especially at lambing time. Mary would help sometimes, too. When the men were busy with the birthing, the yearlings would sometimes feel neglected and wander off. Daniel was getting older, and his legs were not what they used to be. He could no longer go chasing after those stray sheep. One day, after a night of work with the lambs, Daniel took count of the flock. There was one missing. A search party, involving Mary and Jesus, was organized and they set out to find the lost one. Daniel was a wise shepherd, but he no longer had the stamina and ability needed for an extended search.

"Why does Daniel leave the many others for one? Is he not worried that the whole flock will run away?" inquired Jesus.

"Daniel is a fine shepherd. He knows his sheep trust him.

They can hear his voice and they listen to his commands. They trust him because he takes them to good pastures, and he is gentle and kind to them. He knows that they would not

223

wander away too far. The odd sheep may wander off a bit and get caught in a shrub or vines, and Daniel always seeks it out. He never abandons them. All his sheep are precious to him, and he does not give up on them."

Eventually, Jesus found the lost lamb whose foot was trapped between rocks in a broken stone fence. He lifted the frightened and bruised animal onto his shoulder and carried it down the slope and set it before Daniel. Daniel exhaled a sigh of relief and thanked Jesus for being a good shepherd.

Chapter 31
Where is Jesus?

The dawn was breaking on the horizon. From their high point on the foothills of Mount Tabor, the family caravan gazed upon the splendour of the rising sun over the Sea of Galilee. The horizon shone with a soft pink that gradually changed to coral and then a buttery yellow. The cloudless sky beyond the glow of the rising sun was at first mauve and then filled their view with a cerulean blue. The rainy season was mostly at its end and the ground was solid and free from mud. The fields between them and the lake were lush with the green growth of the early shoots of barley and wheat. An array of yellow wildflowers exhibited their delicate glory on the grassy hill in the foreground. It was a magnificent, breathtaking vista of the Lord's artwork.

Mary, Joseph, Jesus and all their extended family had set out on their annual journey to Jerusalem for Passover. Left behind were Jesus' grandparents, Anna and Cleopas, as they were getting too old for this long and difficult trek. Accompanying them, however, were Mary Cleopas and Nathan and their children James, Jude, and Simon. By this time, Joseph's sons, James, Joses, and Simeon, had wives and children of their own and had built additions to the family home. Salome and her husband were now married and lived nearby in Nazareth. She had left one child behind and was in the early months of pregnancy for her second.

They had left before daybreak to travel in the cooler temperatures. As they were a large group, they would take the shorter but more perilous route through Samaria. The men, all bearing walking sticks, would divide themselves to cover the front and back of the convoy and the women and children would walk in between their pillars of protecting males. There was always safety in numbers.

It was the season of Nisan and the weather promised to be clement, and their procession would be able to sleep outdoors and avoid the cost of staying in the various inns along the route. They had loaded their pack donkeys with all they needed to travel. They did not bring lambs for the Passover feast because they were staying with family in Bethlehem and small families would join with others to purchase an unblemished lamb from the local providers. Mary, Joseph, and Jesus would stay with one of Joseph's brothers and partake of the ritual meal with that family.

Before they headed out, Joseph had led them in a prayer for guidance and safe travel. They all joined in the singing of psalms as they made their way toward rockier paths.

Forever, I will sing the goodness of the Lord.

I will sing of your mercies, O Lord, forever, with my mouth.[51]

The rest of the journey was uneventful. The travel was a wonderful time to be with family and to laugh and tell stories around the fire.

One nippy, starlit evening, the families had gathered around the flames to keep warm. Wrapped in their cloaks, they drank heartily of wine libations for the adults and pomegranate juice for the younger set. Everyone loved to be around Mary's fire because she was the best storyteller. After a few rounds of funny stories told by the men and their meeting with strangers from afar, Jesus asked: "Why is it so dangerous to pass through Samaria?"

Mary looked around at the adult family members and nobody seemed prepared to tackle that question. She explained that ages ago, the Assyrians had conquered the Northern Kingdom and many of the Hebrews had married

---

[51] Psalm 89

Gentiles and had forgotten their Hebrew ways. They had stopped practicing the laws of Judaism and were neglecting the covenants ordained by Adonai and were worshipping idols and foreign gods. The tribes of the north were lost and considered unclean.

"Does that mean that they are bad people, Imma?" inquired Jesus.

"They are not of our way, my son, but I'm sure that they are good people who have compassionate hearts and hear the voice of Adonai in their souls."

"Well, tell that to the pilgrims who have been robbed and beaten by the likes of them on this very route," complained one of the men.

Mary's eyes softened and she waited for the tetchy noises to settle before she began her story.

"I heard a woman at the synagogue a little while ago tell an interesting story about a Samaritan." The crowd became silent in anticipation.

"It happened on the road from Jerusalem to Jericho. A man got robbed by bandits. They beat him and kicked him repeatedly and stripped him of everything he had. He was lying there on the ground wearing nothing but his own blood and his many bruises," continued Mary. "He was lying on the dusty road in the heat of the high sun and people just passed him by. They actually stepped over him and made some unkind comments about the obstruction in the road."

"Oh, that was terrible!" interrupted a listener and the others nodded and added their agreement to that comment.

"Was he a Jew?" asked another listener.

"I think he was, but it didn't seem to matter to the passersby. This woman saw a priest go by and ignore the poor, wounded man. Then she saw another man wearing long tzitzits and she thought he was a Levite. He not only ignored him but moved over to the other side of the road to avoid looking at the man."

Mary paused in her telling and let the audience imagine the scene. "The woman who was in a group behind saw a traveller approach the injured man. He got off his donkey and brought his waterskin to the poor creature and urged him to drink to quench his thirst. He then cleaned his dirty, blood-encrusted wounds, pouring wine and oil on them. He bound them as best as he could. He took his own spare linen shift from his side saddle and helped the man cover his naked body. He then hoisted him onto his animal and walked beside the man and donkey until they got to Jericho. He found an inn and he cared for him and then he gave the innkeeper enough money to continue the care until he returned."

All the enthralled listeners bobbed their heads in approval.

"The woman said that everybody in town was talking about it. All the people were surprised as to who it was that made such a kind gesture." Mary waited a moment to bait her hook.

"And who do you think the man was?" she asked. The group collectively shrugged and looked at each other for answers. Mary watched them wonder who the merciful, caring, and generous man was. After a few seconds of leaving them to wonder a little more, she said: "He was a Samaritan. Do you think that he was a good and righteous man?"

Jesus held the story in his heart and pondered the meaning on the remaining leg of the journey.

They arrived safely in Jerusalem, and after bathing and making preparations, the families celebrated the Passover meal together. The children answered the age-old questions about why this night was not like any other night and the other questions that followed. As Jesus had turned twelve years old, this was going to be his last time to respond, because he was soon to be of age and would participate as an adult. The family then attended the Temple for the rituals and worship. And then, because they had imposed on the hospitality of relatives long enough, they left directly from Jerusalem for their journey back home. The weather was again cooperating and this time, they decided to return by way of Jericho and along the Jordan River. Again, the men took the head and tail positions of the procession for the security of their flock of loved ones. They were almost a day out when Mary and Joseph realized they had not seen Jesus in their midst.

Mary fell back in the party to see if Jesus had attached himself to the older males at the back. She did not see her son but did notice Joseph walking with his stick.

"Joseph, have you seen Jesus?"

"No. I thought he was with you."

"I thought that he was with you and your boys."

The alarm set in their faces at the same time. They frantically searched the little convoy of relatives, asking if anybody had seen Jesus. No one had.

Mary was beside herself. Had they left him behind? Was he harmed? Where was he?

"Oh, Joseph. We must go back and look for him!" she cried in a panicked voice.

"Of course, right away. I'll tell the others what we are doing and let them continue to Nazareth without us."

The anxious parents turned away and, leading his donkey, Joseph and Mary retraced the steps they had just taken. They stopped at Bethany to see if Jesus had stopped at Simon and Naomi's place, thinking that he might visit there as they had so many times before. There was no sign of him there and the only boy they could see was Lazarus with his sisters Mary and Martha. The family was sympathetic but could not help. Naomi fully understood the horror of losing a child, even one as clever as Jesus. They prayed for his quick return to the arms of his parents and sent them off with provisions to sustain them in their journey.

Mary and Joseph returned to Bethlehem as quickly as they could and checked with all their relatives to see if Jesus had stayed behind with them. No sign of him anywhere! Now, they were getting frantic. Mary was very afraid. She took a minute to calm her nerves and to remember to trust in the Lord. Surely, Adonai and his angels would not let anything bad happen to Jesus. She and Joseph stopped for a rest and prayed together to find their boy. It brought calm and comfort to their minds and souls. After a brief rest they headed into Jerusalem proper to look into the city and the Temple.

Meanwhile, Jesus had been intrigued by a lesson being taught by a well-known rabbi on the porch of Solomon in front of the Temple. The holy man was surrounded by other rabbis, Sadducees, Pharisees and Herodians. Many boys of scholarly age were also in the crowd listening to the lecture. Jesus took a seat on a step and listened intently. He had not noticed when his family had taken leave of the city and begun the journey back to Galilee.

When he did notice that his relatives had gone, he did not panic; he continued to pay attention to the teachings and to the answers given by the notable academics that surrounded the priestly rabbi. Jesus had even given clever and wise answers to questions. His answers were so insightful that the rabbi had asked him to come forward and then encouraged him to give his interpretation of a law or scripture passage. Jesus spent the night in the woman's court. He was well fed when the temple clerics heard his story about his separation from his family and pilgrim group.

They consoled him by saying: "Do not be afraid, young man. Your parents will notice that you are not with them and will return to fetch you." They had called him young man, and Jesus knew that he had reached the age at which he could be considered an adult and left to make his own choices and to follow his own beliefs and convictions. He slept well on the reed mat that they had provided. He was not afraid. His father in heaven would watch over him.

By the third day, Jesus had made quite an impression among the students of the rabbi's lessons. Feeling confident in his new maturity, Jesus dared to ask some questions of his own. After hearing the verse in Leviticus stating that: 'You shall not take vengeance or bear any grudge against the sons of your own people but you should love your neighbour as yourself.'

Jesus asked: "Who is my neighbour?" This created a stir among the participants. Several opinions were shared before they all turned to the boy-man who had asked the question in the first place.

"And who do you think is our neighbour, young man?" asked a Pharisee.

Remembering the story of the good Samaritan, Jesus answered: "Our neighbour is any person who was made in the image of our Creator God."

With these words, Jesus shocked the learned people in the circle. However, they had to agree that it was true. Jesus had many questions which he put forward for discussion and debate. He asked: "When did sin enter the world? Who is the woman described in Genesis whose seed will crush the serpent? Why were the prophets ignored by the Jews? What do the Shewbread, the Menorah and the Incense altar represent? Where is the Ark of the Covenant? If Solomon's

Temple was destroyed by the Babylonians, would this Temple also be destroyed if the Jews do not listen to the prophet among them?"

The discussion was often heated, and the renowned leaders and scholars marvelled at the understanding, knowledge, and wisdom that this mere boy demonstrated.

One rabbi was seen shaking his head and asking: "How can someone so young give answers like that? He speaks with such authority!"

Mary and Joseph finally spotted Jesus standing in the middle of the learned group, giving a talk to attentive ears. Their fears immediately abated. They blew out their retained breath together. Their son was safe! Knowing he was within their view, they listened to his arguments. They were amazed and the crowd was clearly enthralled by his answers. Mary could imagine the deep questions that Jesus would have asked the scholars as both Mary and Joseph had many times been challenged by their son's keen and eager mind.

At the end of the current discussion and before another began, Mary and Joseph approached Jesus and Mary asked: "Son, why have you treated us so? Behold, your father and I have been looking for you anxiously." Jesus looked at his dear mother and father and wanted them to know that he was now an adult and that they need not worry about him anymore. He was his own person, dependent upon his father in heaven alone.

"Why did you look for me? Did you not know that I must be in my Father's house?" It was difficult to understand Jesus' reaction, especially after the scare that they had just experienced at his absence. Despite this, Mary just smiled and nodded in her relief.

"Come Jesus, let us go home now." She put her troubled thoughts aside but kept all these things in her heart.[52] Mary reminded herself that Jesus was not an ordinary boy.

Their trip home had been marked with sadness. After the Passover, there had been a small rebellion in Jerusalem and the Romans had crucified the rebels. Their battered bodies were hanging from crosses all along the road. It was the Roman way of deterring others who were contemplating an insurrection against the Emperor. It was not a pretty sight, with flies buzzing around the rotting corpses. Crows swooped down to gouge out eyes and other soft tissue while vultures were flying above in circles waiting for the flesh to ripen to their tastes. The whole scene was revolting, and Mary and Joseph, after a brief explanation, tried to distract Jesus from the sight. Jesus had surely lost his youth and naivety on this trip.

When they returned home, Jesus was once again loving and obedient to them and helped his mother in the garden and his father in his carpentry and construction work. He continued to grow in wisdom and stature and in good favour of God.[53] But clearly, Jesus was no longer a boy.

---

[52] Taken from Luke 2:41-51
[53] From Luke 2:52

Chapter 32
The Death of Joseph

It was a brisk day in the autumn season of Tishri. The light was already dim as Joseph and his construction team made their way back home after a day of work in Cana. They had been working with the son of Cleopas to build an extension to his house for one of his sons who was betrothed to a local village girl.

Jesus was almost fifteen years of age and he had just recently had a growth spurt and an amplification of his structure and muscle tone. He was taller than his brothers now. He had long, curly hair that he tied in a tail in back. His hands were calloused and rough from his work with wood and metal. He wore his tool pouch across his shoulders and chest. He was a serious young man who showed an unusual level of wisdom and common sense. Nevertheless, he had a teasing manner and a jovial disposition. To know him was to love him.

James and his brothers were walking ahead, planning the tasks for the next day. Jesus was walking beside Joseph and discussing matters regarding the current job. At one point, he noticed that he was the only one talking. Joseph was a quiet man, but he had been virtually silent all along the walk. He turned to watch Joseph, but he quickly thought that something was not right. Everyone knew that Joseph had a weak heart and he had been showing more and more shortness of breath and lack of upper body strength of late.

"Let me carry your tool satchel, Abba. You really don't look well."

"I will let you carry it, son. It seems to be heavier today."

"We are not far from home, and you can rest there," assured Jesus.

However, when Jesus helped Joseph take his tool bag off his shoulder, he noticed that Joseph's face was ashen and glowing with perspiration. The weather was cool, and the walking pace had not been rigorous. Something was indeed wrong.

"Abba. Let us stop. You are really not well. James!" Jesus called to his half-brother walking in front. "Yalla, yalla!" By this time, Jesus was already needing to shoulder Joseph to support his body. Joseph was breathing with difficulty, and he was holding onto his chest in obvious discomfort. The grimace on his face showed that his father was in considerable pain. The boys finally reached them and they led and half-carried Joseph to his home.

Mary was busy preparing the evening meal. She had made a lamb stew seasoned with rosemary and there was a delightful aroma in the main room of the house. There was plenty of freshly baked bread for her boys. She noted that it would soon be time to press grapes to make more wine, as she was pouring out sparingly the last amphora of the previous season's wine into the cups, when there was a clamour and yelling in the front courtyard.

"Mother, come and open the door for us!" called Jesus.

Mary dashed to the door to meet the family crew. "Oh, my goodness. Joseph, are you alright?" She led them to their room, where there was a bed covered with a sleeping rug. The boys gently placed their father on the bed. He was still short of breath, and pain still marked his features. Joseph was now fully white-haired, and the once-brown patch in his beard had also changed to a charcoal grey in recent years. His forehead was wrinkled, and his cheeks had sunken, revealing prominent cheekbones, hollow cheeks and slack jowls. Nevertheless, he was still a handsome man and his eyes still sparkled with internal light.

While the boys settled their father into these more comfortable surroundings and washed his body from the day's sawdust and dirt, Mary rushed to her apothecary and took out an elixir made of willow bark and foxglove flowers. This last ingredient was poisonous in large quantities, but when used in very small doses, it could help with blood circulation. She spooned some into Jospeh's mouth and flushed it down with water in hopes that this would make him feel better. She had used this combination successfully with other men who were suffering the ailments of the heart. As hoped, Joseph soon showed ease and relief of pain. The present caregivers all breathed a little easier with the noticeable recovery of their dear Abba.

"What happened?" she asked. The boys took turns blurting out their takes on the incident including that Joseph had not been as industrious on the job as usual.

"You boys go join your families and Jesus and I will nurse your father back to health," instructed Mary. "Don't expect him at work tomorrow. He really needs to give his body a rest." The boys reluctantly left to go home. They were all deeply worried that their father's life might be coming to an end.

Mary spent the evening feeding Joseph some of the gravy from the lamb stew and dipping his bread in the wine to build up his strength and energy. Joseph seemed to have recuperated somewhat, but she was still worried. Jesus was in and out of the room, checking on his father and exchanging small conversations with him. Just before it was time to settle down to sleep, Mary and Jesus said a prayer to the Almighty for a speedy and full recovery for Joseph. They both felt that their prayers and God's will might be at odds this time.

That night, Mary crawled into bed beside her husband and held him close to her body. She wrapped one arm across his chest and rubbed his back with the other.

"How are you feeling, Joseph?"

"I am well with you by my side, my dear wife." They lay there together in silence, thinking their own thoughts.

"You frightened me tonight, Joseph," said Mary.

"I know. You must prepare for my passing. I am not a young man and my heart has been failing more and more all these years in little ways."

"You have been such a great husband to me, Joseph. I give thanks every day to the Lord for having chosen you for me."

"Our love has always been different, Mary. We were one in our soul. I was always happy and content with you near me, and whenever you were away, I missed you and your brilliant smile looking so content and approvingly of me. My cup runneth over and I, too, gave thanks to the Lord for having given you to me. Still, you must prepare."

Mary held him tighter and hummed a beautiful refrain until she could hear him gently snoring.

The next day, Jesus visited his father in bed and assured him that his sons were ready to complete the work that they had started. Jesus hugged Joseph and kissed his cheeks three times. He encouraged his childhood mentor to rest and listen to his spouse and take the medicines that she offered to him. He then set out, assured by his mother that this was not Joseph's time, and instructed by her to comfort Joseph's other sons. During the day, Salome and Mary came in to visit their father. They cooed and tutted and helped Mary with his care. Mary Cleopas came in for a shift and they all did Joseph a favour by leaving their rowdy and unruly children at home. Joseph needed peace.

That night, Jesus broke bread and shared some wine with Joseph and they discussed the day's work successes and challenges.

"You have been a wonderful and protective father to me and taught me much. And I have always understood that you have been a wonderful husband to my mother. I thank you."

"Jesus, I have always held you as my own. You were the fruit of my dear wife and our Heavenly Father. How precious you are to me. It has been a privilege and an honour to love you, care for you and protect you. I have been rewarded on earth."

"As you will be in heaven also, Abba. I will be with you for eternity. You have been a good and faithful servant and I love you dearly."

"I'm not sure what the Good Lord has in store for you, Jesus. You are destined for greatness. The way will not be easy for you. You will suffer and your mother will suffer with you. At your presentation, Simeon, the High Priest, told us that.

The father and his adopted son fell into a comfortable and intimate silence.

Joseph was not able to go to work again. His effort to get out of bed and walk around would bring on difficult breathing and pain in his chest and arms. He spent most of his day resting in bed, sitting on a bench in the garden, and praying. Mary and the other women around him pampered him and cared for him, but they knew it was tough for him not to practice his trade with his boys. He enjoyed their camaraderie as much as the creative work of building. He knew that his days were numbered. He spent his time in contemplation of his life. He had no regrets. As he reviewed his memories, he couldn't help but smile. He remembered his childhood with caring parents and boisterous and exuberant brothers. He lovingly remembered his first wife and the beautiful children she bore him. He remembered his life with Mary. He recalled the husband selection process, the surprise mysterious pregnancy, the angels, the warning, the trial by bitter waters, the glorious birth of Jesus, the flight to Egypt, and losing Jesus in the Temple. He remembered it all: the fears, the joys and the pleasure. He focused on his Mary. She was so young when he married her, yet so mature and wise. Her heart spilled over with love and with devotion to her God, her family and for all who sought her help. She was a marvel! The love they shared went far beyond the conjugal expectations. It was even deeper and more complete. It was divine. She was his dove.

Mary held a bowl of broth in her hands. She was on her way to the garden to offer him some sustenance. She stopped and watched her husband for a few minutes. It was a splendid summer day. The light was bright, and the air was comfortably cool in the morning, but it would undoubtedly end up being a scorchingly hot day. Joseph sat on his favourite bench in the shade of the olive trees laden with their unripened fruit. He was solemn and meditative. In his gaze, she saw reflected her own worth and beauty. He was gentle, tender, and enormously protective. Joseph was a happy man. His contentment came from being deeply selfless. The needs of others always came before his own, and the act of continually giving himself rendered great rewards of joy to his soul. There was honour and nobility in self-sacrifice, and he enjoyed the delight he experienced from his gifts to others. People loved him—a great return that. Mary grew all warm inside thinking of what a wonderful husband he had been to her. He had indeed been God-sent.

Mary quietly approached him and handed him the cup of broth. He took a sip and looked at her intimately.

"You know that my time is near, Mary."

"Yes, I have noticed reduced capacity in all your activities, Joseph."

"I have had a wonderful life. I have been blessed with all that is important in this world. I have been especially blessed with you."

"It is I who was blessed with such a wonderful man who loved, honoured, and cherished me. I am so grateful that you came into my life, Joseph."

"I am grateful too. I loved my first wife, but it was the love of household activity, raising children and earning a living. With you, it was a marriage of souls and an intimacy of the heart. I can't explain this communion that we share. Even though we have never had intercourse of the body, we are one in the depth of our essence and in the spirit. I love you passionately, Mary."

"For a person who has always complained about not being able to find the right words, you have touched the core of it very well. I could not have said it more eloquently. You reflect my thoughts and feelings exactly. I love you passionately, too, my dear husband."

It was Joseph's time. He was too weak to leave his bed and the entire family had been called to his side. They stood or sat around his bed and watched the man they loved in his laboured sleep. Only whispers of great sadness could be heard as Joseph's loved ones witnessed the last hours of this nobleman. Mary was often seen wiping her silent tears. They were often accompanied by the whimpers and snuffles of Joseph's daughters, Salome and Mary. Even the littlest children seemed to sense the gravity and the sadness in the ambience and mood of the room.

Joseph's eyes slowly opened, and he recognized his loved ones.

He spoke his words with a weak, reedy and halting voice, "Do not be sad. I am ready." Every statement he made was followed by a moment of strenuous and wispy breathing. I'm going to a good place." His words were punctuated with lengthy silences as Joseph sought the strength to continue. "No more hurt and worries. Do not weep for me."

Jesus, who was close by his side, spoke softly to him, "Shall we pray together, Abba?" Joseph nodded. Mary and others wept.

"All Your works shall give thanks to you,

O Lord, and all your faithful shall bless you,

They shall speak of the glory of your kingdom,

And tell of your power."

At this point, Joseph mustered up strength and a strong voice and answered with the following psalm verse of the Ketuvim:

"They make known to all people your mighty deeds,

And the glorious splendour of your kingdom.

Your kingdom is an everlasting kingdom, and

Your dominion endures throughout all generations."

Then, surrounded by love of the Father, the Son and the Holy Spirit and his family, Joseph closed his eyes, and he breathed his last breath.

The family sobbed but they remembered what their Abba had told them and, led by Jesus, recited:

"He who dwells in the shelter of the Most High,

Who abides in the shadow of the Almighty,

Will say to the Lord, 'My refuge and my fortress.

My god, in whom I trust'."

Chapter 33
Widow Mary

"Thank you for helping me with the barley sowing, Jesus. This is a job that Joseph used to help me do. It's heavier and more labourious work than weeding and so he never let me do it on my own."

Carrying the heavy sack of grain over his shoulder, the fifteen-year-old Jesus smiled at his mother and said, "Rightly so, Imma. We know that women are not up to sowing and they should stick to their sewing."

"Oh, you!" she cried, as she laughed and slapped his shoulder. Jesus made a great gesture to show how she was strong and had nearly toppled him with her clout. He laughed teasingly and hugged her and they enjoyed a light moment together.

Joachim's sheep farm and land in Nazareth had continued to be prosperous and the family had continued to follow Joachim's practice to split the earnings from their estate to the Temple, charity, and their family. The taxes had reduced their income considerably, but they were happy living a simple and humble life.

Mary, dressed in a well-used working linen tunic and a veil tied behind her head, went on to explain. "Now, we must be mindful of where we spread the seed if we want a good harvest. Be careful not to spread seeds on the path because the birds will scoop them up. There are also patches where the earth is very shallow. Here, the seedlings will spring up, but because there is not enough soil, they will wither at the first hot sun. We need to stay clear of the area where there are thorns and nasty weeds, nettles and such, because they will eventually choke the new sprouts and they won't survive."

"I have ears to hear you, Imma. You are absolutely right and I understand to sow only on good soil."

As they were scattering the seed Mary talked to Jesus about his life in the future. She asked him if he had a girl in mind to become his wife. Jesus answered that he was thinking that the only woman he was interested in was Mary, his dear Imma. He would be faithful to her and only her until he died.

He was the man of the house now and, together with his half-brothers, had continued to work at the business. The carpentry and contracting work were doing quite well. Although they were not rich, they wanted for nothing and felt very blessed. Any excess wealth went to those who had little and sometimes Mary would take her robe off her own back to give it to a poor person shivering in the cold. Anna's, Joachim's and Joseph's compassion and generosity were in their blood. They had taught their children well and consequently, their family enjoyed the fullness of life and the joy of giving. Giving was more satisfying than having. This was a difficult concept to understand for untrusting, nervous, and greedy people.

Neither did Jesus need to worry about his mother. Mary, with the help of Mary Salome and various wives of their children, kept the house well furnished with herbs, vegetables, and fruits from the garden. The vineyards and olive orchards were doing well, and the animals were flourishing under the new herder, mentored by Daniel, who, like Joseph, had recently passed away. Mary had suffered numerous losses in her family. Anna and Cleopas had died before Joseph, and other older relatives in Bethlehem had also gone to their maker. Mary could have lived independently because she was a skilled spinner and weaver, and her work was in great demand in local markets and to the passing caravans. Her skills as a healer were often called on and there were often gifts of saffron, honey, spices, chickens, or eggs left at her door after she had ministered to a sick person or assisted in midwifery.

One day, Jesus confided to his mother. "You know, Imma, I am feeling something in my inner self. I do not understand what it is, but it feels like a calling. I feel a power surge in my soul and I'm not sure what to do with it."

"Your destiny and mission in life will emerge eventually, Jesus. Pray on the matter. Leave yourself open to the Spirit and the will of the Lord. He will guide you."

Jesus smiled at Mary. "You are wise as always, Imma."

"You know, Jesus, that you were born under unusual circumstances that are a mystery even to me."

"What do you mean?"

"I think that it is time that I share the events surrounding your birth with you. You're old enough. It is too important a subject to discuss with you while we plant the barley field so we will set a time after prayer tonight to enlighten you."

Later that evening, Mary told Jesus more details about his birth. He had long been aware that his parents had referred to him as the son of the heavenly Father, but he was never fully clear about what that truly meant, or how it had happened. Mary described to Jesus in detail about her betrothal to Joseph, the angel's annunciations to both her and Joseph, the miraculous birth in a cave near Bethlehem and the flight to Egypt. Jesus listened attentively and took in the information in a meditative way. He needed time to absorb and understand what it all meant. He also knew that he could feel a power in himself growing stronger each day. This strength of knowledge and authority and healing force were not experienced by the other boys and men in his life. In the following months and years he would spend a great deal of time asking Adonai for the wisdom to understand what was being asked of him in the service to his Father in heaven.

As Jesus approached his twentieth year, this energy inside grew. He could feel a force course through him in moments of need. He did not yet understand his calling and mission in life but thought that the power that pulsed in him would one day give him the answers he sought. Mary was aware that Jesus was awakening to the divine power that moved in his being but he was still confused and uncertain of his destiny.

One day, he was working atop a scaffolding. The son of the owner was underfoot and bothering the workers on the platform. He was fooling around, and jumping and feigning sword play, and he fell off the edge. He landed on the ground with a thud. The child was barely breathing and he had lost consciousness. His panicked father thought he was dead and beat his breast with shrieks of lamentations and cries of desperation. Jesus first calmed the man and then bent down to the young boy. He heard the shallow breathing and saw the stillness of the little body still holding on to his wooden sword. Jesus went down on his knees and held the boy's head in his hands. What could he do? He could call on his Father in heaven. Jesus closed his eyes and prayed:

"Blessed are you, Lord God of all creation. Through your goodness, we have received life. Great in might and strong in compassion, please restore this child to his full and untroubled existence." He held his hands around his head for a little longer and released. The boy started to moan and move his head back and forth, making a grimace of pain. Suddenly, he opened his eyes looked directly at Jesus who returned his gaze. He sought his father who was hanging above Jesus' shoulder.

"Abba," called the child. His father quickly moved to his side and cried:

"Tawdi, tawdi! Thank the Lord! You are alive, my son. How are you feeling, my dear boy?"

"I want my Imma," cried the boy.

"What is your imma's name, young man?" asked Jesus.

My imma's name is Veronica," answered the boy, still sniffling.

Jesus nodded sagely and told the father, "He is well and he will be playing with his sword again in no time."

Mary never knew about this incident because Jesus didn't know what to make of it. He was not sure whether the power had come from him or from God the Father giving him the authority to heal in his name. He contemplated this mystery for a while. He did not know whether the healing was a result of the energy pulsing in him or just the direct work of the Almighty. It was too soon to tell Mary.

Chapter 34
Mother Mary Mentor

A day can reach a high temperature quite quickly in Nazareth and so the workday begins early. Mary was up while it was still dark and she was beginning to prepare the morning meal. The garden was lit by the ebbing moon and the approaching dawn to the east, and it allowed her to see Jesus' form in the garden. She stopped what she was doing to watch her son as he prayed. He did this every morning. He wore a simple homespun linen tunic and a woollen overdress in the cooler weather. He wore sturdy, well-worn leather sandals that he kept until they practically fell off his feet. His face was a male image of his mother. He had beautiful, soft, twinkling eyes. He had high cheekbones, an aquiline nose, and her dimples. He now sported a beard that was slightly divided into two strands because of the cleft on his chin. His mouth was full but it was his smile that lit up his face. In fact, his smile lit up a room!

Jesus was now of marriageable age. There were several appeals by matchmakers to make Jesus a husband of several girls who would very much like to be his wife. Why not? He had a profitable trade, a home, and a solid Jewish bloodline. He was handsome; he was intelligent, he was kind and caring. He was the catch of the town! And yet all attempts to find him a wife had been refused. He said he was not ready to marry. The reasons he gave were that he still did not fully know who he was himself. He was happy in the company of his mother and his destiny in life was still not determined. He was not sure it would be fair to a wife if his destiny included constant travelling. Truth be told, his role as rabbi in the synagogue should have compelled him to marry, as this was an expectation of their Hebrew faith. Still, Jesus showed no interest and kept saying to Mary, "You're my only girl, Imma."

Jesus was now an authority on Scriptures and the Law and he spent many non-working hours discussing with other rabbis or teaching young people. He had charismatic appeal to people around him who hung on his every word and asked many questions of him. Often, his audience was made up of eyelash-beating, wide-eyed girls who were sighing and flirting with him as he spoke. Unfortunately, the refusal of so many eligible wives did not bode well in his hometown. The town talk reflected their feelings that Jesus was rude and arrogant and thought himself above the people in his community. They whispered and bad-mouthed him behind his back and although they did not dare speak this way in front of Mary, she was aware of their discontent. Jesus felt it, too and consequently started to spend more time in Sepphoris, Capernaum and other villages working on building projects. He spent less time in Joseph's woodshop. Mary was sad about that because she saw him less.

The women had gathered after Sabbath in the courtyard of the synagogue. They contentedly sat around on stone stools.

"That was an excellent lesson that rabbi Jesus gave today, don't you think, Mary?" asked one of the women.

"Not hard to listen to with that smooth voice and certainly not bad to look at, too," laughed Kelilah.

"Dai! Enough! Mary is right here and this is her son you are talking about. For shame," admonished Dinah.

The women all chuckled more in embarrassment than mirth but hoping that this would save face for Kelilah. Mary sat demurely and did not make a fuss and she kept her own counsel. There was a long pause in the conversation and then Dinah exclaimed:

"Truly, I tell you that Jesus certainly speaks with authority and wisdom. At such a young age! I would go so far as to say that he is the best rabbi in all of Galilee. Sorry, Rahab, but he is."

Mary lowered her eyes in humility and said: "Yes. I find him quite captivating, but what can I say? He is my son and in my eyes, he can do no wrong."

"The whole village agrees that he is a very eligible bachelor and they can't understand why he is not married already. My Rebecca would have been a good match, but she is married now to the butcher's son."

"Never mind your Rebecca. My Sarah would be most suitable for a rabbi's husband because she is a rabbi's daughter. And still available as she has her heart set on Jesus."

An older woman who had no daughters opined: "We don't understand, Mary; what is the problem with the maidens who have been offered in Nazareth? Can you explain why such a wonderful man is not married yet?"

"He has his reasons. He feels he may have a calling for a mission that goes beyond Nazareth and marriage. He feels that it wouldn't be fair to a wife who would want to have children and a stable home."

"Is he talking insurrection against the Romans? Oh, dear," asked Tamar.

"I'm sure it is not that, but he is not sure what that mission is. He is a gifted preacher and teacher, so perhaps that is his calling. He must have more time to determine the direction of his life and at this moment, it is not commitment to family and home."

There was a general gasp in the air.

"Do you mean, he would leave his mother for a mission? Mary, you are a widow. It is his responsibility to care for you!" Rahab exclaimed.

"If it is the will of Adonai, then yes." At that statement, all the women were stunned silent and looked at each other with gaping mouths.

Mary read the audience and assured them. "Jesus is a very special man. You know this. You have just told me. But he must do what he must do. And you know that I am an independent woman. I can sustain a living with my crafts and my garden. The farm is doing well and James is quite capable of overseeing the business of our domicile. My sister Mary Cleopas, now a widow, is with me and together we can run our household and keep ourselves company. We won't suffer from loneliness as we have too much to do."

That seemed to put an end to that discussion. One of the women looked around and asked, "Where is Mary Cleopas?"

"For a few weeks, she is visiting her daughter in Cana who is caring for her newborn son."

"How many children does this daughter have now?" asked Tamar.

"This is her fourth child and only boy. She has born daughters before this."

"Good. Every woman needs a son in these times and in this world," averred Dinah.

"Amen," chorused the women.

The years passed. Jesus was now a robust but elegant man of twenty-five years. This year, Mary and Jesus decided to go by themselves on the annual pilgrimage to Jerusalem. They were planning on making several stops to visit friends along the way. The spring weather was beautiful and lent itself to a lovely roundabout journey. Both Jesus and Mary had been working hard and needed a respite from their labours. Their travels would take them around the Sea of Galilee. They left Nazareth one sunny morning and went north to visit a friend named Jacob in Magdala. This was a friend that Joseph, James and Jesus had made when they had been contracted to build his stables. They had promised to visit when they had the occasion, but after Joseph died, things had changed. Isaac and Rachel did not even know about Joseph's passing.

While they were enjoying an evening meal on the canopied section of the roof on a balmy evening fragrant with tree blossoms and wildflowers, they told their hosts about the death of Mary's beloved Joseph. Isaac and Rachel were sad to hear of this loss and asked how the family was getting on with life. They remarked on how lucky Mary was to have such a strapping man in Jesus and asked about James and his family.

Mary and Jesus were saddened to hear that one of the prominent men in Magdala had a daughter who seemed to be possessed. She went into convulsions where her head and body shook wildly. She was aggressive while making animal-like noises and foam would appear at her mouth. Her seizures were happening more and more frequently and the father had to constrain her to her house and garden so that she would not harm herself or others. Jesus was deeply troubled by this and asked if anything could be done. Isaac told him that all the local physicians had been called because the father would spare no expense to resolve the suffering of his daughter and her family. Her name was Mary too, but the people called her Mary Magdelene because of the status of her parents in Magdala.

"Poor woman. I feel for her and her father," said Mary.

Jacob shook his head in solidarity with the family and admitted, "She has been like this for some time now. No man will take her for wife with this malady." Jesus nodded in concern and compassion. A silence fell on the sympathetic group.

Jacob broke the silence by raising a new topic. "Have you heard about the rebel called Barabas?" Jesus and Mary's intrigued faces let Jacob know that he could continue.

"Apparently, he is leading a group of rebel men and stirring things up, causing dissension and trouble everywhere from Judea to Galilee."

Mary commented, "I am aware that people are upset about their poverty, their oppression by the Romans, taxes, and the abuse of power by Herod."

"It's getting worse. Barabas has killed Roman guards and has attacked Roman fortified properties. He has preached directly against Herod."

"He is bold, this Barabas," said Jesus.

"There is a warrant for his arrest and the Romans are searching for him. If I were him, I would be hiding in the hills right now because the minute the Romans find him, they will execute him with relish."

Mary asked, "Should people be worried about their pilgrimage to Jerusalem? Are people in danger?"

"Barabas is not against people like you and me. He is after the oppressors, not the Jewish people... he is a brutal murderer, though. However, he will need to stay well hidden for a while, although his followers will be prowling the land and doing his bidding."

On another stop, in Capernaum, they visited again with Zebedee's sons, John and James. Father Zebedee had recently passed, and his wife, Mary Salome, Mary's distant cousin, was managing the marketing and sales of the daily catches while the boys continued to fish. Their family had joined forces with a family in Bethsaida just across the lake and together they were pooling their resources to make a decent living harvesting the fruits of the Sea of Galilee.

"I think that you should stop in Bethsaida to meet Simon and his brother Andrew before you head back on your journey south. James and I will go with you to introduce you to them. They are great fellows and Simon's mother-in-law is a wonderful and good woman. She manages the business at that end of the lake."

They all set out by boat to make contact with Simon and Andrew, who were mending their nets on the beach when they found them.

"Must have been a great catch if you need to repair the rips in the nets," teased John.

"I only wish. No, I have put the repairs off too long and I was losing as many fish as I caught," quipped Simon. "And who have we got here?" Both Simon and Andrew got up to meet the new arrivals.

"This is Jesus, bar Joseph, and his mother, Mary. They are taking a journey to the Passover and they wish to visit acquaintances to keep in touch and to announce the passing of Joseph to those who have not yet learned of his death."

The fishermen offered the appropriate words and gestures of condolence and asked Jesus if he had taken over Joseph's business. Jesus informed them that although he worked for the business, it was Joseph's son, James who was in charge. He himself was just a worker and a rabbi on the side. They stayed over for supper and enjoyed a meal of fish cooked over a fire with seasonal vegetables, honey cakes, and, of course, wine. They chatted well into the night about the state of affairs with the Romans and the hefty taxes that were being demanded to supply the numerous legions and the lavish lifestyle of the Roman officials and the Prefect, as well as King Herod, who seemed to have an insatiable need to build palaces.

"Ordinary people are poor and yet are continually drained of any small earnings. Many are starving and begging in the streets. It's a horrible state of affairs for the men of Israel," reported Simon. "People are getting desperate and feel they need to take action against their oppressors," added Andrew.

"We have heard that the Romans are building temples to Jupiter, Apollo, Athena, Mars, Diana and so many more 'gods' that I can't keep track anymore. You can see these everywhere--in towns, villages, and cities," lamented John.

"Even worse, they want to violate our own places of worship by sculpting a statue of Caesar for our Sacred Temple. Our Temple! This is an abomination to our one God!"

At that moment, another person approached the gathering. Simon greeted the newcomer.

"Shalom, Mark. How nice of you to drop by to see us. Come sit around the fire. Let us introduce you to our new friends from Nazareth, Jesus bar Joseph and his mother, Mary."

"Mary and Jesus, this is Andrew's friend Mark. He's too good for the likes of us fishermen. Mark is an educated man of means, but we won't hold this against him, will we, James?" teased John.

John went on to explain to Mark that their guests were related to their mother, Zebedee and that Joseph had been a fine carpenter and builder who had become a great friend to their family.

"Shalom," responded Mark with a smile. "I wonder why you would want to keep the company of these two lazy, good-for-nothing gut-spillers. Their mother, though, is a truly clever woman who keeps these two boat-drifters in line." They all broke out in laughter at the jovial bantering.

Mary Salome said: "Welcome, Mark and please have some wine."

The conversation turned again to the terrible things happening in their homeland. During this discourse, Mary and Jesus said little and kept the disheartening news in their hearts. They, too, wondered how long this could go on and how to put an end to this catastrophe.

Their next visit was in Bethany, at the home of Lazarus' parents. They arrived in the afternoon. The day had been very warm and they were sweaty from their trek. Naomi was now a widow suffering from some ailment that had stripped her of energy and greatly affected her mobility. Her daughters Martha and Mary had not married and had opted instead to care for their mother and for their brother Lazarus. Their father had died from abdominal pain on the right side. He took to his bed in pain and died within a couple of days. It was a terrible way to leave the world and the family was still reeling from the loss.

"Shalom, Lazarus!" exclaimed Jesus as he hugged his boyhood friend.

"Shalom, Mary and Martha," he added as he hugged each of them in turn.

"Peace to this home," Mary added as she greeted her friends with affection.

"We would be lying to you if we did not admit that times have been rough with the passing of our father, and our mother being in a bad way," admitted Lazarus.

"Your visit will be a wonderful distraction and will be greatly appreciated by our mother, who still mourns her beloved husband," contributed Martha.

"Bless his soul," said Martha's sister Mary. "You must miss Joseph terribly, too." Mary nodded and tears welled up in her eyes. Jesus put his arm around his mother's shoulder and squeezed her close to himself.

"Come, come. Let us bathe in the mikveh," urged Mary. "Martha will prepare the evening meal for us."

During the course of the meal, Lazarus talked about the growing unrest among the Jews. "There is a whole faction of discontented... no, I mean enraged rebels out there stirring insurrection."

"Has there been retaliation by the Romans?" asked Jesus.

"Yes, and there is a great pressure on Herod to control his people and to quash these violent political skirmishes."

"Sadly, we see the consequences all along the road to Jerusalem," said Martha.

"What do you mean?" inquired Mary, mother of Jesus.

"There are more crucifixions. The Romans have been crucifying the guilty and then letting their bodies rot on the crosses as an example to others. There are so many!" exclaimed Sister Mary, her sadness mixed with anger.

"It is sacrilegious to leave humans exposed to the elements in that way. It is a terrible injustice!" cried Naomi.

Lazarus added somberly, "The innocents get caught up with the guilty. They get grabbed, accused, jailed, given a sham of a trial, and then are put to a horrible death on the cross for just being in the area of the arrests."

"The walk to Jerusalem will be very smelly and unpleasant, I'm afraid. The skies will be black with scavenger birds making quite a squawk around the rotting corpses," admitted Martha.

"Not pleasant, indeed," agreed Jesus.

"It is time for a Messiah," stated Mary, the mother of Jesus.

Before settling down for the night, Mary examined Naomi and provided some tinctures and herbs that might ease her pain and limber up her joints. There was nothing more to do but try to bring her relief from her suffering, because healing

Naomi was not in Mary's skills and it was now up to the will of the Lord. The family prayed together, led by Jesus. They prayed for their people, they prayed for peace and they prayed for Naomi.

The next morning, Naomi and Martha waved god-speed to Mary, Jesus and Lazarus and his sister Mary as they headed to Jerusalem for Passover. The last leg of the journey south of Jericho was difficult as they entered the rocky hills toward the Sacred Mound.

The trek was more unpleasant than they had imagined, but no imagination had prepared them for the horrendous cruelty toward human beings that they witnessed along the route. The skyline was lined like a fence of crosses. The scavenger birds cast ominous shadows on the scene and the air was tainted with the nauseating aroma of rotting flesh and blood.

Mary's heart was heavy. "What a terrible way to die," she cried.

"So much pain and suffering," added sister Mary.

"No Jew is safe!" exclaimed Lazarus. "Fortunately, women have been spared this gruesome treatment, thank the Lord. But be on the alert. Run away from any skirmishes as you might be caught with the group by accident. Do not expect a trial or justice. He stopped and looked about him. "What a shame, what an abomination!"

The saddened and heavy-hearted party continued their journey in solemnity and sadness, and with respect for Adonai's creatures.

Mary reached for her son's hand and said, "There must be another way." Jesus squeezed his mother's hand and nodded in agreement.

During the sacred holy day, Mary and Jesus shared a Passover meal with family, although, sadly, many of the older generation had passed away. They remembered their elders in their prayers and told stories, serious and comical, about their dearly missed loved ones. Many new children would be named after their beloved ancestors.

In keeping with their travels to see friends and family, Mary and Jesus set out to visit John, the son of Zachariah and Elizabeth. Both of John's parents were no longer. Zachariah had been murdered by Herod's men and left in the Temple. His blood still stained the stone floor. Elizabeth had escaped with John to the rocky, caved-peppered hills in the wilderness. She had remained there with her Essene relatives until she died. She had mourned Zachariah until her last breath. Zachariah had sacrificed his life and the Hebrew women had witnessed the butchery of their babies. It was hard to shake the memories of the massacre and the great loss to the Hebrew people.

John had grown into a large and strong man. He wore camel-hair clothes cinched with a belt--the mark of a holy man-- but he was too humble to recognize the important role he was called to play. He held a leadership position among the Essenes and remained influential as he preached. He did not preach insurrection and violence. He called for repenting and making way for the Messiah. He announced to all who would listen that the time of the Messiah was near. "Prepare the way of the Lord!" he would cry out.

Mary and Jesus spent the rest of the spring season, from Nisan to early Sivan, with this reclused population of austere desert wilderness dwellers. John and Jesus would, on occasion, go deeper into the desert and harvest locusts and honey. On several occasions, the two cousins went away to pray and to share many conversations about the political situation, the corruption of the Pharisees, the degrading faith in God among the Hebrews with their attraction to idols and to the Roman and Hellenistic ways of life. They discussed how these problems would affect the Jewish people. They discussed the Messiah and how he would change their lives. They both agreed that the Messiah would choose a peaceful way. John taught Jesus where to find water and how to survive on the stingy desert harvest.

"I feel it will be soon, cousin," claimed John.

"The coming of the Messiah, you mean?" asked Jesus.

"Yes, I will be leaving this community soon and entering my mission to prepare the way of the promised Saviour," confessed John.

"What do you think he will be like, this Saviour?"

"I'm not sure, but Isaiah talked about a 'Prince of Peace, and a Wonder-Councillor'."

This statement set Jesus to thinking about the meaning of this prophecy. He remained quiet and meditated upon it.

John took the conversation up again and said, "I don't think that the Messiah will be a violent rebel like Barabas and the likes. His mission will be heavenly."

"I agree", said Jesus. "And something tells me that the Messiah will not meet the political aspirations of the Hebrews."

"I think the 'Son of Man' will be talking about another kingdom. Not the earthly Jerusalem, but a new Jerusalem," asserted John.

After a pensive moment, Jesus replied, "Adonai's will shall become clear to us in His own time."

"I feel the call to go to Judea and see if I can discover my mission. The urge to go is strong," admitted John.

"Peace to you, my dear cousin. May Adonai be with you."

This conversation gave Jesus much to ponder. His sense of his own calling and mission was forming, as hints of illumination and enlightenment from the Holy Spirit were presenting themselves to him spontaneously without solicitation. The sleeping divine embers in his soul were sparking and bursting into increasingly frequent revelations.

At the same time, Mary was noticing a difference in her son. He seemed to be more pensive and meditative. He seemed to be slowly discovering who he was and his vocation—and it wasn't woodworking. There was no firm commitment just yet, but she felt it would be soon.

Chapter 35
A Wedding in Cana

"Come and dance with us, Auntie Mary," called the little girls to Mary as she sat in the shade of a sycamore tree. It was the season of Av and it was very late summer hot. She had just sat down to rest for a minute.

"I just sat down," laughed Mary.

"Please, you must 'hul', dance with us, Auntie! Come whirl with us," cried one girl with bits of honey cake still on her cheek and hair, while another had pomegranate juice staining her lips.

"Come whirl with us and show us the steps, Imma of Jesus!" chorused the others.

Another girl chimed in, "Remember what the prophet, Samuel, said, 'Before the Lord, I will make merry'. Ple-e-e-a-s-e."

Mary couldn't help but think how tired she was. This was the third day of the wedding festivities of Nathan's granddaughter in Cana. Mary was now forty-five years of age, and although she was still quite spry and light in her step, she was feeling her age when it came to the endless dancing that came with a wedding feast. It was very hot at the end of the day, but the children didn't seem to feel the heat the way the adults did.

She was slow to respond and get up, but the girls were relentless:

"The musicians are playing their instruments and it is the girls' turn to 'hag', to celebrate and dance. See, Jesus just finished a 'chagog' dance with the boys, and he was marvelous in his energy and spirit."

"You know, dear nieces, that Jesus is fifteen years younger than me. He does dance well though, and he loves to make children happy. You are lucky that like him, I am fond of children or otherwise, I would give in to my fatigue."

Mary got up and proceeded to whirl in a circle with the girls, showing the grapevine step and a few other dance moves.

When the music came to an end, Mary stopped and clapped and laughed with the young lasses and said, "I'm good for one more but... let us slow down the pace a bit." She left and consulted with the musicians and returned.

She showed them the flowing motions of a lyrical dance that she had learned in the Temple. They gracefully and poetically moved through a softer version of the dance to a psalm.

'I will give thanks to the Lord with my whole heart,

In the company of the upright, in the congregation.

Great are the works of the Lord,

Studied by all who delight in the...

He sent redemption to his people;

He has commanded his covenant forever.

Holy and awesome is his name.

His praise endures forever.'[54]

---

[54] Psalm 111

By the end of the creative dance, all the people had stopped to watch, and they clapped in appreciation. It was a great honour to Adonai and to the bride as well.

The oldest of the girls spoke on behalf of the others and said, "Thank you, Auntie Mary. That was beautiful and we have learned new steps and ways to move our arms and hands." They all came together to hug Mary. She smiled at them and kissed each one of them on the head. She made her way to see Mary Cleopas and noticed Nathan and Mary whispering to each other with a concerned look on their faces.

"What is the matter, Mary?" asked the mother of Jesus.

"Oh, Mary, we miscalculated how much wine we would need and we are running short. We did not anticipate this many people would show up. But the day is fair and it has brought out our many neighbours and friends."

"And I guess it did not help that Jesus brought his friends and disciples," added Mary.

"They are most welcome; however, we don't know what we shall do. We are only in the late afternoon. The evening meal has not been served yet."

Mary was silent for a moment. "Leave it to me."

Mary sought out Jesus. He was not hard to find because his friends were surrounding him, teasing, and laughing. There were the Zebedee boys and their fisherman partner, Simon, and his brother Andrew. Mark, Andrew's friend, was also with them. As she approached, she heard them teasing their friend about his fish breath in a light-hearted manner. "You had better chew on mint before you kiss a girl with that mouth!" bantered Jesus.

"Nothing useful comes from that small, good-for-nothing village of Nazareth. And these fishermen from Galilee cannot escape the smell of fish on them!" ribbed a citizen from Cana, called Bartholomew.

"I'd rather smell like fish than stink like tanners."

"You've got a point there, but we need the leather," said a more serious Philip, a Bethsaidian like Simon and Andrew.

"Jesus, may I speak with you?" asked his mother.

"Of course. I can refuse you nothing, my dear Imma." He came to her. Lifted her off her feet and twirled her around, smiling into her face. He put her down and they walked away when he noticed a worried look on her face.

"Jesus, they have run out of wine and the day is still young."

"What can I do about it, Imma?" A look of realization crossed his face. "Oh, mother, why do you involve me?"

"They are our kin. And they have no wine, Jesus."

He frowned. "It is not yet my time," he said quietly. Nevertheless, Jesus, always unable to refuse his mother, followed her to the serving area.

Mary called over some servants and told them, "Do as he tells you."

There were six stone jars standing there, for the Jewish rites of purification. Each held a capacity of twenty or thirty gallons.

"Fill them up with water," instructed Jesus. They did as he asked and filled the jugs right to the brim.

When they finished the task, Jesus looked up towards the heavens and prayed quietly. He felt the power bestowed on him. Then, he asked the servants to draw some out and take it to the steward of the feast. The steward tasted the liquid and his face broke out in a huge grin. "This is marvelous!" He continued to drink. He called the bride and groom and their parents and announced to them, "Every man serves the good wine first; and when men have drunk freely, then the poor wine, but you have kept the good wine until now." He shook his head incredulously and walked over to his friends to brag about the taste of this fine wine.

The disciples had witnessed the reaction of the steward and stood bewildered. This Jesus was a manifested glory to Adonai! They were mightily impressed with their rabbi leader.

Mary Cleopas and Nathan looked at Mary and at Jesus and didn't know how to react. They were not quite sure what had happened. For Mary, this was the first clear sign that her son Jesus had manifested. His mission had begun at this wedding in Cana. She knew that it was indeed his time. Jesus became fully aware of his calling as well. They finished celebrating the marriage of their relative until the stars came out and the night grew cool. The next morning, Mary and Jesus headed out to Capernaum with his brethren and his disciples who felt compelled to follow him. What was to happen in the coming days and weeks was still a mystery, but they all felt that they were being called.[55]

---

[55] Taken from John: 2:1-13

Chapter 36
Mother Mary, Disciple

Mary watched the small plume of blue smoke rise towards the heavens. She had collected driftwood and broken branches from a nearby scrub patch on the beach on the Sea of Galilee. Mary, Jesus, and his friends had left the wedding at Cana, rested in Nazareth for the night, and then headed for the fishermen's home in Capernaum which was to become their centre of operations. She followed her son. He liked having her around. His mother was meek, yet full of wisdom. She was a humble woman who always considered herself a handmaid of the Lord. And angels were always with her.

The boys had been fishing all night and she was preparing a fire to make their breakfast as soon as they arrived at shore with their catch. She enjoyed the fragrance of the burning wood. The bundle of brushwood must have included some pine and cedar in order to produce such a pleasant aroma. Her thoughts moved to her new circumstances. She realized that her life was at a turning point. Jesus was soon going to leave her for his grander mission. She herself had prompted it in Cana with the miracle of changing the water into wine. She was somewhat sad, knowing that he would not be at her side anymore. But she understood that he was no longer hers, if he even ever was. He belonged to the world now, and to his heavenly Father. When circumstances would permit, Mary would be at his side, or perhaps just be part of his group of followers. She sighed. Hope. She was full of confidence and trust in the Lord. Jesus would do great things, but she knew he would also suffer for his trouble. So would she. Simeon had prophesied that fact when he said, 'Behold, this child is set for the fall and rising of many in Israel, and a sword will pierce through your own soul also.' Mary was feeling the initial point of that sword now. She would need to become a self-sufficient woman. But she was fortunate; her circumstances were better than most widows. She smiled to herself and realized how blessed she was with many home comforts and a prosperous family around her. She had her skills and she was still young enough to be of service to Adonai.

She stood up and gazed out at the water, holding her hand over her eyes to shadow the bright light of the rising sun. She could see the boat slowly moving toward her, silhouetted in the pink and mauve hues of the horizon. The boys were on their way back and would soon be on shore.

"Did you catch anything?" called Mary to the tired and motley crew that disembarked from their fishing vessel.

"Of course, Mary! A day's wages. We had Jesus with us and he seems to bring us good fortune," Simeon hollered back with a grin.

"Come and join me for breakfast."

The fishermen secured the boat to the shore. They left their catch in the boat and washed their hands in the lake. As they sat around the fire Mary had prepared, they continued their banter of mockery and ribbing.

"Philip caught nothing. He's more curious than fisherman. He asks too many questions. He is an empty netter," teased John.

"His head seems to be somewhere else, but certainly not on the sea," laughed James.

"Remind me again, isn't Philip from Bethsaida? Isn't fishing in their blood?" asked Jesus as he nudged Philip in the shoulder fondly.

Philip took the teasing without reply. He merely laughed and made faces at them and shook his fist out at them. They all laughed together.

Not to be outdone, Simon and Andrew added to the banter. "What of these two?" Simon was referring to the two brothers, John, and James.

"They caught the most fish in their nets today. They would not shut up! They couldn't stop the boasting and swaggering. Almost tipped over the boat with their cockiness," added Andrew.

"Yes, I guess you could call them the sons of thunder," kidded Jesus.

They all laughed as Mary passed around loaves of bread to her left. She bent her head and couldn't hide a smile as she passed to Jesus, to her right, a stone that was the same colour and shape as the bread. She had found the stone on the beach while looking for wood and had remarked on how like a loaf of bread it was.

"What is this?" asked Jesus. "I ask for bread, and my mother gives me a rock. What is the world coming to?" Jesus looked at Mary with a serious look, but he could not take away the smile from his eyes. Mary laughed out loud and gave him a nice, soft loaf instead.

Mary wrapped her arm around her son's shoulder and declared, "I found a scorpion in the eggs the other day; be happy that I didn't give you that by mistake, my dear son." Jesus put his arms around her shoulder and brought her close to him and planted a kiss on her head.

Andrew cleaned a couple of large fish from their day's harvest and placed them in a basket to contribute to the morning meal.

"Careful, make sure there is no snake in that basket because my imma might just cook it up and try to pass it for a fish."

They all laughed in hilarity. And the merriment continued because they were glad to be with each other and they were thankful for their success today.

"Let us give thanks to the Lord, our Father in Heaven." The men got calm and serious as Jesus looked up into the morning sky and said, "Adonai, we bless your Holy Name. We thank you for the gift of this beautiful day, a re-creation of your love for us. We thank you for our catch today. We thank you for the meal that you have provided and that has been prepared for us by imma. Thank you for the gift of each other. May we be worthy of your kinship. We ask that the rest of our day be a sign of our love for you, dear Father."

"Amen," chorused the others.

After having enjoyed the breakfast, Jesus looked at the men in the circle of friendship. The razzing had stopped and Jesus took a softer and more serious tone. Mary knew that this was a moment of decision. She would diminish in the life of Jesus and be merely a witness. She would do this gladly. She understood the role of women in the affairs of men. She would be happy just to be part of his life. She would follow.

"I need to leave you all now. I'm not quite sure what my mission is yet, but I know that I have a calling. I will be heading to Jerusalem to discover what Adonai's will is for me. My Father's plans with regards to my work here on earth will be revealed as I seek his will." The men looked at each other, a little bewildered as to what Jesus meant. Joseph had been dead for years now. "I will count you as my friends always. If you follow me, I will make you fishers of men."

All the men stood up, rounded their arms about each and put their heads forward. Mary remained seated. Simon said, "You are our teacher, our master and our friend. You can count on us. Whatever mission is assigned to you, we will be there for you. Go in peace, Jesus. We are here for the little woman, too. We will treat her like our own imma. From now on, we will call her Imma Mary." The other men nodded in acceptance of this promise.

Jesus smiled broadly and said, "My friends, if that is the case, check your food for rocks, scorpions and snakes." The fellowship of Galileans all laughed heartily. Mary, too.

Jesus turned to his mother and invited her to join the circle. Together, they sang a psalm of thanksgiving.

Chapter 37
Nazareth Town Talk

Eliana, Rachel, Alona, Dinah and Maraha had gathered at the well in Nazareth. As they waited their turn to dip their bucket in the well, they shared the news of the town.

"I hear that Mary is back in town," announced Dinah.

"Yes, and I hear that Jesus was not with her and that he has quit the business," contributed Maraha.

"What a disappointment that man has turned out to be. We had such great expectations for him," said Alona.

The women all nodded and Rachel went on, "He was such a good speaker at the synagogue. Such a handsome man with nice manners and a gentle and caring demeanour."

"Many girls have tried to attract him. The matchmaker has all but given up as Jesus has dismissed all marriage candidates she has brought forth. It seems that he is satisfied with no woman in this town," claimed Eliana.

Putting her full bucket on the ground, Dinah responded, "Thinks he's too good for the likes of us."

"Mary must be angry with him. No wife, no children, no job and no care!" cried Miraha.

Rachel, who always looked for the best in people, countered, "Mary will do fine. She is a very skillful cloth maker; she is a healer and keeps a good garden. Everybody around Nazareth has called on her generous spirit on many occasions—for illness, for birthing and for comfort in the loss of a loved one. Mary has a good family and they will be good to her as she has been good to them. Mary will always be a saint, in my opinion. I will not speak ill of her."

"Well, Jesus is not well viewed in Nazareth, I can tell you," added Alona. "Any man who lets his half-brothers look after his mother is not to be trusted or well-regarded. I, for one, don't care if I never see him again."

"Alona, you've been holding that bucket on the edge of the well while you shared your opinion. 'Yalla, yalla!' The rest of us have things to do."

The women completed their task and slopped their water containers down the road.

Indeed, the people of Nazareth were not thrilled with their homeboy's decision to leave and become an itinerant rabbi.

Chapter 38
Witness to a Baptism

For her part, Mary followed Jesus whenever she could. She loved this way of life. Her admiration for her son and his ability to reach people continued to grow, and she enjoyed hearing him speak with such deep authority on the laws and the faith of the heart. People would flock to him and listen, sometimes for hours, about peace and compassion and forgiveness. It was such a contrast to the hell-bent rebels and their violent solutions to the problems of injustice and oppression.

At times, however, she needed to return home to practise her crafts of spinning and weaving. She shared many chores with Mary Cleopas and enjoyed minding and teaching the grandchildren of her stepchildren. Mary kept many things in her humble heart.

One day, Jesus made a brief stop at his home and told Mary he was going to Jerusalem. She asked if she could accompany him and he told her that she was always welcome. Mary had become a frequent member of Jesus' audience as he preached along the way in various small villages and communities, especially those towns that did not enjoy a synagogue. Mary stayed in the background like one of the listeners and participants. She was there to care for her son and to witness his growing power and influence over the Chosen People.

Jesus and Mary were now well used to the journey to Jerusalem. They had their regular stops and layovers but now had many more stops along the way to allow Jesus to preach. When Mary travelled with Jesus and the disciples, they were accompanied by a donkey carrying all the trappings required for the journey. Jesus, for himself, travelled light. On his own, he only had the clothes on his back and what he could carry in a leather over-the-shoulder satchel.

The day was bright and the weather was balmy. Mary and Jesus arrived at the Jordan River, not far from Jericho. There was a crowd of people gathered around a grizzled and scruffy-looking man who was submerging people under the water of the Jordan. People were lining up for their turn. When the man spoke, Jesus recognized who it was. It was his cousin, John. He held Mary's hand and nodded forward. She recognized him too, in spite of not having laid eyes on him for nearly a decade. They both stood and watched. Among the people in the crowd, there were a few Pharisees and other religious officials. They looked more pleased with themselves than with what they saw. The shadow of dark clouds dimmed what had been a sunny day. The air was heavy and oppressive. The haughty Pharisees, full of their self-importance, challenged John, the baptizer.

"Who are you?" they demanded.

"I'm not the Messiah if that is what you think," John confessed.

Looking at his hairy, unkempt appearance, they continued to question him. "You look like Elijah. Are you he?" John shook his head. "I am not," was his response.

"Are you the prophet?" Again, John shook his head.

"Then, who are you?"

John answered, "I am the voice of one crying in the wilderness, 'Make straight the way of the Lord.' "

"Then why are you baptizing?"

"I baptize with water, but among you stands one whom you do not know, who comes after me, the thong of whose sandal I am not worthy to untie."

At that moment, Jesus stood up and walked toward John. John knew then the Messiah had arrived. The baptizer took one look at the familiar face and announced surely and clearly, "Behold the Lamb of God, who takes away the sin of the world! This is the man of whom I have been talking."

"Baptize me, John."

"No, Jesus, I am not worthy. I need to be baptized by you, yet you come to me?" retorted John.

Jesus put his hand on John's shoulder and answered, "Allow it now, for it is right for us to fulfill all righteousness."[56] John bowed his head and acquiesced. Jesus removed his overclothes and when he was dressed only in his linen tunic, entered the water to be baptized. The ceremony lasted but a few moments and a fully drenched Jesus thanked John and walked out of the water. At that moment, the sky opened up, the clouds cleared away and the day shone with light. The world went still and silent. There was something strange in the hush. The crowd watched as a dove landed on Jesus' shoulder and a booming voice came from above saying, "This is my beloved Son, with whom I am well pleased."

After a long moment, the birds and insects began to perform again with their happy noises. People were astonished and buzzing with each other. In contrast, Mary was serene and still in the realization of what she had witnessed. Jesus had confirmed what she already knew in her heart. The redemption of the world had begun.

Jesus rejoined his mother and said to her, "I will take you to the Temple where you can rejoin the Daughters of the Hebrews. I need to go to the desert to seek my Father's will." And so Jesus hugged his mother and placed a kiss on her forehead. He touched his nose to hers and looked deeply into

---

[56] Matthew 3:15

her eyes and finally said goodbye to his mother at the gates of the Holy Place. And Jesus, filled with the Holy Spirit, began his lengthy trek to a forsaken wasteland.

Jesus was gone for forty days. During that time, Mary resided at the Temple. As a former graduate of the Temple daughters, she was readily accepted as an instructor and mentor to acolytes. Mary's reputation there was well known and the High Priest and other officials welcomed her. They felt honoured that Mary would give her time and skills to train new girls. Mary loved being back within the walls of the Holy Place and remembered the smells and sounds of her childhood. Many of her colleagues and friends were missing. Anna, the prophetess, Simeon, Zachariah, her teachers, and her mother's friends had all passed away by now. It was a new group of staff and officials now and the women from her time there were few in number and quite elderly. Most of the girls had gotten married and had families. It was impossible to know where everybody had landed after leaving the Temple sphere. She enjoyed letting her light shine amongst the new girls. It brought to mind all that she had learned during her time between the holy walls. Mary did whatever duties were asked of her, but mostly she found time and privacy to pray. She prayed for the girls. She prayed for Jesus and John the Baptist and she prayed for the world.

Chapter 39
Witness to a Miracle

Mary was in the women's court in the Temple in Jerusalem, ministering to some young beggars. The needy seem to be younger and younger these hard days, she thought. Most people gave them small change, or threw hard, moldy crusts of bread to them, or ignored them entirely. However, Mary's generous spirit brought them food like olives, figs, cheese, and fresh bread, and she took the time to sit down beside them and speak to them. Mary's experienced healing hands would see to their sores and ailments in the best way that she could. She would sell the works of her refined skills, fine and expensive tablecloths and scarves, to interested vendors and then buy cheaper and warmer wool material to make things that the poor people in the streets needed. The measure of thick, warm cloth could be used as a covering or as a sleeping mat. Her quiet kindness and compassion did not go unnoticed. When she was applauded by her peers and superiors, she accepted the praise respectfully but dismissed it as just a small thing she could do to right the wrongs of those poor creatures' misfortunes. These people were created by Adonai. After all, had it not been written in the Book of Micah that we should 'act justly, love tenderly, and walk humbly with your God'? It was her duty. Not only that, it was also her nature.

It was at a moment such as this that Jesus saw her when he returned from his stay in the wilderness. He found her ministering to a poor, ragged woman and her child. He smiled. She was such a ray of sunshine to those she encountered, bringing light and warmth to their day.

"Shalom, Imma. It is nice to see you again."

"Oh, Jesus, my beloved! How good to see you!" she exclaimed, and she ran into his open arms.

The hug emphasized his bony structure. Mary stood back and examined her emaciated son. "You are much thinner. And you definitely need a bath! I can see you washed your hands and feet but your hair is matted and you are covered in dust."

Jesus laughed. "Typical mother, always finding fault. But I was in a hurry to see you just to discover where else I could improve." He continued to grin at her.

Mary gave him another lookover and smiled. "Nothing, my son. Absolutely nothing! You are perfect! But I sense that something has changed in you."

"I was mightily tested in the desert, Imma. And I passed the test, but more importantly, I have learned more about my Father and his kingdom."

"Then you are ready."

Jesus nodded once, solemnly.

"Then let us feed you! Tomorrow is the Sabbath. We will give thanks to the Lord for your safe return and pray for your future purpose." Mary hooked her elbow into his and they each sought their own 'mikvey' bath with a promise to meet later for a catch-up meal and Sabbath preparations.

Jesus and Mary headed back to Galilee. His work would begin thereby amassing a team of trusted men to help him in his ministry. But before going to Capernaum, Jesus wanted to make a stop at Magdala to visit his father's friend Jacob.

"Salom, Jacob."

"'Barakh ha-ba', welcome, Jesus and Mary," greeted Jacob, kissing each on both cheeks.

"Peace to this house," responded Jesus.

Jacob and his family broke bread with their visitors. Hebrew people were always hospitable to friends and even strangers. It was an unwritten law in their community ever since their long journey through the desert with Moses. Their house was opened to those who knocked.

During the course of the conversation, Jesus explained that he believed he was called to a special mission. When Jacob questioned Jesus on the care of his mother, Mary assured him that she was in no fear of danger or destitution. She would be occupied and safe in Nazareth. She planned on participating in Jesus' work, albeit in the background. She knew that Jesus was called by the Father and bound to do wonderful things.

"So, what brings you to Magdala, Jesus?" asked Jacob.

"The last time we were here, you mentioned the plight of a poor girl possessed by demons."

Jacob shook his head in sadness and sympathy for the family, "Yes, her name is Mary and she suffers yet."

"May I see her?" asked Jesus.

"Indeed, I will take you there," was Jacob's answer.

When they arrived at the home of the afflicted woman, Jesus and Mary were well received by the homeowner, Cyrus, the woman's father. The home was elaborately and richly decorated. It displayed four tall and beautiful columns at the front, leading to a large marble hall with marble floors surrounding a pool exposed to an open sky. The floors brandished luxurious rugs from Persia, and beautiful tapestries hung on the walls. Everything was gilded and demonstrated opulence, affluence, and influence. Jesus felt sure that every available effort had been made to heal the daughter of her disorder.

The afflicted woman's wealthy father was beside himself. When he discovered the reason for the visit, he heaved a heavy sigh and blew out a breath. "I am desperate and will do anything for her." He welcomed Jacob and the two visitors. Jacob introduced Mary and Jesus to Cyrus' wife and family members and indicated that Jesus thought he might be of some help to Mary.

"She is in a bad way, Jacob. And she seems to be getting worse!"

"Lead me to her," requested Jesus.

"Of course. You know that no wealth on earth can compensate for the suffering of her condition—on her and on us. It wrenches my heart out of my chest every time I witness an episode. What you will see is not my daughter. It is an evil spirit. I would even say that there is more than one demon in her, if the different personalities she expresses are any indication."

Jesus listened attentively, and Mary followed him into a room. What they saw was a ghastly scene.

"Whatever you can do for her to relieve her of such an affliction, I would be eternally grateful," sobbed the victim's father. "Her mother can't witness this anymore. She just cries and wails much of the day. It is hard to get away from the horrible sounds my daughter makes."

Jacob's daughter, also called Mary, was chained to a chair which was nailed to the floor and wall. She was dirty and disheveled. There was food splattered around and excrement all over her clothes and the wall and floor around her. The room was disordered and showed signs of a recent row. The female slave in charge of her care sported a black eye. In spite of her injuries, the woman seemed more sympathetic and anxious for her charge than frustrated and angry. The caregiver nodded and moved out of the way, saying, "This is not my Mary. My Mary is sweet and loving. This is a vicious demon, Lord. Help her if you can, please." They could hear Mary's mother sobbing in another room.

"As we will have a problem distinguishing our two Marys, I will refer to your daughter as Mary Magdelene." Cyrus agreed with that decision.

The possessed woman was not fully dressed because the exercise of changing her clothes had resulted in a battle that left her caregiver with bruises and injuries due to the thrashing and punches. She was gowned in a simple linen shift covered with foul-smelling debris. The sounds that came out of the sufferer's mouth were inhuman. At times, they were bass guttural grunts and growls. At other times, high-pitched wails pierced the atmosphere with screeches, squeals, and serpent hisses. She yelled, howled, and roared. However, between the terrifying utterances, there were occasional soft moans and murmurs. Jesus and his mother, Mary were moved with sympathy and compassion.

Jesus approached the woman but as he got closer, he was met with increased screams and uproar from the inhuman spirits that lived in her body. The spirits were angry at Jesus' advance and presence. They fiercely thrashed about in fury. They twisted and distorted her body and shook her head violently. The spirits (because Jesus was convinced that there was more than one invading this dear girl) howled and wailed all the more as Jesus got closer to the woman. The fiends both wept and laughed. It was a most disturbing outburst to all who witnessed this frightening attack. Unperturbed, Jesus looked up towards heaven and prayed silently while the affected victim threw a fit and convulsed and finally passed out with a foamy drool hanging from her misshaped mouth. Jesus placed both his hands on her head. He held them there until the unconscious but restless body began to calm. He seemed to be quietly mouthing prayers, and then he spoke aloud, commanding the demons to leave the girl's soul. Nothing happened at first and then there was a mighty spasm followed by a tremor and Mary Magdalene loudly belched out a foul and odorous breath. She did this seven times. The demons were gone. Her body visibly returned to looking normal and tranquil.

She was at peace. Cyrus burst into tears of joy, still in disbelief as to what had happened before his very eyes.

"Unchain her," commanded Jesus.

"Are you sure, Master?" queried the slave woman.

"Yes, you are safe; the demons are cast out." Jesus exited the room with Cyrus.

Jesus' mother approached the victim and sat on the floor and let the girl's beaten body cradle in the nest of her own body. She caressed the woman's shoulders and stroked her head and brow. The afflicted woman breathed easier and her breath became soft and regular. Mary asked the servant for a warm, wet cloth to wash the face of her patient. The slave cleaned her body with perfumed water and changed her shift to a clean one. All this time, Mary Magdelene sheltered in the embrace, serenity, and safety of Mother Mary's arms. She awoke and looked up, gently smiled in greeting, and said, "Where have I been, and who are you?"

When Mary Magdalene had been made decent and respectable, Jesus and her whole family, as well as Jacob, re-entered the room.

"Shalom, Abba and Imma," greeted a normal-sounding voice. They were all amazed at the transformation.

Mary Magdalene's father said, "Shalom, sweet daughter. 'Barak ha-nimza', blessed be the one already present."

"L'chaim!" cried out the servant.

Mary Magdalene learned what miracle had just transpired. She looked upon her saviour with adoring eyes. Their eyes locked and there, a deep relationship based on recognition, gratitude, and praise emerged. It would grow and last unwavering for a lifetime.

Before Jesus and Mary departed, Mary's father, Cyrus, expressed his gratitude and gave Jesus a purse of money.

"This is to start you on your mission. I will sponsor you and your work. Count me and my family among your disciples. You are always welcome here, Jesus. You too, Mother Mary."

"I would ask you and your household to go to the river Jordan and be baptized by John the Baptist," responded Jesus.

A few minutes later, Mother and son set out for Galilee to recruit a team of faithful and humble men.

Jesus' mother did not accompany her son to Capernaum. First, they returned to Nazareth. Mary had been gone a lengthy time and there was some catching up to do. Jesus spent the night and broke bread with his extended family who were all anxious to hear the news of what had happened on their long trip. Jesus recounted his Baptism and declared that he now clearly understood who he was and what he was meant to do. They shared many stories and enjoyed many laughs on the roof of their home in Nazareth on this fragrant and balmy evening in Galilee.

Joseph's sons told Jesus not to worry about his mother because their imma Mary was in good hands with them. They would provide all the necessities. Besides, as the family all agreed, Mary, to her own credit, could make a living on her own as she had many personal skills that she could employ. The family would be there for company and safety. And because they loved her.

While she was at home, Mary took on a new project. She wanted to gift Jesus with a new robe. A robe that would keep him warm as well as enrich his austere lifestyle with a garment that was befitting his status as a teacher and preacher. She knew that he would accept the work of her hands because she knew he could refuse her nothing. So she began.

The skeins that she had on hand were the fine purple thread that was left over from her creation of the Temple veil.

Her part of that endeavour had been to weave lengths of purple strips into the veil. The Tyrian purple pigment was a deep, rich and rare dye made from the mucus of three different varieties of Murex snails. She also had skeins of the dye made from the 'tholaath' or crimson worm. This magenta pigment was extracted from an insect that lived on oak trees. In the latter part of her life cycle, the female would bloat up with a red dye that coloured her eggs and excreted onto the tree bark. After she died, workers would scrape the dead worm off the trees, dry it and grind it into the powder that produced the beautiful crimson dye. It took many worms to make the dye, so it was only used by royalty and the very wealthy. Mary had traded many of her woven fabrics to obtain a few skeins of this beautiful hue. She skillfully wove the two colours within the warp and weft of her seamless garment. It was her last great work before she would go to join the disciples of Jesus and spend much of her days journeying in the land. She wrapped it in a simple linen sheet and had it delivered to the Temple and asked that they keep it for her. She would not give it to him yet. She would know when it was the right time to present it to her beloved son.

Chapter 40
Mary Was There

And so Jesus went on to begin his mission. He began to recruit his team of apostles in Capernaum. He decided to make his home base in that town by the sea as he sensed that he had lost favour in Nazareth. He had obviously outgrown his hometown and they resented the fact that he seemed to know more than the local rabbis and scholars. He had outdone his welcome. Mary realized that Jesus would never be properly understood in Nazareth. Therefore, she was not surprised when Jesus set up home base in the fishing community and asked his friends Andrew, Simon, John, James, and Philip to accept him as their master and teacher, walking the same path of life that he walked. He said he would make them fishers of men. Without hesitation, they left their boats and nets behind and joined Jesus.[57]

At the same time, Mary, mother of Jesus, and Mary Cleopas took on the work of domestic life in the peace of their garden, enjoying the solace of spinning and weaving and the household chores. The boys managed the farm and the carpentry business. The two women were blessed with many grandchildren and great-grandchildren running around the house compound. Mary was in charge of their education in Hebrew, the Holy Scriptures, and the laws of their faith. She had a way with children and they not only loved her as a teacher but they loved her as a person who could play with them and be silly with them.

Mary was there when Nathan, husband of Mary Cleopas, died. He had been part of Mary's life for so long that she was

---

[57] Taken from Matthew 4:19

as devasted as her sister. Thankfully, there were sons to take over the affairs of their estate and they were financially very secure. Mary Cleopas took a long time to get over her grief. She mourned her husband for many months, and Mary was there whenever her sister went into a state of depression. It increased the workload for Mary, the mother of Jesus, and she was not always able to accompany her son when he travelled to various communities around the Sea of Galilee and beyond. However, she went whenever she could get away from her family responsibilities.

James, the youngest son of Mary Cleopas, was a quiet and pensive child. He had grown even more pious as he got older. He was more at home with the holy writings and with prayer than he was with hammers and chisels, trowels and calipers. He loved to hear the lessons that Mary taught the children and he put himself forward to accompany Mary and his own mother to places outside the village of Nazareth. He enjoyed the art of selling and was very astute in the business of bartering the spun and woven goods to the various buyers and foreign markets. He could describe different weaves and materials and argue their value with the best merchants. He had also become a disciple of Jesus and accompanied both women, mother and aunt, to places where Jesus spoke to the crowds that were amassing to follow the well-spoken itinerant rabbi. On these trips, James could take along a supply of merchandise and peddle it for additional income. That way, he benefitted from both worlds—listening to the words of Jesus and marketing the textiles.

On one such occasion, Mary, Mary Cleopas, and James were getting ready to listen to Jesus speak to a large crowd. The crowd was waiting for the rabbi Jesus to speak and were talking amongst themselves and were discussing and anticipating what he would say.

Mary was tapped on the shoulder and turned to see a beautiful woman before her.

"Shalom. Do you remember me, Mary?" inquired the young woman who was richly dressed and coiffed.

Mary looked over the pretty face and sought out her eyes and replied.

"Of course, I remember you. You are Mary of Magdala. You look much different than the last time I saw you; however, I can clearly see the sweet maiden I met in your father's house that day. How are you, Mary?"

"I certainly remember the woman who held me in her arms and brought such tranquility to my soul after the demons were cast out by your son."

"I was very taken by that beautiful soul, my dear girl."

"Since then, I have been following Jesus. I hang on to his every word. He is different than the others trying to lead people to a different world. May I sit with you as we listen?"

"We would be blessed, Mary," answered Jesus' mother.

After introducing Mary Magdalene to Mary Cleopas and James, they all settled down in the grass to listen.

It was a glorious day. Jesus had positioned himself on the top of a hillside where his voice carried as in a natural amphitheatre. Jesus was dressed in a simple white garment, cinched with a woven belt of many colours that Mary had made for him. His hair was blowing slightly in the breeze off the sea of Galilee.

Jesus began his talk with, 'Blessed are the poor in spirit, for theirs is the kingdom of heaven....'

The people were spellbound. In the current politically intense climate, they had never heard someone speak of meekness, mercy and peacemaking before. It was refreshing to hear that their mourning would be comforted and that their thirst for righteousness would be rewarded. Jesus' tone was soft, smooth and heartwarming. He filled their souls with comfort and solace. There was a tremendous charm and allure to this man from Galilee. Even the children remained passive and attentive. Mary's son appealed to the core virtues of people and they were captivated by this new interpretation of how they should lead their lives. Mary looked admirably at her little boy, now a grown man of influence. He cut an attractive figure against the waving grasses on a rocky knoll. He was handsome of face for sure, but Mary knew that it was his smile and his lively and sparkling eyes that made him so personally compelling.

At the end of the sermon, people clambered up to speak with Jesus and tell them of their woes. He healed many of them spiritually and physically. The people had witnessed numerous healings and miracles where the blind could see and the cripple walk, that Jesus' reputation had grown immensely and so did the crowds and the demands for his healing power. Mary knew that the draw on his power was exhausting for him and that her son would require solitude to pray to build up the strength to repeat these wonders time and time again.

"Wasn't he splendid, your son?" asked Mary Magdalene with awe and enthusiasm in her voice.

"Yes, he is perfect! However, I am his mother and not very unbiased on the subject," Mary declared with a laugh.

From this time on, the three Marys became fast and close friends and were often seen together at the Jesus assemblies. The women and Jesus and his apostles often stayed at Cyrus' house when touring the area. It was obvious to Mary that Mary Magdalene was head-over-heels in love with her son. She was sure that the woman wanted more from Jesus than Jesus was able to give in the midst of his ministry. Regardless, this beautiful, besotted woman was kind and good and she followed Jesus everywhere. She became like a daughter to Mary and like a sister to Jesus.

288

Mary was there when Jesus fed the masses. The people had gathered again in the countryside in the late afternoon when the chores were done and it was too hot to work. Jesus chose a place where the large group could find shade by the hill at that time of day. Many had travelled some distance to hear the new 'rabonni' speak. They had been listening for a long time, and they were completely mesmerized by his words. It became late and they had not eaten. Jesus felt compassion for their hunger and asked his apostles to find food to feed the crowd.

Jesus had added to his band of close disciples to now number twelve. It included Levi, now called Matthew, who had previously been a much-hated tax collector. Matthew had been impressed by what he saw in Jesus when he witnessed the miraculous healing of a leper. When Jesus asked Matthew to follow him, he willingly abandoned his lucrative endeavours and joined the followers of Jesus. Matthew was educated and quite different from the simple fishermen of Jesus' earlier roster of recruits. He was a great storyteller and he remained steadfast, devoted and committed for the rest of his days. Jesus had also recruited Bartholemew, Thomas, Judas Thaddeus, James, son of Alpheus, Judas Iscariot and Simon the Zealot in a variety of synagogues inside and outside of Jerusalem. They all called him Master. There appeared to be a natural leader among the group. All of the disciples seemed to look up to Simon. Jesus called him Simon-Peter, and then eventually, it became just 'Peter'.

Mary loved this assorted group of devotees and supporters. They had adopted her as their travelling mother. They were quick to tease her but always reverent and respectful to her. They had learned how clever, knowledgeable and insightful she was. They had learned early that Mary could win any challenge regarding Jewish law and scripture. They came to trust her mind and insights and often sought her counsel.

However, there was still the problem of providing food for this large crowd of people on the hillside. They did not have the resources to do this. All they had was a couple of fish and a few loaves of bread. Mary was not shocked but wonderfully pleased when Jesus took the two fish and five loaves of bread, blessed them and then fed the many. Like the wine at Cana, she did not know what he had done, but the twelve baskets were never empty. She helped the apostles serve the hungry and even though they had all eaten their fill, there was still an abundance of fish and bread left over.

Mary was there when Jesus called the thief and swindler, Zacheus, down from the sycamore tree. Another convert for her son, and a nice meal at Zacheus' house! Mary was there when a hemorrhaging woman touched the tassel of Jesus' prayer shawl. He was aware of a loss of power and asked who had touched him. The woman admitted to being the guilty one. This was made a grave situation because her touching Jesus in her state would have made him unclean. Jesus was unfazed by this phenomenon and cured the woman of her affliction. The followers of Jesus witnessed many such cures and conversions.

Mary was there when a very large crowd had gathered in Judea, just beyond the Jordan, to hear Jesus speak. Jesus' peace message included loving your enemies. Unheard of! In this time of political insurrection, the idea of turning the other cheek was revolutionary after centuries of "an eye for an eye and a tooth for a tooth." How would the Hebrews reconquer and regain their land and faith with that attitude? Many Hebrews thought that Jesus was going to be their deliverer. His talk about the kingdom of God further confused the flock.

On one occasion, after he had spoken and turned to move on, a bevy of children raced to him to hug him around the waist and to ask him questions. The apostles, knowing that Jesus was dead tired, tried to stop them and steer them away. However, Jesus laughed and said, "Let the children come to me, and do not hinder them; for to such belongs the kingdom of heaven." He took some smaller ones in his arms and hugged them and gave them back to their parents. He did not rush but spoke to them gently and made them laugh, and blessed them one by one.

Mary was very pleased with her son. She loved that he was inclusive, kind and compassionate to everyone. She would smile when she would hear a family experience in the parables he told. But Mary wasn't blind. The large crowds that Jesus drew and the unorthodox message he delivered made the Pharisees, Sadducees and Scribes both jealous and resentful. Jesus' message of mercy, kindness and justice made them look bad. She must warn Jesus that he needed to be careful, because the Jewish authorities felt threatened by him.

Mary of Magdalene was smiling beside her, admiring Jesus' playful way with the little ones.

"He certainly is good with children," she observed.

"But, of course, Mary Magdalene. I told you he was perfect," quipped the mother of Jesus with a smile.

Mary was not blind with regard to her friend Mary Magdalene. It was obvious to anyone with eyes that Mary had lost her heart to Jesus and would have no other.

Chapter 41
Worries and Woes

Jesus was well into the second year of his mission when he and his apostles hopped into their boats in Hippus and crossed the Sea of Galilee to escape the increasingly pressing and demanding throngs of people. The crushing pace of the preaching, healing and expelling of demons was very wearing on the body, mind and soul. It was time to take a few days of rest in his hometown in Nazareth.

Mary welcomed the boys to her home and she and Mary Cleopas began immediately to prepare a homecooked evening meal for them. First, the men spent some time in Joachim's mikvey for a ritual bath.

While they were enjoying wine, bread and a lamb dish with mint, the apostles and Jesus discussed their experiences on their journeys to new communities. They noted that they seemed to be attracting Gentiles who were welcomed by Jesus but not so well regarded by the Jewish authorities.

Galileans were accustomed to foreigners because the trade routes from faraway lands often intersected in their communities. Caravans, Roman legions and people from the eastern regions often stopped in the villages of Galilee to have something repaired, seek water, buy provisions or sell their wares. These community members did not have the same dim regard for strangers as did the people living closer to the larger cities who had developed a disdain for their ways. It was another bone of contention between the Temple officials and Jesus.

Mary had finished serving the food when the men invited her to sit with them to hear the stories. They continued to regard Mary as their second mother and welcomed her keen mind and good humour.

"Mother Mary, did you hear what Jesus did last night?" asked Simon.

"No, tell me," she replied. "I need to hear this.

"Well, we were out in the boat fishing when, out of nowhere, the wind picked up. The most violent that I can recall," recounted John.

"Our fishing boat was tossing and heaving in the waves the height of a man," recalled James.

"Oh, you exaggerate, John! They were at least twice that and swamping the boat," corrected James with a wink.

"We had to take down our sail or the storm would either have blown us over or we would have been thrown way off course," added Philip.

"We were really afraid for our lives, and what is Jesus doing?" asked Thomas. "He's asleep in the stern of the boat!"

"Sleeping like a baby, undisturbed by the turbulence," recounted Simon. "I woke him up because this might be the last time we would see each other."

Bartholemew blurts out, "And do you know what he says?"

"Nothing, because he's still sound asleep. Can you believe it?" added Philip.

"We yelled at Jesus to come and save us, that we were going to die!" cried John and James together and on top of each other.

"You won't believe it, Mary, but your son wakes up, rubs his eyes and says, 'Why are you afraid, oh men of little faith?'."

"He could hardly keep his balance when he stood up and a great big wave came up over the boat and soaked him to the skin. But is he even nervous? No. He rebukes the wind and the sea and calms the whole lot with his mere words," retells Andrew.

"What sort of man is this that even winds and seas obey him?"

"I, for one, am not going to defy him or even disagree with him!" expressed Matthew, shaking his head in disbelief.

"I will bow and call you Master, Lord, for you have power from heaven," vowed Thomas as he acted the role of a slave.

While this dramatized story was being told, Jesus and Mary were chuckling to themselves, smiling and shrugging their shoulders. The evening continued in well-earned merriment and camaraderie. They drank, ate, told stories and made plans for the morrow.

On the day of the Sabbath, the whole group attended in the synagogue in Nazareth. Jesus was asked to read. He asked for the Isaiah scroll and read:

"The Spirit of the Lord God is upon me, because the Lord has anointed me to bring good tidings to the afflicted; he has sent me to bind up the broken-hearted, proclaim liberty to the captives and the opening of the prison to those who are bound..."[58]

Eyebrows went up on that reading and the rabbi made a harrumph sound and quickly got up to take over the readings. Jesus closed the book and gave it back to the attendant and sat down, and all the eyes of the synagogue were fixed on him. In response to their inquisitive stares, Jesus said, "Today, this Scripture has been fulfilled in your hearing."[59]

Mary listened to his words and her heart stopped for a second. She knew in her heart that this would not bode well for

---

[58] Isaiah 61:1
[59] Taken from Luke 4:16-21, Mark:6:1-6

Jesus. The Nazarenes were already prone to hold him in disfavour, and this would yet again make them feel that he thought that he was better than them and above the religious authorities. He had as much told them that he was the Messiah, the anointed one. They would not understand and this would harden their hearts and make them hostile towards him. They would not accept him or believe in him. The Evil One was at work, polluting their hearts and minds with bitterness, spite and hostility. What would happen to her beloved son, now, she asked herself. Her heart was heavy with sorrow because he was telling the truth, even if it would bring him trouble.

As Mary had predicted, the congregation gathered in their usual social circles and talked about what they had heard in the service that day. She overheard some talk and the apostles overheard other conversations among the men. At first, they were impressed and spoke well of him and then they started to question where the words of wisdom which proceeded from his mouth came from and then it took a bad turn.

"Is not this Joseph's son?"

"Isn't he not the son of Mary and brother of James, Joses, Judas and Simon? And his sisters live here too."

"He is merely the son of a carpenter. He gives himself airs and thinks he is the Redeemer."

"We do not see you doing all those miracles of healing here like in Capernaum. Why don't you show us what you can do, here right now!"

"Better than that; why don't you fix yourself, you little pup!"

Jesus responded to their doubts and accusations by reminding them that Elijah could not perform miracles in Israel but only in Sidon and Syria during three years of drought and famine.

"Truly, I say to you, a prophet is not without honour, save in his own country, and in his own house," declared Jesus.

At this, they were gravely offended and were filled with wrath. And they rose up, grabbed him bodily and led him out of the city, and to the brow of the hill on which the city was built, so that they might throw him down headlong. The apostles got involved to rescue their Master and in the midst of the melee, Jesus was loosened and they made their escape.

Mary now realized that she would not be able to see her son at her home again unless it was clandestinely. This saddened her greatly and she felt less at home in her own village. She made the decision, then and there, to make more time to follow Jesus.

Chapter 42
Following the Way

Jesus' reputation was growing. The gossip was not always good. It did not help that the Pharisees claimed that Jesus was not from God. He was not formally anointed as a rabbi. Jesus' preachings were unfounded and blasphemous. His miracles were mere tricks.

These stories had reached Nazareth, but Mary hoped that Jesus would not venture back again. He did try one more time and had performed a couple of healings and had hoped to convert his own people to repent and accept the new kingdom. The crowd had gathered again to see him in the synagogue. When the family heard that he was back they were worried for him because it had not gone well on the previous occasion. They needed to remove him from a dangerous situation. People were already claiming that Jesus was out of his mind. Scribes from Jerusalem were present and accused him of being Beelzebub and ruled by the demon. His power came from Satan, they said. This was ridiculous! Why would a demon cast out demons? It made no sense.

When Mary and the family arrived at the gathering, the people noticed it and told Jesus that his mother and his brothers were outside and were asking for him.

Jesus replied, "Who is my mother and my brothers?" And looking at those who sat around him, he said, "Here are my mother and my brothers! Whoever does the will of God is my brother and sister and mother."[60]

---

[60] Mark:12:46-50

People took a collective intake of breath and stared at Jesus.

His words had done nothing to endear him to the Nazarenes. Who would dare treat his own mother like this! Jesus was unkind and insulting to his family and his own house. While they were aghast, Mary was not offended in the least. She fully understood what her beloved son had meant. He was not excluding her and his family; he was rather including all people in his family. He was making of them heirs to the kingdom that he preached about. He wanted to include all the mothers, the brothers and sisters, Jews or Gentiles, the rich, the slaves, the righteous and the sinners. However, the Jews would not understand that because they thought they were God's chosen people and only the righteous were accepted into heaven. They were like the 'stiff-necked people' and they refused to believe. Jesus could do no real miracle there and he wondered at their unbelief. This fact confirmed Mary's plan to leave her town and follow Jesus. Her son knew the way.

In other communities all around Galilee and Judea, Jesus was seen as a prophet. Some even went so far as to say he might be the Messiah. And in spite of the adverse gossip many people still believed because they had witnessed the signs for themselves. They had seen a blind man's sight come back; they had seen a man who had not walked all his life get up and walk. How could they not believe?

Mary discussed her plans with Joseph's and Mary Cleopas' family and told them of her intentions to follow Jesus. They tried to talk her out of it because Jesus was stirring up much animosity among the higher ups and he was being resented for all the good works he was doing. And doing it without status and in complete poverty. It made the Pharisees, Sadducees, and Scribes look bad. They felt that Mary could support Jesus much better from home under their protection. However, Mary was not persuaded and she was resolved to be with her son. She promised that she would stay in the background and stand with all the other disciples. In consequence of this, Mary Cleopas' and her son James decided to accompany Mary to follow Jesus. First, they had to make inquiries about where he was preaching because Jesus could be anywhere in the land.

The two Marys were joined by another Mary in Magdala. From then on, the three Marys went together. James, Mary Cleopas' son, and Mark, Andrew's friend, often escorted the women for their safety. Sometimes, they stayed at Mary of Magdala's house when they were in Galilee, and sometimes, they stayed at Lazarus' house when they were closer to Jerusalem. Mary and Martha would often be part of their party as well. Most of the time, they pulled out their bed rugs and slept in the open air with the rest of the apostles and disciples. With any funds raised, Jesus fed the hungry and gave drink to the thirsty, both physically and spiritually. Mary and her group of women ministered to the lepers and the beggars along the way. It was a different lifestyle, but they were happy doing good works. They felt that they received more than they gave. They were in awe of Jesus and they marvelled at the miracles. And Mary's angels kept watch.

The more good Jesus did, the more trouble he seemed to find. The Pharisees were always trying to trick him. There was a time when they asked him if it was right to pay taxes to Caesar. They had not expected to receive a clever answer when he held up a coin and said, "Pay unto Ceasar what belongs to Ceasar and to God what belongs to God." They accused Jesus of healing or for eating grains of wheat on a Sabbath. They were always trying to catch him in a mistake and when it never happened, they falsely accused him of blasphemy out of jealousy. They faulted him for eating with sinners and for not living up to the Jewish laws. Jesus would push back and call them hypocrites and vipers. He rebuked them for using the laws to make things hard on their faithful but not living up to the laws themselves. They lived richly and held to the glory of their lofty priestly positions and had little regard for the welfare of the sheep of their flock. They were not good shepherds. He accused them of cleaning the outside of the cup while the inside was left unclean. The hypocritical leaders loved to make a great show of how religious they were while being prideful, self-righteous and unkind. While they were concerned about what went into the mouth, Jesus was more concerned about what came out of the mouth. Indeed, he did not make friends with the religious authorities. The Sanhedrin Council would meet to discuss the Jesus effect. They felt that it was "better that one man die for the people than the whole nation perish."[61] With that, they began scheming to find a way to get rid of Jesus.

Mary learned to love her son even more as he gathered the crowds and gave them hope for a better way of life that would lead them to the new promised land, the New Jerusalem. However, she was growing more nervous about his boldness and 'huspa' towards the authorities. It was around this time that Jesus began to state to his apostles and disciples that he would die and come back three days later. He said it in more hidden and mysterious forms like 'Destroy this temple, and in three days I will raise it up,'[62] and more overtly when he told them, 'The Son of Man is going to be betrayed into the hands of men. They will kill him, and after three days, he will rise.'[63] The apostles had a hard time understanding the meaning of this and would not give the statement any credence, but Mary understood and she was filled with dread.

---

[61] John 11:50
[62] John 2:19-21
[63] Mark 9:30-32

It was early morning at the Temple. Jesus and his followers had just returned from the Mount of Olives. Pharisees and the teachers of religious law brought a woman who had been caught in the act of adultery. They shoved her in front of the crowd.

"She was caught with another man! The law of Moses is clear; she must be stoned for her sin," shouted one of them.

A group of men were surrounding the poor woman on her knees with her veiled head down and her arms protecting it, whimpering and begging for mercy. The men all had stones in their hands, the size of grapefruits, at the ready for the signal to throw.

Jesus and his disciples arrived on the scene. The crowd split and made a pathway for Jesus. The Pharisees, still trying to trap him, asked, "This woman was caught in adultery. The law says that she should be stoned; what do you say?" Jesus stood in silence and looked right at the accusers. Mary Magdalene whispered to Mary, "There was a man involved in this act of adultery; where is he and why are we not stoning both of them?"

Mary's eyes filled with tears and she whispered back, "It is such a cruel way to die."

"How is Jesus going to respond to that trick question designed to catch him breaking the law of Moses or Roman law? He is between a rock and a hard place himself," contributed Mary Cleopas, shaking her head.

Mary of Magdala, answered confidently, "We know Jesus to be a compassionate man. He is also a clever man. He will think of something."

Jesus bent down and started to write in the dirt with his finger. Some people closer to Jesus started to see what he was writing and quietly dropped their stones and walked away. The authorities kept barking the question at him, "It is the law, Jesus of Nazareth! She is a prostitute! Answer the question!"

Jesus stood up and declared, "Let any of you who is without sin be the first to throw a stone at her."[64]

Some stood there poised to hurl their projection, but when they heard this statement, they knew that they could not do it—they certainly could not be the first. Eventually, they dropped their rocks and went away.

"Where are your accusers? Didn't any of them condemn you?"

"No, Lord," she answered.

"Neither do I condemn you. Go and sin no more."[65]

The three Marys went up to the woman. They straightened her up and brushed off her clothes. Two of them held her by the elbows and spoke to her in a gentle and understanding manner. They invited her to join them in following Jesus. They would provide her with a means of care so she could abandon her trade. The holy women knew that often, when a woman is left destitute with no means of survival, they would resort to this way of living. Compassion filled their hearts and another convert to the Way was made.

Jesus was continuing to preach throughout the region when the news arrived that John the Baptist had been beheaded by the order of King Herod. Herod had fallen under the spell of his stepdaughter Salome and he foolishly promised any boon and she had asked for the head of the Baptist.

---

[64] Taken from John's gospel and quoted from John 8:7
[65] John 8:10-11

Jesus and Mary were very much aggrieved by this news. John was kin. He was innocent of any crime except for pointing out Herod's sin. He had spent his life in poor and humble circumstances, baptizing willing subjects and teaching repentance from sin. It was a cruel end for a great man, a chosen man, a prophet.

Mary bowed her head in teary remembrance of John and his parents, her cousin and friend Elizabeth and her husband Zachariah. Jesus called on them to pray and they all bowed their heads to remember John and to pray for him.

While the crowd gathered around Jesus, he talked to them in parables. He told them that the kingdom of God was like a mustard seed, or a found pearl. He used many agrarian metaphors like vineyards, bread, or wineskins. Mary remembered that many of these parables were derived from the experiences and stories that she had shared with Jesus in his childhood. Her favourite was the story about forgiveness with the son who wanted his inheritance early, squandered it, and when he found himself homeless and starving, returned to his father to ask for forgiveness. The father opened his arms to him. Mary knew that Jesus meant the heavenly Father who would happily receive his repentant children into the kingdom of heaven. If the people were looking for a political revolutionary who would free them from Roman domination, they would not find that in Jesus. They would instead find a religious revolutionary who came to fulfil the scriptures by liberating people from sin.

During a break in the sermons, a messenger came to find Jesus. He was out of breath but managed to spout out a message from Martha and Mary. The message was thus: 'Lord, he whom you love is ill.' Jesus nodded his thanks and signalled that the messenger was to be fed and given some coin for his trouble. Jesus did not leave right away. He continued to minister to his flock. Mary spent some time pondering her son's inaction on this grave matter. Lazarus was one of Jesus' longest and closest friends. He loved the two sisters, Mary and Martha, like his own sisters. If Lazarus died the two women would have no protector. Why was he not heading to Bethany with all speed? Jesus must have some plan. Thinking deeper on what the motive was, Mary remembered that Jesus' miracles had become more and more amazing. He was curing people without even being there, like the centurion's slave, and he had raised a man from the dead in Nain. She wondered if he knew that even after death, he could raise Lazarus, which would glorify his name even more emphatically as a true miracle worker. Mary thought she had the answer to Jesus' hesitation. Jesus stayed in place another two days. He then ordered that they head south towards Jerusalem and to Bethany. The apostles reminded him, 'Rabbi, the Jews were but now seeking to stone you and you are going there again?'

"My dear friends, Lazarus is dead. And for your sake I am glad that I was not there, so that you may believe. But let us go to him."[66]

Martha heard that Jesus was coming, she went and met him, while Mary sat in the house. She was clearly troubled.

"Lord, if you had been here, my brother would not have died. And even now, I know that whatever you ask from God, God will give you."

"Your brother will rise again in the resurrection on the last day."

Lazarus' sister Mary joined the group and she was weeping for the loss of her beloved brother. Jesus was deeply moved in spirit. He wept for his friend.

---

[66]John 11:15

"Where have you laid him?" he asked.

"Come and see," they answered. The mourning Jews were impressed with his compassion towards Martha and Mary. They felt the love that Jesus had for this family who had been close friends for decades.

They arrived at a cave tomb and Jesus ordered that they remove the stone. The sisters were aghast, "Lord, by this time, there will be an odour, for he has been dead four days."

Jesus prayed to his Father and called out, "Lazarus, come out!"

Lazurus came out with the funeral wraps still hanging on his person. He was whole and very much alive.

Mary smiled. Jesus had raised Lazarus from the dead, had rewarded the two women with the gift of their brother and had shown to all the power that he wielded by the hand of his Father in Heaven. However, this miracle may have been the last straw for the people who were seeking his demise. Had her son gone too far this time? Her spirit was very troubled.

The news of Jesus' raising of a dead man spread all over Judea. It was the time of the Passover and many pilgrims were arriving to participate in the annual feast of Unleavened Bread. The city was teeming with the faithful. When they heard that this miracle worker was entering the walled town, they rejoiced and cried out, "Hosanna. Blessed is he who comes in the name of the Lord." When Jesus entered the gates on the back of a donkey the people were very enthusiastic about his arrival. They threw palm branches and garments on the road before him. "Blessed is the kingdom of our father David that is coming! Hosanna in the highest!" the crowd cried.[67]

---

[67] Taken from all four gospels.

It was the 14th day of Nisan. Arrangements for the Passover had been made ahead of time through Andrew's friend, Mark. Mark's mother had an upper room in the city and she invited Jesus and his apostles to participate in the feast there. Her name was also Mary and she never called her son Mark but rather John Mark. The apostles had shortened the name. So now there were four Marys. The women stayed behind and prepared the food and acquired the wine necessary for this important feast in Jewish life. It was in memory of their exile from the Egyptians and their journey to the promised land. They never wanted to forget this life-changing event in their history and lives. The women enjoyed each other's company as they prepared the unleavened bread, the maror of horseradish, and chazerit. The bitter herbs remind them of the bitterness of enslavement. The fragrance of the lamb roasting on a spit in the courtyard poured into the open windows of the upper room. Tonight was the first night of the Festival and they would enjoy the Passover meal. The women went busily along at their tasks, not realizing that this would be the last supper for Jesus and that he would soon sacrifice himself like the Passover lamb.

Jesus and his friends sat together and enjoyed their meal. They dipped morsels of meat into the well-prepared sauce. They shared the cups of wine. The twelve laughed and observed the rituals of the memorial event as it had been celebrated for centuries.

"I have earnestly desired to eat this Passover with you before I suffer, for I tell you I shall not eat again until it is fulfilled in the kingdom of God."

Jesus announced that someone among them had betrayed him. After a lot of questions, denials and astonishment on the part of the apostles, Judas Iscariot left the supper table and went out.

"Well, I could never betray you, Lord," exclaimed Simon, whom Jesus had renamed Peter.

"Truly, I say to you, this very night, before the cock crows twice, you will deny me three times," replied Jesus.

Peter was not to be so easily dismissed and declared, "If I must die with you, I will not deny you."

The women were in the preparation room bringing out the food and as they finished serving the meal, they stood at a distance and watched. Jesus held out a large round of unleavened bread and he raised his eyes towards heaven and gave thanks.

He broke it and gave it to them saying, "This is my body which is given for you. Do this in remembrance of me." The women shared in this bread as well.

Again, Jesus took the chalice of wine and said, "This is my blood of the covenant, which is poured out for many."

They passed the cup around and drank. The women were included in this rite as they were part of the many. After, the cup was passed back to Jesus, empty.

Jesus said, "Truly, I say to you, I shall not drink again of the fruit of the vine until that day when I drink it new in the kingdom of God."[68]

All the participants looked at each other, not knowing what he meant. They were baffled. In spite of the fact that Jesus had told them many times that he would die, they didn't really understand. They did not want to hear it. Their disbelief was based on their desire to have him with them always, and in believing that the Master was so mighty and powerful that it could not happen. He was a miracle worker! They could not believe that someone so young, so good and so innocent would be taken from them. They believed that he was the Son of Man, after all. But Mary knew the outcome and she kept her

---

[68] Taken from Mark, Matthew and Luke

wisdom in her heart and suffered alone the thought of losing her beloved son.

This was the time, she decided. Mary unwrapped the linen covering of the beautiful seamless robe she had woven for Jesus. It was in perfect condition. She had fetched it from the Temple's keeping just today. The dual colours had made it look purple to some and scarlet to others. The hue shifted according to the angle of the viewer.

It would at least keep Jesus warm from the spring night air.

She approached Jesus and presented her handmade robe to him. He was moved by the gesture. He stood up and she placed it on his shoulders. It was beautiful and he looked so handsome and royal in it. He was innocent, noble, and without blemish. He was the perfect sacrificial lamb.

All the people present in the upper room made admiring sounds that paid compliments to the fashioner. Mary was embarrassed by the praises and humbly lowered her flushed face. The vermillion cloak fell almost to the ground and Jesus wrapped it around his arms over his elbows. He turned to face his mother and looked into her eyes for a long time, absorbing the depth and breadth of her heart, and the grace and goodness of her soul. Tears swelled up in those eyes and he wished that he could spare her the sorrow that he knew was coming. He was truly aggrieved. He put his face very close to his mother and held his hands on each side of her head. He held her there within his grasp for a while and then placed a long kiss on her forehead. He squeezed her shoulders, took one last look, and let her go.

The last cup of wine, the cup of praise, had not yet been served to mark that the meal had come to an end, when Jesus rose and began the singing of the Hallel psalms, songs of praise:

"...O Lord, I am your servant;

I am your servant, the son of your handmaid.

You have loosed my bonds.

I will offer to you the sacrifice of thanksgiving

and call on the name of the Lord.

I will pay my vows to the Lord

in the presence of all his people,

in the courts of the house of the Lord,

in our midst, O Jerusalem.

Praise the Lord..."[69]

The apostles were puzzled. Leaving before the meal was over? This night was truly different from other nights. As the twelve followed their Master without question, they went with him as he made his way to Mount of Olives, and Jesus stopped to pray in the garden of Gethsemane. The apostles could see that Jesus was deeply troubled; however, they were sleepy from the eating and drinking and left Jesus to pray in agony all alone. The women stayed behind but, not sure whether or not Jesus was finished, had left the table the way it was. They, too, wondered why Jesus had not fully completed the ritual meal. It was unusual, but with Jesus, they were used to a different interpretation of the laws and rules of their traditional rites. They waited patiently. Jesus' mother's heart was heavy with worry.

It was not quite dawn yet. The women were dozing on the rugs and cushions when they heard a commotion on the stairs

---

[69] Psalm 116:16

and Mary's son Mark came bursting through the door yelling, "They have taken him. They have arrested Jesus!"

"What happened?" asked Mother Mary with a very worried look.

Mark retold the story that he had been told by the apostles who right now were lurking in the shadows, wondering what was happening and hoping they would not be caught in the net as well.

Chapter 43
Death of an Only Beloved Son

Mary Cleopas wrapped her robe around her sister, who was struggling to stand. Although she had not said a word, the tears coursed down Mother Mary's face and her expression was contorted with pain. She had been through so much for a young woman, but she bore it with humility and grace. Her dear sister was stronger than she looked. Nevertheless, witnessing the brutal cruelties carried out on her only son must be excruciating. How much more could a mother take, as she was his imma. A mere mortal and human, after all.

Mary looked up at her son, bleeding and struggling for breath. Jesus, in turn, painfully looked down towards his mother, his aunt, and his faithful and dear friends, John and Mary Magdelene. They were the only ones who had shown enough courage and loyalty to be here at the foot of the cross. Women, the most lowly, dismissed and disregarded humans, yet there they were, while his apostles had scattered in fear and were nowhere to be seen. In the end, it would often be the women who would remain steadfast and fearless in their faith.

Mary knew that her Jesus', her dear little boy's, suffering would be ending soon. How much more suffering could a body take? He had been hanging on the cross for several hours now, dripping with blood from his head, his hands and his feet. In pain and in agony. His back was a mass of lacerations from the brutal scourging. Mary knew her son and his compassionate nature. She knew Jesus was worried about her and would wonder how he could spare his mother the anguish that his suffering brought her and the grief and sorrow that would follow his death. He was the son of God, but in this, he was powerless. It needed to be done. She had been such a lovely mother, kind and good. So good and so obedient to the Father. Faithful in everything! How it pained him to see her in such anguish. He could feel the life draining from him, so with as much strength as he could muster, Jesus called out to his mother. "Woman, behold your son." And turning to his disciple John he cried: "Behold your mother."[70] He felt better knowing that John would care for her and love and honour her as he himself did.

Without being told exactly, Mary knew that this was a symbolic gesture. Jesus knew that she could look after herself as she had the resources to do so. However, Jesus was making a perpetual and enduring legacy in her. He was making her the mother of his new church. She was the new Ark of the Covenant. The apostles would protect this new Ark as they set out to build the new church, the New Temple and the New Jerusalem. Mary was to be John's mother and by extension, mother of all human beings that believed in Jesus. The revelations were clear to her and she understood her new role. It did not make watching him suffer and die any less agonizing.

The little group of faithful below the cross could see that the effort to connect with his mother and John had drained Jesus almost completely. The end was very near now. With a gasping breath, her beloved son cried out in anguish: "Eli, Eli, la'ma sabach-tha'ni, Father, why have you forsaken me?"[71] Her heart was pierced as if a sword had been thrust into her breast.

To fulfil Scripture, Jesus called to one of the guards below and appealed to him: "I thirst." One of the guards looked around and found a jar of soured wine and he put a spongeful of the vinegar on hyssop and held it to his mouth.

---

[70] John 19:26-28
[71] Matthew 27:46

When Jesus had received it, he said: "It is finished."[72] His head fell forward and he surrendered his spirit. Mary was stunned by the impact that her beloved Son was no more.

In a short while, two black-clad men, members of the Sanhedrin Council who were secretly following Jesus, came staggering up the hill. The wind was fierce, their clothing was blown against their bodies, and their head covers did little to protect them from the torrential downpour. They were followed by servants with a ladder, tools and a pallet. Nicodemus was carrying the myrrh and the oils needed for preparing Jesus' body for burial.

Hardly heard over the din, Joseph of Arimathea called out to the Centurion. "I have here an order from Pontius Pilate granting us permission to dispose of the body."

The Roman soldier examined the document, now soaked with rain. However, it did bear the seal of the Governor, so he let them pass.

Joseph and Nicodemus approached Mary and explained that they would help prepare his body and place it in Joseph's tomb not far away. "We must hurry because the time is late, and it will soon be the Sabbath," claimed Nicodemus.

"We must do this quickly, as I'm not so sure that Caiaphas, the Chief Priest, isn't up to something. He is so threatened by Jesus' power that he is capable of doing anything at this point; he may even try to remove all evidence of Jesus' person," declared Joseph.

"I am very grateful to you, Joseph. It is kind and generous of you," Mary returned.

---

[72] John 29-30

"Mary, if you only knew what cowards we both were and how little we did to prevent this outcome, you might not be so forgiving."

Even in her unfathomable grief, Mary was able to summon comfort for the two Pharisees, "My son has always been in Adonai's hands. I believe that he has fulfilled his destiny and what God had planned for him. Do not be too harsh on yourselves. Good will come from this, you will see."

"Mary, you are blessed among women. Pray for us," begged Nicodemus.

In the midst of the storm, they took a moment and kissed the other mourners, and offered their sympathy for the vicious and untimely death of their beloved and innocent sovereign. But, as time was of the essence, they began to give instructions for the removal of the body from the cross. "Be careful with that man! Let us treat his body with dignity. Be gentle, be gentle!" ordered Joseph.

It wasn't an easy task, especially in the fury of the storm, but the men, as gently as they could, pried the nails from Jesus's hands. While one of them supported the body over his shoulder, the other released the spike from his feet. They carefully carried him down the ladder. The rain had mercifully washed the blood from his body and his hair had been rinsed of all the crusted blood in its strands. The servant closed Jesus's eyes before he presented him to his mother and placed his battered body on her lap and in her arms.

There was a loud wail from Mary Magdalene. She was so distressed by the sight of Jesus' mother holding her dead son that she could no longer contain her grief. She folded upon herself and sobbed inconsolably.

Mary, the mother of Jesus, had always kept things close to her heart, but even she could not help but express her anguish. Her tears joined the rain and ran down her face in a flood of sorrow. She looked at the brutalized body of her only son. He had been so beautiful. He had been such a good son. He was so smart and so wise. He was gentle and kind. He had been strong and forgiving. She remembered what the angel had told her when he visited her on that day long ago. "Hail Mary, full of grace, the Lord is with you!" She had been quite frightened by Gabriel and had cowered. He assured her: "Do not be afraid, Mary, for you have found favour with God. And behold, you will conceive in your womb and bear a son, and you shall call him Jesus. He will be great and will be called the Son of the Most High, and the Lord God will give to Him the throne of His father, David and He will reign over the house of Jacob forever, and of His kingdom, there will be no end."[73] She had not understood how things would happen, why she was chosen or what the future would bring. She had just known that she trusted God, and she was obedient to him always. She had done God's will. Somehow, her husband Joseph had understood, and he had become fiercely protective of both Mary and her child. In the silence of her heart, she had always known that Jesus was a very special child. But to come to such an end, she was not prepared for that. Yet, she trusted God and his plan for her son. Nevertheless, the emptiness and the pain she felt was unbearable. She placed tender kisses on his cheek as she had done many times before. She embraced his body to herself, and hugged and rocked him until she had completely drained her emotions.

In her numbness, memories flashed in her mind. She saw Jesus as a baby lying in swaddling clothes in a manger. That had been the best they could get as travellers during a very busy time in Joseph's hometown, where they had been ordered to appear for the census. She smiled at recalling the times that Jesus would scrape his knees and hands and she would deliver a hug and kisses to make everything better. She had once

---

[73] Luke 1:30-33

covered his little face in kisses when he had gathered wildflowers on the hillside outside of Nazareth and presented the broken and withered bouquet to her as a gift. She remembered their time in Egypt. She remembered him apprenticing with his father, Joseph, to work with wood. The memory of losing her twelve-year-old son on the way back from a pilgrimage to Jerusalem also sent a shiver down her spine. They were greatly relieved to find him in the synagogue, deep in heavy discussion and debate with the rabbis. They were in awe and admiration for his abundant knowledge and wisdom. She recalled the tears that they had both shed at the loss of their saintly head of the family, Joseph.

She remembered when Jesus discovered that he had some powers that could not be explained. She had warned him not to call on those powers until it was time. She felt it had been his time when, at a wedding in Cana, the hosts had run out of wine. Jesus's power had transformed urns of water into fine wine. She also remembered the tears she had cried when she had bidden him goodbye as he set off on his mission. As a mother, she had known in her heart that not only would she lose him to his work and his journey, but that it would eventually get him into trouble and conflict with both the Roman and Jewish authorities. She had been prepared, but no amount of preparation could ease the agony of this brutal and agonizing death.

The others watched Mary in her grief and their hearts broke at witnessing such a tragedy. They, too, were moved with pity and deep sorrow. The scene of pathos before them was forever set in their minds. Nothing could be worse than a mother losing a child. And losing him in such a violent manner. It was devastating.

Another show of lightning and a huge crack of thunder broke the tender and poignant moment, and the task at hand was resumed. They removed the crown of thorns from Jesus's head and rested him on the litter. He was then taken to the vault offered by Joseph of Arimathea. The women led the funeral procession; all were weeping with sorrow for their loss.[74]

The time was limited, so a full burial ceremony was not an option. They had to work quickly. Mary personally prepared the body. Nicodemus and Joseph helped her wrap the linens and the ritual ointments and placed him on the marble altar table. The two rabbis concluded a brief burial ceremony and then with the help of the servants they rolled a huge stone in front of the cave crypt. Grinding, gritting and grating noises insulted the ears and then there was a final clunk and all went dark in the tomb and in the hearts of the attendants.

---

[74] Adapted from *D.L. Hawkes, Descent Into Hell*

Chapter 44
What Now?

The weather was gloomy. The rains and winds had stopped but it was dark with brooding clouds and misty air. The citizens of Judea were still shaken from the earthquake that had occurred yesterday at about the time Jesus had died on the cross. Or so they were told. They also learned that the veil that covered the entrance to the Holy of Holies was rent in two. The eleven apostles, the four Marys and Mark, were all huddled in the upper room where the final supper had taken place. The windows had been shuttered with heavy drapes and the occupants were showing their fear and nervousness in their different ways. Some were pacing; some could not stay still, others ranted and raved, others were sullen in a corner of the room. Mary was sitting quietly on a chair, her hands folded on her lap, and she was in a contemplative state of prayer. She had no more tears; she was empty.

It was now the evening of the Sabbath but none of them had wanted to go out to worship. None of them wanted to eat the food that lay before them. All of them were unsure what to do. All of them were very afraid and in a state of shock at how quickly the fate of Jesus had turned. One minute, they were having a Passover meal and the next, Jesus was arrested, and the very next day, he was crucified and died. Just like that! They knew that Jesus had made enemies but they did not see a crucifixion coming. They remembered that Jesus had predicted his death and something else that did not make sense to them. They were in shock and did not know what the future would bring. They grieved the loss of Jesus. They missed him already. He was their Master and they had relied on his wisdom, his courage and his steadfast loyalty to Adonai and to them. They believed that he was the Son of Man and that he had loved them. Imagine, he had loved them—humble fishermen and sinners. All of them were in deep mourning. The mix of fear and grief was devastating. Their emotions were ready to explode. What now?

They were startled by a heavy and rapid banging on the door.

Who could that be? The authorities? It could be Romans or Jews. They were frightened of both. The banging continued insistently. They heard the call, "Let us in; we mean you no harm!"

Mark ran to the door and opened it a crack to see who was there. He saw two Pharisees clad completely in black with very few vestments or adornment of their priestly position. He hesitated a moment and evaluated the risk that they had been followed.

"Let us in, Mark; we are in grave danger of discovery while we wait outside."

"Come in, Nicodemus and Joseph. I'm so sorry it took us so long to decide whether it was safe. We are very nervous about what will happen to those of us who were so close followers of Jesus."

"I understand," said Joseph. "We are nervous and afraid, too. Know that we are on your side and feel as devastated as you about the crucifixion. Is Mary here?"

Mark nodded and led them to the room where they had sheltered. As they entered the silent room, there was an atmosphere of fear and anxiety.

"Peace to this house," assured Joseph.

"We come with news," declared Nicodemus.

Joseph bowed his head low and spoke to Mary. "Mary, we are so sorry for the loss of Jesus. We come to ask forgiveness for our shameful inaction at the trial of your dear son. We had no idea that they were looking to crucify him overnight like that. Yet we were cowards and did not defend him and protect him from the lies and injustice he suffered at the hands of his own people. The very people Jesus had healed and ministered to. He spoke only of peace! And to arrive at such a violent end..."

Mary looked at them with a soft, forgiving look. Tears filled her eyes and they silently fell down her cheek.

"Thank you for your kind words, my friends. Thank you for the care you gave my son after taking him down from the cross. I will forever be in your debt for this generosity. You are always welcome here." The room visibly relaxed.

Joseph of Arimathea shook his head in sadness. "It was the least we could do."

Mary spoke again, "Something good will come of this, you will see. The man who did so many wonders and walked on water, cured lepers, and raised the dead, was no ordinary man. Dying was what he willingly did for us. He will not leave us orphaned. I know this in the depths of my soul."

The two priests nodded their heads and Nicodemus disclosed a major confidence, "We have secretly been following him because we know that he is the Christ—the Messiah promised in the Holy prophecies."

"We are so ashamed of ourselves for our contribution to this great injustice that we will no longer serve at the Temple. To think that we contributed by our silence. Both of us have decided to remove ourselves from the council and return to our homeland, where we hope to atone for our sins," articulated Joseph.

"You have our blessings," offered Peter. "Go in peace."

The two humbled men embraced each of the men and Mary, and pledged to her their aid and support when she needed it. They swept their arms around the room to include the supporters of Jesus. They left as surreptitiously as they had entered.

"What now?" declared several of the men in chorus.

"We can't hide here forever. They know who we are and they'll come after us!" cried Thomas.

"Who? The Romans, the Jews? I fear someone will come after us," added Matthew.

Peter nodded his head. "They do indeed know who we are. Haven't we been following Jesus for the last three years?"

"Yes, Jesus made enemies, especially in his last year. He reproached and accused the Pharisees of hypocrisy and cleared the tables in the Temple. I'm afraid that we may all be included in their vengeful wrath! Because I gave up collecting taxes for them, the Romans are still angry with me. The Jews that I collected from and cheated are not fond of me either," admitted Matthew.

Simon the Zealot was fidgety and restless. He was up and down from his place and raised his hands up in the air and yelled, "I say, let them come. We'll show them that we aren't just stupid country folk and fishermen. We walked with Jesus.

He healed, he cured, he taught. We can defend ourselves. We have friends!"

"What we should do now is do nothing but lie low until things blow over," opined James.

"Well, I know what I'm going to do. Tomorrow, at dawn, I'm going to the tomb to give Jesus a proper preparation for his interment. It was done so quickly; it was not done right. He, of all people, deserved a respectful burial and funeral. I'm preparing the spices and oils now," said Mary Magdalene.

"It's still Sabbath, Mary. You shouldn't work at that now!" Philip voiced in a whisper.

"Mary of Magdala! You can't go out there! You were seen with him, too. You were there under the cross. They will recognize you. Do not be foolish!" admonished Bartholemew.

"Mother Mary. Make her see reason!" added a worried Matthew. "She may even lead them here, to our refuge."

Mary of Magdala shrugged her shoulders and continued to put crucibles, lamps, vials and other supplies in a leather satchel.

"Philip is right, Mary. There will be Roman guards and possibly Jewish authorities there. They might accuse you of sedition, too, simply by association. They might see you as abetting a criminal. You mustn't risk it," coaxed John.

"Still, I am undeterred," declared Mary Magdalene forcefully.

All heads turned to look at Mother Mary as they all deferred to her. They had started to call her that name for two reasons: it helped sort out the two Marys and they had adopted her as their common mother and they would all share in her care and submit to her wisdom.

"Let her go. After the festival, things will have settled down. Angels will protect her. She will be safe from harm. But Mary, please take other women with you. You will be less noticeable and the work will be lighter."

"You don't want to come with us, Mother?" asked Mary.

"Today, I will mourn."

Bang, bang. "Let me in," called Mary Magdalene. As the door was locked, somebody had to unlatch it before even a resident could come in.

"He is risen. He is risen!"

"What are you talking about, woman?" asked Peter.

"The tomb is empty. I tell you, it is empty. The linens are there and his face cloth is folded upon the altar," beamed Mary of Magdala, out of breath from her run ahead of the other women back to tell everyone.

The men all looked at each other with questions on their faces. Their wrinkled brows, their subtle grimaces and their hands in the air all showed confusion and incredulity.

"Can that be? I saw him die, with my own eyes, two days ago. The Roman soldier pierced his side and only a bit of blood and a water gushed out. No, no. It is impossible. He is dead and buried. Someone took his body!" cried John.

Simon, the Zealot, chimed in, "It must have been the Jews. They wanted no trace of the man and they certainly didn't want a miracle of his resurrection. He raised Lazarus; they must have thought that he might be able to raise himself."

"If this is so, why did Jesus show his greatest miracle to you mere women, instead of us?" asked Peter. Mary Magdalene looked at the speaker and wasn't surprised by the question. She did not answer.

"That doesn't matter," replied James. I can't get my mind around the notion that he is risen from the dead. It should be impossible! No one has resurrected himself from the dead before!"

The apostles all looked at Mother Mary at the same time, wondering what her reaction was to this news. Mary had listened to the news but she was not as surprised as the apostles had been because she understood, without doubt, that Jesus was the long-awaited Redeemer.

Mother Mary looked at each one in the eyes and questioned them, "Why should you be astonished at this news? Were you not his close friends and followers? What did he tell you in the last few days prior to his arrest? Think, my dear children."

The faithful servants of Jesus took a moment to ponder the question and suddenly, it dawned on them. He had told them many times what would happen. They had ignored and dismissed that part because they did not want to face the world without him, and because rising from the dead was beyond their comprehension. They all admonished themselves for having forgotten who Jesus was. They knew he was the Son of Man and that God was all-powerful, but they thought that his work was not finished and that God would not have led him to such a horrible, horrible humiliation and terrible death on the cross. On the cross, for pity's sake! It took a moment for them to come to the realization and conviction that it was indeed possible. He was the Christ, the Pascal Lamb. Of course, he could. He had risen!

By this time, the other women had arrived and confirmed that the tomb was indeed empty and that beings in dazzling white garments had told them that he was not there.

Peter remembered and declared, "He warned us that the Son of Man must be delivered into the hands of sinful men, and be crucified, and on the third day rise."

"I didn't want to think that he was serious," cried John.

In one synchronized motion, the apostles got off their feet, dashed out the door and ran to the tomb. It was empty. They believed.

They returned home, asking themselves many questions as to the circumstance of this rising from the dead. The women had the answers.

All together, they began to question Mary Magdalene. Excited questions tumbled out, one after another, until they needed to take a breath before they began to pepper these mere women about what they had witnessed.

"The tomb was empty, but did you see Jesus?" asked Thomas.

The women, Mary Cleopas, Mark's mother, and a servant named Joanna, all shook their heads.

Mary Cleopas spoke first, "The crypt was empty. The linens were lying there. And standing there, two bright, shining, lightning-white beings asked us why we were seeking the living among the dead. They said that he is risen. And even though these magnificent beings said that we should not be afraid, we were so astonished and so excited that we set out as quickly as these old bones could go, to report to you what we had seen."

"Oh, we almost forgot to tell you. The glorious men, I think they were angels, said that Jesus was going ahead of you to

Galilee and that he would see you there," added Mark's mother.[75]

Mary Magdalene entered the conversation and divulged that, "The other women started ahead of me. I let them because I was distraught, and because I was younger of legs, I would be able to catch up. I was devastated that they had taken his body. I was weeping when I had another look into the tomb. There, sitting at both ends of where the body had lain, were two angels in white. They spoke to me and asked, 'Woman, why are you weeping?' I told them that I was afraid that someone had taken Jesus away and I didn't know where. I turned around and saw a man standing outside the tomb, but I didn't recognize him. His figure was in shadow in the rising sun. I thought he was a gardener. I asked him where they had laid the body and I would take him away. Then I heard, 'Mary.' I recognized that voice and cried: 'Rabboni!' "It was Jesus!

"He said that I should not hold him because he had not yet ascended to the Father but to go tell his brethren and say to them that he will be ascending to his Father, your Father, to his God and your God."[76]

"Incredible!" exclaimed Philip, full of awe.

"I have seen the Lord!" shouted Mary Magdalene.

While they all danced for joy and relief, Mary smiled and kept her elation close to her heart.

---

[75] Women's story taken from all four gospels
[76] Taken from John's account
326

As soon as the coast was clear, Mary and all the close disciples set out for Galilee.

Jesus appeared to his beloved apostles on several occasions. He appeared to two disciples on the road to Emmaus. They did not know him at first but recognized him in the breaking of the bread. On another occasion, Jesus spoke to some of them when he appeared in a room. "Peace," he had said. He ate with them and spoke to them about the kingdom of God. Thomas wasn't there the first time, and he had doubted and questioned the others' testimony. However, Jesus appeared on a later occasion and insisted that Thomas place his fingers in his nail wounds and spear wound on his side.

The disciples were delighted that he was with them again. Jesus was glorious! He explained their role of preaching and teaching all that he had commanded them and to baptize all who asked in the name of the Father, the Son and the Holy Spirit. He instructed them on how to proceed with their commission beyond Jerusalem, Judea and Samaria and to the end of the earth. He told them to await the promise of power from the Holy Spirit. He told them that he would be with them always.

It was never written that Jesus visited his mother; however, knowing how much Jesus loved her, it is quite probable that he did. If he did, Mary never spoke of it and kept it close to her heart.

Forty days after his Resurrection, near Bethany, Jesus blessed his disciples. He was then carried up into the heavens on a cloud, not an ordinary cloud but one that appeared luminescent, lively and vibrant as though there were invisible celestial beings within it, energizing the atmosphere with glory, honour and victory. The Apostles and Mary watched him ascend into heaven. While they watched, two men stood by wearing white robes. They had to be angels! They spoke to them, "Men of Galilee, why do you stand looking into heaven? This Jesus, who was taken up from you into heaven, will come in the same way as you saw him go into heaven." [77] They thereupon returned to Jerusalem with great joy. [78]

They would miss him desperately but they had seen the Lord!

They were happy and knew that he was not far from them. He was in the breaking of the bread. Jesus had promised to send them another Counselor to be with them forever. He had said before he died, "I am still with you. But the Counselor, the Holy spirit, whom the Father will send in my name, he will teach you all things, and bring to your remembrance all that I said to you." He had promised that he would not leave them desolate, that he would come to them, and be in them. "Let not your hearts be troubled, neither let them be afraid." [79] The apostles had not understood at the time and they had no idea what would happen next, but they were sure that Jesus was with them as they were with him. Their hearts were light and filled with life.

As for Mary, she had been a witness to it all, but she understood in the wisdom of her soul. As she had been pregnant with Jesus, the world would soon be as well. She was grateful that she had played her part in fulfilling the will of God Almighty.

---

[77] Acts 1: 10-11

[78] Taken from Luke 24:50-53 and from all four Gospels

[79] Taken from John 14:15-30

Chapter 45
Mary After Jesus

Life was still risky in Jerusalem. People had heard that Jesus had risen from the dead. Some believed and rejoiced. They could not hurt Jesus anymore; however, the apostles and other disciples were still feeling threatened by the Jewish authorities. The latter seemed to be hell-bent on destroying all memories and signs of Jesus. But the Jesus movement, sometimes called 'The Way', was gaining vigour among both the Jewish and Gentile populations. And, as always, there was no talk like town talk and it was spreading like wildfire. Some of it was positive, and some was very critical. This uncertain state of affairs made the followers of Jesus extremely nervous. They moved quietly in public these days.

Meanwhile, Mary returned to Nazareth. The townspeople there left her alone. She was a mystery. But, of course, the women still talked at the village well. It is interesting that talk that was once critical and adverse becomes more positive and kind after a person dies.

"I heard that Mary was there when it all happened."

"Poor thing, I heard they chose Barabas, the criminal, over Jesus, the innocent one."

"I don't think I could have borne my son being so publicly humiliated. Whipped and a crowned with thorns and then made to carry his heavy cross across town to be crucified."

"Sounds like his friends abandoned Jesus. They were nowhere near the crucifixion. In fact, I heard that the supposed leader of the pack had denied knowing him outside the trial."

"Such a shame. As a mother, I wonder how she managed to keep it together when her only son is treated in such a horrible and disgraceful way."

"She is a very strong woman, that Mary. I feel sorry for her. She is a good, good woman who didn't deserve this dishonour and punishment."

"She was always kind to me. She brought over medicines and stayed up all night with my daughter who was suffering from a fever. She only left when the fever broke. I will always be thankful for her compassion."

"We all have stories like that in the village. She was a lovely person. Full of grace. The best amongst us, that's for sure."

"I hear that Jesus' followers, especially the one named John, have taken responsibility for her. She is well cared for and that is a good thing."

"Apparently, all the men have adopted her and call her Mother Mary. Mary Cleopas' son, James, has taken charge of accompanying her anytime and anywhere she wishes to go."

"Such devotion."

"She comes home now and then to rest and to continue her work as a spinner and a weaver. She has told people that she finds solace in the work and is able to pray alone and remember her son."

"She does that when she is home in Nazareth; however, she spends her other time with the apostles. She and that Mary from Magdala spend much of their time with them."

"I heard from James that they want to learn more about Jesus from her. She does not preach or teach but serves them meals and looks after them."

"They're not doing much, I hear. They are still feeling persecuted and plan their moves in an upper room in Jerusalem. They often seek Mary's counsel on matters."

"Well, I for one, wish her well. She is a righteous and holy woman and I hope that the Lord is good to her from now on."

"Me too!" chorused the other women. On that note, they headed home.

It was in the season of Sivan and the weather was blistering hot. It was the festival of Pentecost in Jerusalem. It was the feast called Shavuot when the Jewish people celebrated this holy day in gratitude for the harvest and the first fruits of their labours. They also remembered the occasion when they received the tablet of commandments given by Moses from Mount Sinai.

The followers of Jesus had agreed to slip into the city from Galilee one by one surreptitiously. They had not moved as a whole flock but had entered stealthily, like thieves in the night. They had agreed upon a secret knock to give them passage into the upper room. Over the passage of a couple of hours, all the apostles and close disciples including the Marys, were finally gathered in their secret meeting place. The air was heavy and oppressive. Though it was unusual at this time of year, brooding, black and threatening rain clouds had collected in the western sky. This weather seemed to replicate the mood of gloom in the room. The people present were sighing, somber and sullen. They were still nervous about the political and religious dangers in the holy city. They refused to admit their fears to each other because Jesus had emphasized to them that they should not be afraid. Yet here they were, morose and troubled. Mother Mary seemed to be the only one at peace. She had such confidence in Jesus and in the will of God that she spent her time praying or serving. She brought comfort to their souls.

The sky got very dark over the city. Thunder broke the silence, lightning split the sky, and the rain fell in torrents. People below the window were all scrambling for shelter. Those, lucky enough to be indoors, were praying for the storm to pass without causing harm. Hopefully, the rain would actually bring in cooler air and rid the atmosphere of its stifling humidity. Suddenly, there came the rush of a mighty wind, and it filled the house. The windows were open but covered with lattice-work shutters, letting air in but keeping most of the rain out. Almost as soon as the thunderstorm struck, it quickly passed. The sky regained the bright light of the sun. The shining, radiant light replaced the gloom with a golden hue. There was still a little rain in the air and the light of the rainbow it created broke into its band of colours and entered the upper room. The rainbow light, split and broken into its various hues by the latticed screens on the windows, appeared like little dancing tongues of flame over the heads of the people therein. There was a moment of sudden realization within the group. The Holy Spirit had descended upon them! The Promise.

The drops of light soon disappeared, but meanwhile it must have penetrated their hearts, because they all felt a surge of courage and wisdom. They were suddenly gifted with the ability to speak many tongues. Not bad for a coarse and crude crew of fishermen and tradesmen! They were filled with energy, courage and drive. They now knew what they needed to do and were empowered to do it! Most of all, they felt the presence of the Son of God, fulfilling his promise to be with them as they were about to undertake their evangelical pursuits.

"Do you feel it, Mother Mary?" inquired Peter.

"Yes," she said demurely. "My spirit is on fire. I feel enlightened. I feel a divine power within my soul."

"Yes, yes! That is exactly it! I'm not afraid anymore!"

"You were afraid? Well, I wasn't, not one little bit," said Andrew sarcastically.

The apostles all scoffed at that last remark and jumped up to hug each other and share the joy of their newly given confidence and conviction.

"He came through for us, as I knew he would!" exclaimed John joyfully.

"Now, what do we do?" asked Philip and Bartholemew together, looking at Peter.

"We go out and face the world, and tell all who will listen about Jesus the Christ who was born, lived among us, was crucified, died and rose again to save us and show us the way."

"Chada!" shouted James in Aramaic.

"Allelouia!" added Judas in Greek.

"Praise Jah!, echoed Matthew in Hebrew.

They were astonished to find that they were all able to speak the praise in different languages! They immediately fell to their knees and recited the prayer that Jesus had taught them.

In the months following Pentecost, the servants of Jesus the Christ went out and served the Lord by their words and by their lives. They converted many. The many miracles and good works that they wrought and the many adventures and dangers they accomplished were described later in the writings of a physician named Luke, an acolyte of Paul.

Paul was originally a persecutor of the followers of Christ. He was born Saul, in Tarsus; he was a Zealot Jew, a Roman citizen, and he spoke fluent Greek. He hated the movement of Jesus the Christ. He argued that this was a blasphemous sect and should be irradicated. He was shameless in his pursuit. He watched the stoning of the falsely accused holy man Stephen and did nothing to stop it because he consented to this murder. He continued to round up Jews of the Way to bring them to Jerusalem for an unfounded and unjustified accounting of their practices and disregard for Jewish laws.

For every verbal abuse, imprisonment, lashing, torture and killing that was perpetrated on the faithful supporters of Jesus Christ, Mary felt the piercing of her heart. She lived in complete sympathy with their plight and prayed to her Son to intervene for these poor souls, if not here on earth, then in the Kingdom of God. She felt the pain personally and helped the apostles as well as she could in service to their work and in prayer. It was too dangerous to remain in Jerusalem, so John sent her back to Nazareth to pray and to stay out of harm's way. Mary spent hours on her knees praying. She was doing this one day when she was startled by a bang on the door.

James looked out the window and said, "It is Saul, the persecutor! He has come to drag us off to prison!" The banging continued insistently.

"What shall we do, Mother Mary?" asked James frantically.

"Let him in, James. If it is the will of God that we should be martyred for our faith, then so be it."

"You have more courage than I have, Mother." The banging at the door continued. Finally, James opened the door a crack and faced the man himself—Saul.

"What is it that you seek?" demanded James. His own mother, Mary Cleopas, and other servants were huddled in fear at the other end of the house.

"I have come to seek Mary, the Mother of Jesus."

"Well, she might not be wanting to see you, Saul. Yes, I know who you are!" snapped James.

"I am no longer Saul. I am now called Paul, now that I have converted to the faith."

James was stunned and stared at the man before him.

"I understand your fright and disbelief, my friend, but I mean you and Mary no harm."

"Let him come in, James. We will offer him a Nazarene welcome."

"Shalom, Mary. I am Paul. Peace to this house. Be not afraid." The other women slowly crept out of their hiding places and entered the room and began to prepare the food and provide hospitality for such an august convert to the faith.

Over honey cakes and herbal tea, Paul explained to Mary what had happened on his route to Damascus to persecute Jesus' followers. In blindness, he saw Jesus standing before him, and was completely infused with the faith of the Father, the Son and Holy Spirit. He related his regained sight by Ananius' laying of hands, his baptism and his change of name to Paul. He was now a complete devotee of Jesus and he and his new friend Peter were leading the Way. Peter concentrated on the Jewish population while Paul attended to the Gentiles. He explained that he was invigorated with the joy and the exaltation of the Spirit and was delighted to be a faithful servant of God the Son.

Mary nodded and expressed her gladness at his total conversion. "I have prayed for this, Paul, and my prayers have been answered."

"I come to ask your forgiveness for the atrocities that I have committed towards your people, Mary."

"If my son can forgive you, then so must I."

Together, they sat and talked about Jesus. Mary told him many stories about the mysteries of his birth and the stories of his childhood. Paul listened attentively to the stories that Mary told. Finally, he stood up and announced, "I must go now, Mary. I thank you for your hospitality, and most of all, for your forgiveness. I may stop and consult with you from time to time, especially if Peter and I disagree about issues."

Mary nodded solemnly and led him to the door with a warm smile. Afterwards, the entire household knelt in a prayer of gratitude for the miraculous transformation of the persecutor Saul into the apostle, Paul.

Mary continued to participate with the apostles on their journeys around Galilee and Samaria. At other times, she stayed home and helped the people of the villages around Nazareth. During this time, more and more people came to believe that Jesus was indeed the long-awaited Messiah-- the Christ. There were many converts and the church of Jesus grew. They now called the followers of Jesus, 'Christians'. They included all varieties of men and women, well beyond merely the Chosen People of God. God may have chosen the Jews, but now the Jews and people of all nations were choosing the Son of God, Jesus.

Chapter 46
Final and Heavenly Reunion

"Jesus said, 'A new commandment I give to you, that you love one another; even as I have loved you, that you also love one another. I am the vine and you are the branches. He who abides in me, and I in him, he it is that bears much fruit, for apart from me you can do nothing.'"[80]

John was preaching to a large group of people in Colossae. They had been on the road for many months now. After a rest in Damascus, John and Mary and James, son of Mary Cleopas, had journeyed to the churches in Asia Minor and remained for a time. Mary Cleopas no longer accompanied Mary, as she had preceded her sister Mary in death. The resultant trio had made trips to various villages along the way. Many cities had appointed bishops in their churches established by Paul on his previous visits. On the whole they received a good reception at all these places. The Word had spread incredibly fast and people were hungry for the message of Jesus the Christ. The disciples were ministering to the Gentiles now. 'The Way' was catching on, and more and more citizens of Cilicia and Syria, Cappadocia, Galatia and Pisidia were asking to be baptised. It was at Antioch that the name 'Christians' first appeared.

The apostles encountered many problems in the process of conversion, such as the question of circumcision and whether one needed to be circumcised to be Christian. Paul finally won that argument on the basis that Jesus had wanted his followers should come from all nations, and thus he was favouring the 'circumcision of the heart' over the traditional Jewish rite.

---

[80] John 13:34, 15:5

It had been a long journey and Mary was not young anymore. She was still a strong woman, and the Holy Spirit continued to give her strength, courage and wisdom. She continued to minister to the sick and to troubled minds and souls. She also nurtured and cared for the disciples, providing for them by cooking and baking bread in the field camps. Sometimes, she would stay at someone's home and enjoy the hospitality of faithful followers. In spite of her role as mother of Jesus, she always considered herself a humble handmaiden of the Lord. In the evenings, after the work of the day was done, John, James and Mary often discussed the challenges they faced in preaching the good news. The men had confidence in Mary's views and were respectful of her opinion on matters. For her part, Mary relied on the wisdom given to her by the Holy Spirit and seemed to always have a sensible and enlightened response to issues.

They had made their way across the land from Antioch to Tarsus, Derbe and Lystra. Unbeknownst to John and James, Mary had concealed her declining health and weakening body. She was easily fatigued and often opted to stay in place while the men went out to the smaller hamlets to minister the word. It was at Colossae that Mary could no longer hide her discomfort and lack of energy. James, the most alert to her needs, noticed her slowing down and struggling to breathe.

"How long has this been going on, Mother Mary?" James asked.

Mary shrugged her shoulders and said, "It has been progressing very slowly, so I'm not sure I can answer that question accurately, James."

"Well, you must not keep up this pace with us. I think we should head over to the house that John was given to use in Ephesus. Can you manage that? We will get you a donkey and there will be no more walking and working in the villages. "

"That is very kind of you, and I think that you might well be right, James. I will only slow you down."

John and James discussed the matter. While John was very concerned about Mary's condition, she was able to persuade him to continue his work and she would gladly go with James to the lovely home on a lush hillside near Ephesus.

Ephesus was a town on the Aegean Sea; however, the house found itself nestled close by on a modest hill. The rather large house was built of stones and had vaulted windows to take in the breeze from the nearby sea. It was nicely sheltered by a variety of shade trees and boasted a private courtyard where pomegranate, fig, orange, lemon and lime trees grew. When villagers knew that John and Mary were in house, they would parade up the hillside with baskets of provisions for them. They loved Mary because she was so kind and thoughtful. They brought along their children who were suffering all kinds of ailments for Mary to treat. Mary still had healing power in her hands—some came from her skills and some came from her laying of hands and prayers. It did not go unnoticed that she had a true love for them and they loved her in return. So Mary slowed down her work of proclaiming the word and made fewer trips outside of the home. People came to her and that way, she could continue her ministry until she took to her bed. This reduced her activity a great deal and she instead spent her time in meditation and prayer, listening to the birds outside her window during the day and the singing insects at night. She was content and filled her heart with memories of her beloved Joseph and her son, Jesus. She was looking forward to meeting her loved ones again soon.

Mary progressively became more feeble. Family members were sent for, and many made their way to visit their aunt and grandmother or great-grandmother. The sons of Joseph and their children and grandchildren made the long journey to Ephesus to see their cherished relative. One of the wealthy families in Ephesus sent a servant to minister to her needs and to keep her comfortable. James provided her protection from over-enthusiastic visitors who would insist on seeing her, demanding that she tend to their issues. John had been in and out several times during his rounds and visits to Ephesus. He did not stray far from Mary now. He had sent out a message to summon the apostles to make their way to Asia Minor to pay their respects to the mother of their Lord and Master. Slowly, the others, including Mathias, who had been chosen to become the twelfth apostle after Judas Iscariot had committed suicide, trickled into the village and set up camps not far from the house.

The original group of disciples was happy to find themselves together again. The reunion was overdue as they had all been travelling to all corners of their world to evangelize and spread the good news. This visit would be a respite from their missionary work and from the nomadic way of life. It would be an opportunity for them to reinvigorate themselves for their ongoing missions. They had lots of news to share and many matters to discuss. Paul was in Rome at the moment and it was unsure whether he could make it in time.

One day, the servant Claudia called out to the men. "Come, Mary is calling for you."

They all hurried in after washing and they circled around her bed. Paul had managed to arrive just the day before. It was as though Mary was waiting for him to arrive to share her end of life with all her adopted children and friends.

It was not a big room, so they were shoulder to shoulder and elbow to elbow. All wore a mask of grief as they looked upon the mother of Jesus—the Theotokos. She had been their mother since the death of their Master. They loved her dearly and she loved them as her own children.

Mary was breathing sporadically and with great difficulty. There was a sullen mood in the room and so Paul uttered these words,

"There is therefore now no condemnation for those who are in Christ Jesus. For the law of the Spirit of life in Christ Jesus has set [us] free from the law of sin and death. If the Spirit of him who raised Jesus from the dead dwells in you, he who raised Christ Jesus from the dead will give life to your mortal bodies also through his Spirit who dwells in you. The creation will be set free from its bondage to decay and obtain the glorious liberty of the children of God."[81]

The devotees present in the room responded with a resounding "Amen!"

Mary asked that her cot be taken outside so that she could see the miracle of creation one more time. She longed to lie under the heavenly dome and listen, hear and smell the beautiful life that the Lord had breathed onto the earth. The sun and a gentle breeze softly kissed her face. She smiled when she heard a set of birds sing a harmonious duet. She breathed in deeply of the collection of flowers that lined the house foundation. After taking in the beauty and splendour of the

---

[81] Romans 8: 1-3, 11, 21

new day, Mary acknowledged each one of the disciples and said something particularly attributed to them alone. She took their hands in hers one by one and let them say goodbye. She knew them well. She knew their faults and she loved them in spite of them. Each grown man left with tears in his eyes.

Mary spent a little more time with Mary of Magdala. The two of them had spent a great deal of time on the road sharing the chore of feeding the boys. The two women had shared many a sleeping space, and lodgings when they had them. Mary and other females had often been guests at the Magdala home. Moreover, they shared their special love of Jesus. There was a bond there that linked their souls by the ties that women alone experience. Later in history, a papal leader would say: 'From the beginning of Christ's mission, women showed to him and to his mystery a special sensitivity which is characteristic of their femininity... that was especially confirmed in the Paschal Mystery, not only at the Cross but at the dawn of the Resurrection.'[82]

She was now 64 years old and she had lived a blessed life. The apostles, led by Peter, set up an altar on a nearby rock and the disciples, remembering the last supper, and what Jesus had taught them, said prayers, sang psalms and broke shared bread as Jesus had taught them. Jesus was present to them in the form of the fruits of human hands. After sharing the blessed bread and wine with Mary, the men held out their hands in a unified blessing over Mother Mary. Then they bowed their heads to say a personal prayer of thanksgiving to the Father who had blessed them with such a noble woman. At the end of her individual farewells to all the disciples present, she

---

[82] Statement of St. Pope John Paul II from the encyclical Mulieris Dignitatum

closed her eyes and fell into a peaceful sleep. Her breathing became soft, shallow but steady.

"I always thought that angels surrounded her at all times," whispered Andrew. "I could feel their presence. I can now!"

"You know, in all the time that I have known her, I have never known her to sin. She was a sweet, sweet person full of life and hope, " declared John.

This was affirmed by James, Peter and Andrew. "She always was blessed among women and perpetually full of grace."

"She had to be. She was the mother of God!" proclaimed Peter.

Mary's eyes were closed, and a slight smile appeared on her lips. In a glow of peace and tranquility, the Mother of God stopped breathing. She lay there in complete harmony with nature for a long time while the persons present regained their composure. Luke, Paul's friend and physician, approached the body and announced that she had indeed, passed to the other side. Suddenly, something happened. None of the people knew what it was. They all backed up at the presence of a force in the atmosphere. They presently felt an energy in the room around the body of Mary. She lay in what appeared to be a state of a glorious, divine serenity and her face appeared youthful once more and shone like the moon. Silence filled the hearts of all present and the world stood still for a moment. Even the chatter of birds had stopped.

All of a sudden, there arose a small wind as tender as a whisper. It swirled around the prostrate sacred body of Mary, mother of Jesus, and picked her up to an upright position. Mary was wearing a simple linen sleeping shift, however the zephyr spun around her as to make an immaculate flowing robe of shimmering, radiant light. The light amplified itself and sent streamers of iridescent multi-coloured light energy. The air vibrated with profound mystical liveliness and a sense of

343

goodness and love that was palpable. Mary's face now shone like the sun and her expression was one of absolute ecstasy.

All the witnesses fell to their knees.

Mary Magdelene cried, "Glory to Mary, the bride of the Creator. Father, mother of God, and forever, our blessed mother!"

Peter said, "Pray for us, sinners, Mary."

Angels! Choirs of angels! Before their very eyes, the angels carried her from her bed higher and higher in the firmament and other celestial beings around her danced and sang in a harmonious chorus of voices. The air was pregnant with joy and rhapsody. The singing was celestial and magnificent. It was so beautiful that the humans below were stunned into awe. Never would their ears hear anything so splendid on earth. They watched as Mary rose higher. She seemed to look down at them and gave them a look of unreserved love. She moved her hands from a prayer position to a wide span which seemed to embrace all below her. She rose higher and then gradually disappeared like a fine mist.

The speechless beholders remained amazed as they marvelled at the scene they had just experienced. It was a long, long time before the group gathered to discuss and marvel about the occurrence and to celebrate such a glorious death. They were still in awe as they left Ephesus to continue their work in Jesus' name.

Mary finally joined her Beloved. Her Creator and her Redeemer, bound by love, the Father, placed her in a position of honour in the Kingdom. But Mary's work in heaven had just begun. She accepted the role of pouring grace and blessings on her children. The Mother of God intervened with the petitions and prayers of the earthly children. And as it had always been, Jesus could refuse her nothing. Mary became the mother of miracles.

Historical Notes

The story is imagined by the author but is based on research that includes the Jewish traditions and rabbinic rulings of the time, Scripture, beliefs of Church theologians and scholars, as well as the writings of recognized mystics liked Anne Catherine Emmerich and Mary of Agreda.

I have relied predominantly on two Bible versions: *The Didache Bible* (RSV) and the *New American Bible*.

There is much that is unknown about the life of Mary. More is written about Anna, Joachim and Mary in the Quran than in Christian Scripture. The New Testament is rightly the story of Jesus. Hence, Mary is only mentioned a few times in the New Testament: the annunciation, the nativity, the flight to Egypt, the loss of Jesus in the Temple, the wedding at Cana, the rejection when she and family members called on him during his preaching, and finally the Pentecost. This does not necessarily follow that Mary was not an important holy person ("blessed among women") in our faith development. Therefore, to discover more about the life of Mary, I have also consulted other Gospels—those Apocryphal books like the *Protoevangelium,* the *Pseudo-gospel of Matthew*, and *Thomas.* There are too many sources that have contributed to the story to cite all of them here. Some of these other sources include many bible study courses, magazine issues, and photos and internet articles, films, YouTube videos and lectures. Resources such as: *Aramaic Light on the Gospel of Matthew* by Rocco A. Errico and George M. Lamsa; *The Urantia Book,* Author unknown; *Palestine in the Time of Jesus: Social Structures and Social Conflicts,* by K. C. Hanson and Douglas E. Oakman; *Jesus and the Jewish Roots of the Eucharist; Jesus and the Jewish Roots of Mary;* a Bible study course titled *Mary, The Bible and the Mother of God* by Brant Pitre; *Hail, Holy Queen* by Scott

Hahn; and *The Parables* by Gary Inrig. All contributed to my knowledge foundation.

My research has shown that there is very little consensus and, indeed much disagreement regarding dates and places within the various sources. For example, there is controversy surrounding whether Mary Salome was Anna's older daughter by Joachim (thereby Mary's sister), or whether Anna had more husbands after Joachim, also known as Heli. There are many common and frequently used names, especially as in the case of Mary. Spellings vary from source to source. There are questions surrounding Mary Cleopas or Cleophas. Was she Mary's sister or sister-in-law? When Mary met Joseph, was he an eligible young man or a widower with his own children? The historical Mary is a mystery, so there is much room for the imagination within the context of the first century.

Moreover, family relationships in those days were not always as clearly delineated as they are today, as there often were multiple families living in one household. Second marriages and the housing of widowed mothers, sisters and their families by male family members was common practice. Often, the cousins were considered brothers and sisters. The definition of siblings was loosely considered within members of the same household.

Alas, choices had to be made regarding these unknowns and uncertainties and which versions should become part of this story. Faced with this challenge, I put various pieces together to form what I believe is both a plausible and reasonable narrative. It is a work that combines both research and imagination, hopefully put together with the help of the Holy Spirit. I'm sure that more knowledgeable people will discover many errors, inconsistencies and inaccuracies. I would encourage them to remember that this is a novel, not an academic work, so therefore, just enjoy the story of a beautiful woman, mother of God. It was never my intention to offend any person or any faith, but rather to celebrate a holy life about which we know very little. Any errors, of course, are mine and mine alone.

Acknowledgements

The journey of discovery for me was one of wonder and joy. I was thankful for the Internet which was often used to quickly check for basic information, especially about locations and distances.

However, as handy as those tools were, none was as important as those who were part of my lifetime journey leading to this writing adventure! They would include my grandparents, my parents, and the many priests, nuns, teachers and colleagues who have contributed to my faith formation over many years.

In addition, I could not have written this novel without the help and encouragement of my husband, Chris, who was a sounding board for me. He generously listened, discussed and debated with me. I also thank him for the many hours he spent proofreading my manuscript and advising me on form, style and structure and correcting my many spelling errors.

I am thankful to my brother-in-law, Tom Chapman, for all his patience with my technical ignorance and for his expert technical support and advice. My sister Monique Chapman deserves my gratitude for contributing many hours of beneficial consultation about the novel.

I am thankful to all who read and reviewed my manuscript and gave me such helpful feedback: Father Robert Poole, Monique Chapman, Christina Murdock, and Barbara Day-Wills.

I am grateful for my faith community, who challenged me and assisted me with my questions and theories. God bless you all.

About the Author

Ms. Hawkes is an experienced educator and author with a passion for learning and storytelling. She holds a BA in Psychology and Sociology, a Master of Education, and an Ontario Specialist Certificate in Religious Education. Over the years, Ms. Hawkes has taught a wide range of students, from young children to adults, and has also served as a school principal.

Living in Ontario with her husband and near her family, Ms. Hawkes has written several works, including two novels. Her debut, Descent Into Hell, explores deep moral questions and is complemented by a Teacher Guide designed for intermediate and senior classrooms. Her latest book, Holy Bible, Nana!, is written for younger readers, showcasing her ability to make complex narratives accessible to children. Ms. Hawkes has also written five Christmas plays for children.

With a strong interest in history and storytelling, Ms. Hawkes continues to incorporate her diverse experiences into her writing, crafting stories that appeal to a wide range of readers.

The photograph featured on the back cover is by Angela Flemming.

For more information about her work, visit dlhawkes.com."

www.ingramcontent.com/pod-product-compliance
Lightning Source LLC
Chambersburg PA
CBHW051131120626
46547CB00012B/762